Cathedral Architecture

other books by the author

—

ENGLISH ABBEYS
PARISH CHURCHES
OLD ENGLISH HOUSES
AN INTRODUCTION TO ENGLISH MEDIAEVAL ARCHITECTURE
THE STORY OF ENGLISH ARCHITECTURE
HISTORICAL ARCHITECTURE

CATHEDRAL ARCHITECTURE

HUGH BRAUN

FABER AND FABER LTD
3 Queen Square, London

First published in 1972
by Faber and Faber Limited
3 Queen Square, London WC1
Printed in Great Britain
by W & J Mackay Limited, Chatham
All rights reserved

ISBN 0 571 09962 9

Contents

Notes on Plates

All the plates have been supplied by the National Monuments Record who hold the copyright

1. ELY. The remaining portion of the late twelfth-century west front. The northern wing of the transept has fallen and a thirteenth-century porch obscures its original central element with the west doorway. The bell-tower stands complete except for its timber steeple which has been replaced with a stone octagon. The richness of the arcaded wall-decoration is typical of twelfth-century elevational design.   *facing page* 36

2. NORWICH. The original lantern tower has been raised late in the twelfth century to provide a belfry. The great apse of the cathedral can be seen with its original fenestration replaced by large Gothic windows. Round the base of the great apse can be seen the clustering chapels of the twelfth-century chevet. The Gothic spire replaces the original timber steeple.   37

3. PETERBOROUGH. This splendid nave illustrates the great height achieved by the twelfth-century builders and the effect of this before the introduction of high vaults. The gallery arcade with its bifora treatment plays a large part in the design; above it is the triforium which provides an internal treatment to the clearstory cleaning passage. In the distance the great apse may be seen, its fenestration expanded during the fifteenth century.   44

4. NORWICH. A great twelfth-century nave with its original height no longer seen owing to the introduction of a Gothic lierne vault. The two stories are clearly indicated, the gallery arcade completely echoing the main arcade below it. A Gothic screen provides an entrance façade to the bishop's church; above it rises a fine Renaissance organ case. *facing page* 45

5. DURHAM. The most splendid example of Anglo-Byzantine architecture. The 'duplex bay' system, in which circular pillars divide great bays indicated by massive piers, is clearly seen, the pillars being ornamented by carved motifs probably transferred from contemporary timber architecture. The gallery arcade has been subordinated in scale to the great arcade below it but the biforas are linked together to provide an elaborate architectural treatment. Note the transverse arches indicating the great bays. The very simple 'quadripartite' vaulting may be compared with the far more elaborate ceilings of later centuries. 48

6. DURHAM. One can detect the twelfth-century west transept with its design of three large arches the central one of which has been filled with a late Gothic window. On the wings of the transept a pair of richly-arcaded towers has been raised to create a twin-towered west front, a prototype of a feature later developed by the Gothic architects. The central lantern tower, rebuilt in the Gothic era, has been completed with the addition of a belfry story. 49

7. ELY. The towered and turreted silhouette of one of Europe's greatest churches. To the left is the arcaded bell-tower of the twelfth century crowned with its Gothic octagon while contrasting with this tall feature is the mass of the central octagon with its timber lantern. 64

Notes on Plates

8. ST. ALBANS. One of the largest churches in the world, begun in the eleventh century with bricks collected from the ruins of a Roman city. The great mass of the central tower, looking like the keep of a Norman castle, is clearly seen in this photograph taken before the disastrous restoration of 1879. It has been raised by a belfry story and was originally finished with an enormous timber steeple. *facing page* 65

9. ST. ALBANS. The original work was constructed of Roman bricks plastered over and covered with painted decoration. The screen is not the choir screen but that set west of it to serve as a reredos to the nave altar. The crossing, still lit through its eleventh-century lantern, can be seen beyond. The south side of the church fell and was rebuilt in Gothic style. 80

10. SOUTHWELL. The interior of this church illustrates more clearly than most the twelfth-century system of building a tall structure in two stories. The main arcade is carried upon the circular pillars which under 'basilican' influence began to replace the compound piers of the great Anglian churches. The eastern arm was rebuilt during the thirteenth century; its entrance screen may be seen in the photograph. 81

11. WINCHESTER. Probably the oldest surviving example of the Anglo-Byzantine style employed on cathedral scale, seen here in the angle of the transept of the eleventh-century church. The 'loggia' construction was to have been carried across the gable end of the transept and its main arcade was actually built, but the idea was abandoned after the aisle vault had been constructed and the basement stage of the building completed. It may well have been realized that the gable end had no roof to carry as was the case with the aisle walling. 96

11

12. GLOUCESTER. An attempt to build an Anglo-Saxon basilica. The huge pillars, intended to represent Classical columns, raised the main arcade to an unusual height and left the blind story, where the aisle roof abutted, to be covered with an architectural treatment formed of a pair of biforas in each bay. Above this level all is later and includes an undistinguished high vault. *facing page* 97

13. OXFORD. An attempt by the Augustinian Order to create a basilica which may have been more successful than is now apparent, for much of the nave has been pulled down and the effect of perspective thereby destroyed. We can see the aesthetic arcade with its Corinthianesque capitals and behind it a structural arcade carrying the aisle vault and a simple blind story contrived beneath the main arcade. The glory of this cathedral is its elaborate vaulting system, a poem in masonry designed with great skill and incorporating with it the clearstory treatment and the wide transverse arches around which the whole structure with its stone pendants is woven.   112

14. GLOUCESTER. A remarkable example of a late-Gothic 'conversion' of a twelfth-century eastern arm. What we see today is a system of stone panelling which has been applied to the ancient walling, the new design carried up to develop into a vaulted ceiling of impressive elaboration. The whole of the east wall is filled with a window in the panelled style of the period. The expanse of glass is so vast that the stonework of the window tracery has been bowed outwards to resist wind pressure.   113

15. WELLS. An early essay in Gothic which has not yet attained the stature of later cathedrals but has made full use of Gothic mouldings in the orders of its dainty arcades. The gallery story has been entirely omitted—

perhaps in deference to 'basilican' influence—and the blind story has been treated somewhat unimaginatively as a simple arcade, the usual bifora having perhaps been omitted as having too Byzantine a flavour.   *facing page* 128

16. LICHFIELD. This beautiful cathedral illustrates the richness of early Gothic with its clustered pillars carrying arches having their structural orders completely concealed by systems of deep mouldings. The gallery stage above the main arcade has a pair of biforas to each bay, their jambs fitted together so as to produce a continuous band of architecture. It will be noted that the vault which joins this story across the building absorbs the whole of the clearstory and thus reduces the apparent height of the nave when it is compared with those of the twelfth-century cathedrals. Beyond the crossing arches may be seen the long choir ending in a polygonal English apse.   129

17. WELLS. The two lowermost stages remain of what was to have been a splendid Early Gothic façade the complete design of which we shall never know. The architect who added the towers, however, treated the work of his predecessor with great sympathy and joined his work to the old with notable skill. The buttresses of the towers are tapered towards what were probably to have been stone spires surrounded by crenellated and pinnacled parapets. The arcading of the original work makes no secret of its descent from that of its twelfth-century predecessors.   144

18. HEREFORD. The interest of the design of this eastern arm lies in the transept which is set across it. Planned in two cross aisles, the eastern of which contains a series of chapels entered from the western aisle which also serves as an ambulatory. The windows are late Gothic insertions. The late tower is of the panelled Western type.   145

19. LINCOLN. The photograph illustrates the growth of one of the most stately of English cathedral façades. In the centre can be detected the original west transept with its wings raised at the end of the twelfth century to form a pair of towers. Thrown across the whole front is the thirteenth-century arcaded screen. The west towers were later greatly increased in height. Behind them, on the stump of St. Hugh's great lantern, soars the enormous central tower. All three towers carried tall steeples. *facing page* 160

20. PETERBOROUGH. This great thirteenth-century architectural feat is unique in the world. It is a Gothic portico, the inspiration of a visionary which seems to have no architectural predecessor. 161

21. SOUTHWELL. The thirteenth-century choir of a church only recently raised to cathedral rank. Its architecture is that of one of the lesser monastic churches. The gallery stage has been omitted and the triforium treatment of the clearstory lowered to clear the springing of the high vault in order to bring the whole feature more into the open. Note the stone screen framing the entrance to the choir. 176

22. ELY. Perhaps the finest survivor of the long choirs which were added in the thirteenth century to the great churches of medieval England. The usual clustered pillars support richly moulded arches. The biforas of the gallery story are elaborately ornamented with carving, above which splendid band of architecture the clearstory is buried amongst the ribs of the high vault. 177

23. LINCOLN. One of the most stately of the surviving early-Gothic churches of England. The main arcade rises to a considerable height, the gallery story above being correspondingly reduced. To fill this narrow band, pairs of biforas set in each bay have their supports gathered together to form a continuous band. 192

24. WORCESTER. A fine early-Gothic nave, raised, however, in a city removed from the most productive
masonry regions. The main arcade is low in stature but
lacks nothing in richness of moulded ornament. The
gallery story shows an interesting bifora treatment but
lacks the detailing seen in the great churches of the
East. Nevertheless with its simple vault to complete it,
the interior of the cathedral presents a notable example
of a great Gothic cathedral. *facing page* 193

25. YORK. This is nearing the culmination of Gothic
architecture. The main arcade has achieved a monumental height and the gallery stage has disappeared
except for a blind story architecturally incorporated
with the clearstory. The height of the building has been
increased by twenty feet so as to make up for the
amount of walling absorbed by the high vault. The
arches of the crossing have now assumed a truly monumental scale while between them the light from a huge
lantern tower still illuminates the centre of the building
and the entrance screen to the bishop's choir. 208

26. WINCHESTER. The new architectural scheme applied
to the interior of an ancient nave. The arcade appears
loftier than it is as its supports incorporate the pillars of
the original gallery arcade as well as those of the main
arcade itself, so that the arches are very tall and narrow.
There is a blind story partially absorbed into the clearstory and enabling this to emerge below the deep cones
of the high vault. This is a very heavy one, made more
so by the network of lierne ribwork. The flattened
curvature of the main arcade, the effect of lead roofing
upon Gothic arches, is clearly seen. The ordered Gothic
arch is still employed but with its mouldings greatly
coarsened. 209

27. CANTERBURY. One of the last of the great towers of
Gothic England, illustrating the ultimate perfection of

the two-storied arrangement with the lantern story still serving its original purpose of lighting the centre of the church, and a belfry stage above. The vertical punctuation perpetuates the duplex system of a pair of normal bays to one great bay, which in this case is the width of the building and its tower. The group of narrow buttress-like projections at the angles are carried up above the parapet and worked into pinnacles.

facing page 224

28. CANTERBURY. The ultimate in the English cathedral interior. The pillars of the main arcade are seen to sweep up the whole height of the building and join overhead to expand into the rib system of a high vault, the height of the nave having been raised to allow for the reduced height of the walling due to the vault. The dissociation of the clearstory from a very dull blind story provides an unhappy illustration of the loss of skill in elevational design since the days of the superb treatments introduced during the thirteenth century. The strainer arch thrown across the west arch of the crossing takes the thrust of the aisle arches and prevents their straining the crossing piers and causing them to bow inwards towards each other. The entrance screen to the archbishop's choir is lit by the light falling from the lantern.

225

29. ELY. One of the most notable achievements of the English Gothic architects is this magnificent antechamber to the choir of the cathedral. The whole of its vaulting, with the lantern above it, is the work not of masons but of carpenters and can leave no doubt that it was they who devised the high vaults of the Gothic. A portion of the twelfth-century church in the heart of which this fine hall was constructed may be seen to the left of the photograph. Beyond the octagon the end of the original transept displays its pair of twelfth-century bays.

240

30. SALISBURY. This strangely austere building may reflect the Cistercian tastes of its founder-bishop. The pillars are built in drums of hard stone with their surrounding shafts separately attached. The main arcade is of simple design with the mouldings of the arches lacking the depth of most contemporary work. The gallery stage is an ingenious arrangement of pairs of biforas in each bay, gathered together under broad flat arches springing rather uncomfortably from their imposts. The triforium is a simple development from the twelfth-century system and echoes triplets of lancet windows in the clearstory beyond. The vaulting is simple quadripartite and has as yet no ridge ribs.

facing page 241

31. SALISBURY. With the exception of the central feature, this great church represents the English cathedral of the year 1220 when it was begun. The best illustration of contemporary bay design, once visible in scores of great monastic churches now lost to us, is seen in the transept. The west front, a screen thrown across the end of the nave to provide a rectangular façade, is a descendant of the arcaded fronts of the previous century but with the Gothic bifora much to the fore. The central tower is of the normal late-Gothic two-storied type but the great lantern no longer lights the crossing as the high vaults of the nave and choir were joined together across this to stiffen the strained thirteenth-century work below. The belfry story is a sham, the bells having been hung in a detached campanile contemporary with the cathedral but since destroyed. The stone spire rising from a cluster of pinnacles forms a rare example of this one-time common parochial feature expanded to cathedral scale.

256

32. EXETER. One of the world's loveliest church interiors. Basically it is a twelfth-century building the original pillars of which remain enclosed within the

Gothic ones, which are simply designed but support richly moulded arches. The gallery stage is indicated by a rather unenterprising arcade barely filling each bay. But above it are splendid clearstory windows which light the tremendous high vault, the principal architectural feature which sweeps across it like the branches above a forest glade. The great scale of this vault absorbs much of the clearstory. It is this fact, coupled with the antique proportions of the main arcade and the lack of a notable gallery stage, which deprives the interior of the normal soaring effect of the contemporary Gothic interior. The high vault, however, by the splendour of its conception, completely makes up for this loss of height. Above the entrance screen to the bishop's choir a charming Renaissance organ case helps to punctuate the cathedral into its two component portions without in the least obstructing the vista down this splendid church. *facing page* 257

List of Line Drawings

Preface—The Architectural Historian

The history of architecture has generally been written by clergymen, scholars and other professional people or distinguished amateurs lacking, however, the elements of an architectural training, let alone any practical experience of architectural design. This is perhaps unfortunate.

During the last forty years or so the art historian has occupied an increasingly important place in relation to the art critic.

Criticism of any branch of art is essential to its healthy existence, even though an art critic may be unable to wield chisel or brush. Architecture is equally open to criticism and for the same reason, that only through a keen interest being taken in it can it survive as a viable art-form. But the historian of architecture will find that it is an applied art associated with a number of extremely complicated matters, and that its aesthetic appeal is but the third and last of the 'Conditions' laid down by Sir Henry Wotton at the beginning of the seventeenth century and followed by all English architects including Sir Christopher Wren.

Whether the art critic should like it or not, the architect designing a building has to consider how it will serve its purpose, how he can get it to stand firm and defy the assaults of gravity and the elements. And only then can he make it a work of art.

'To talk of Architecture', said the eighteenth-century writer, 'is a joke . . . 'til you can build a chimney that won't smoke!'

Thus a reliable critic of architecture needs more than a little knowledge of the technicalities of any subject he may be discussing. The art critic may include in his discussions on the history of painting and sculpture the applications of these forms of art to the decoration of buildings. But if he attempts to discuss the buildings themselves he is certain to be hampered should he have no knowledge of the planning and structural problems connected with architecture.

For architecture is building. And not merely rough 'do it yourself', or even jobbing building. It is what Sir Henry Wotton called 'well building'—building on the highest scale—and this requires training and experience. Thus for anyone to try to write a history of a profession of which he has no knowledge must be an impossible task.

The architectural historian should preferably be an historian, that is to say, a scholar trained in a particular discipline. But scholarship itself is a profession, and few of us can find the time or the energy to be members of more than one. Thus the technical architectural historian has perforce to avail himself of the information which has been laboriously extracted, classified and recorded for the use of the student.

The writer is fortunate in having been able to profit from the researches of the late G. H. Cook, whose book *The English Cathedral through the Centuries* is packed with historical data of the greatest interest and value to the architectural historian.

For another reason altogether, any writer on an aspect of Gothic should read Mr. John Harvey's *Gothic England*. An indefatigable historian, he devotes himself to the beauties of that world which is his realm, seeking out and honouring the memory of its architects. Perhaps no other writer has so caught the spirit of transcendency which, above everything else, inspired the Gothic achievements.

Because, lamentably, so much of the world's great architecture has vanished from above the ground, the architectural historian is greatly indebted to the laborious excavations of the archaeologists. This is especially true when he is dealing with English medieval architecture in view of the fact that such a large proportion of the great churches of this country was swept away after 1539.

Men like St. John Hope and Harold Brakspear devoted their lives to the excavation and planning of many of these buildings and have thereby rendered a great service to students of English architectural history. Since their day, however, vast sums have been spent by academic and government bodies on the meticulous examination of similar sites, accumulating mounds of those potsherds so beloved of the modern archaeologist, without, however, the excavators knowing anything at all about the archaeology of buildings. For this is not taught at the universities.

The writer knows, from personal experience, that expeditions arranged by other countries for investigating the sites of ancient buildings always include an architect amongst the various experts assigned to the director for his guidance. In this country, however, the scholars seem to mistrust the tradesmen and thus not only mis-construe much of the evidence but are also likely to spoil their own work by burying features which if examined by technical experts could provide valuable information. And the models of ancient structures one sees in museums have for many years past been a source of harmless merriment to visiting architects who can see at a glance that such constructions would have been quite imprac-ticable.

While confessing to a lamentable lack of scholarship, the writer pleads an excellent training in his trade and many years of experience in the planning and design of buildings as well as the restoration of those of his predecessors. As a critic of art as represented by archi-tecture, the writer feels able to comment with confidence upon building aesthetics, having been taught the elements of the Third Condition at a period when the dictum of Sir Henry Wotton was still respected. So, from his grounding in the elements of design, he ventures upon more authoritative criticism than a modern architectural education would have made possible.

It is doubtful whether the architects of medieval England were taught any rules of design. But to them building and integrity were inseparable, and confidence in divine inspiration unshakeable. . . .

So they managed!

The Cathedral Vision

The word 'cathedral' conjures up a vision of a building of transcendent dignity and beauty. To the modern ear it suggests what in classical times was meant by the word *Basilica*—a structure of regal aspect, architecture's most splendid achievement.

That is its architectural meaning today. But in its original conception it signified nothing of architectural moment. A cathedral church was a church among many others, the adjective cathedral merely indicating that a bishop had set up his see within it.

The cathedrals of England are the enduring monuments of our country's architectural achievements. While to the average person the cathedral must always be a great church and one of superlative dignity and beauty, in reality this represents only a stage reached by a building originally of quite humble character—not perhaps without a dream of one day achieving the splendour of the Hagia Sophia, but in the beginning just an ordinary church in which a bishop took his seat. For the cathedral is the embodiment of that ecclesiastical district known as the diocese.

In order to examine the architecture of any building it is necessary to understand the purpose for which it was commissioned. The actual see or headquarters of the diocese was originally a missionary station from which the countryside was converted and its priestly organization administered. The actual missionary activities were conducted by monks. The bishop himself was not working alone but with an entourage of priests, known as his *familia*, who formed a body of clergy maintaining the character of the see as a religious headquarters by organizing the singing of the daily offices in the cathedral church. These priests eventually formed, of course, the cathedral chapter.

In theory the bishop's seat could have been set up in any church, such as an ordinary parish church. Indeed this was often the case, so that one might search today in vain for signs of a church of cathedral scale on the site of an ancient see such as Ramsbury in Wiltshire, for example. But the presence of his *familia* meant that the bishop really needed his own private church in which his little court could assemble at the appropriate hours and sing their offices to the perpetual glory of God.

This is the purpose of the cathedral: to provide a church devoted exclusively to the bishop and his family of priests. Nothing else was needed. But as the cathedral expanded in architectural scale and magnificence far beyond these simple requirements, the bishop's church became represented by a screened enclosure—the bishop's choir—lost in the heart of a great building which had far outgrown its original purpose.

The medieval bishop was a peer of the realm and as such was appointed by the King from amongst senior clerics whom he considered would be likely to serve him and the country well in parliament. Each bishop had his endowment of manors in the same way as any other noble and from their revenues he maintained the dignity of his see and cathedral.

Adjoining the cathedral was the bishop's house with its great hall, the bishop's chamber on an upper floor above his vaulted treasury, and, invariably, a fine private chapel. It was planned as any other great house of the period and developed down the centuries along the same lines. In outlying manors belonging to the see the bishop might build other fine houses, centres from which he could maintain the administration of his diocese. In order to endow episcopal residences with a special dignity they were referred to as palaces. The bishop's estates were not of course his own to dispose of but at his death passed to his successor.

While some cathedrals were staffed with their 'canons', others were attached to a monastic house called a 'cathedral priory', provided with all the conventual buildings of a great abbey but governed by a prior who sang with his monks in the choir as in any other monastic house, the only difference being that at the east end of the southern range of the choir stalls rose the throne of the bishop.

This was the medieval arrangement of the English cathedrals and the social position of their bishops. After the Reformation the bishops found themselves shorn of their ancient dignity but were able with their revenues to maintain their social position in a Protestant world.

With the creation of modern sees the new bishops with their endowments were ill equipped financially to sit beside the descendants of the great medieval nobles of the Church in the House of Lords, and in recent years the revenues of the old dioceses have been gathered into a common fund from which all bishops are paid an annual stipend. They have been relieved of the responsibilities connected with the maintenance of their sometimes vast, sometimes medieval palaces which have been taken over by the Church Commissioners or the diocesan authorities and converted to other uses, the bishops being provided with more convenient residences nearby.

It is interesting to follow the development of the English sees from earliest times. Canterbury was of course the missionary centre founded by St. Augustine. London, receiving its bishop in 604, might have taken its place had it not relapsed into paganism soon after and lost its chance. The Kingdom of Northumbria had long been provided with bishops by the Celtic Church, but the first Roman bishop built his cathedral church at York in 627. In 635 the bishopric of Lindisfarne was founded and in 678 that of Ripon where a cathedral church was built.

When Theodore of Tarsus—not a Roman, but an Asiatic Greek—became Archbishop of Canterbury in 668 he found the country still a group of six kingdoms with its heart-land covered by the then paramount Kingdom of Mercia. The Mercian capital, Lichfield, had its bishop, linked to Canterbury by others at Dorchester-on-Thames, London and Rochester. What was then probably the busiest port in the country, Dunwich in Suffolk, a link with the Anglo-Saxon homeland, was the seat of a bishop; but even at that time the port may have been showing signs of its eventual erasure by the sea and the bishop soon moved his seat fifteen miles inland to Elmham where the ruin of his cathedral still stands.

Before the year 680 the two western dioceses of Worcester and Hereford had been created and another northern one at Hexham in Yorkshire. A diocese called Lindsey had been formed in what is now Lincolnshire but it is not known today where the bishop had his seat. Another Mercian bishop was installed at Leicester. The Channel port of Selsey in Sussex, which has long followed Dunwich into the sea, became the seat of a bishop. A bishop was installed in the Wessex capital of Winchester, while the remote south-west of England was administered by a bishop seated in another Wessex town at Sherborne in Dorset.

The ninth century witnessed the disruption of the north-eastern parts of England by the Danish invasions which in the end resulted in some reorganization of the dioceses. Isolated Lindisfarne was replaced by Durham, Lindsey seems to have been abandoned and the see of Dorchester-on-Thames was swept away north of the Fenland to the Roman city of Lincoln. The diocese of Sherborne was divided, a bishop being installed at Ramsbury in Wiltshire and later removed to Salisbury, another at Wells in Somerset, and a third at Crediton in Devon, later removed to Exeter.

After the Norman conquest bishops were installed in the churches of the important Fenland abbey of Ely and the priory of Carlisle in the far north-west.

In 1075 the Conqueror decided to enhance the dignity and authority of his bishops by removing some of the sees to fortified places, Selsey being removed to the Roman city of Chichester and Ramsbury to the ancient walled town of what is today called 'Old Sarum' where he built a castle.

Some of the cathedrals remained staffed by secular clergy; others were organized into 'cathedral priories' and the surroundings of the church laid out as in any other monastic house. Some secular cathedrals were provided with cloisters in imitation of the cathedral priories but such cloisters merely served as promenades and led to the cathedral's only appendage, the chapter house where the governing body of the cathedral, known as the chapter, met to discuss the affairs of the diocese.

The secular cathedral is surrounded by an area known as the 'close' which contains the bishop's palace—this of course being much larger than an abbot's house—and lodgings for the canons of the cathedral. At Salisbury the chapter was headed by the 'Four Persons': the Dean of the cathedral, the Precentor who organized the services, the Treasurer who was responsible for the building and the Chancellor who directed education and missionary activities throughout the diocese. Today you may still meet the Four Persons in Salisbury Close.

The affluence of the sees and the unpopularity of some of the bishops—who after all were a part of the crenellated nobility of the Middle Ages—made it desirable for them to surround their closes with walls and gates as at Salisbury or Wells, and by the latter part of the thirteenth century this was being done. Some of these military-looking *enceintes* are most impressive today, and that at Lichfield actually stood siege by the Parliamentary forces during the Civil War.

While one can appreciate the economic necessity for Henry VIII's inauguration of the Reformation in this country by suppressing the obsolete monastic houses, one may wonder what his thoughts may have been as he watched the fabric of the English Church, of which he was now the Head, being converted from a series of some of the most beautiful buildings the world has ever seen into heaps of rubble. Even one of his cathedrals, that of Coventry, a huge building of Anglian type with a towered west front, seems to have been caught up in the riot of destruction which left him at the end with seventeen scattered cathedrals as memorials of a glorious era of church-building.

It seems to have occurred to him to found twenty-one new cathedrals, saving some of the old monastic churches for the purpose. We have a list of these in his own hand and this is interesting as presumably indicating the King's own familiarity with the churches concerned. At the same time it suggests that the King had a somewhat limited knowledge of the topography of his realm.

Reading through his list we are reminded of some of our great lost churches, such as that of Waltham Abbey, revered by Englishmen as the burial place of the last of their Saxon kings. It was to have been saved as a cathedral for Essex, but today only a mighty fragment of it remains.

St. Albans, sharing with Westminster the right to call itself England's premier abbey, was to have become the cathedral for Hertfordshire. It was, however, bought by the town to be their parish church and did not achieve cathedral rank until Victorian times. Only twelve miles away in Bedfordshire the priory church of Dunstable was to have become a cathedral and nineteen miles further on that of Newenham in the town of Bedford was to have been similarly elevated. The uncertainty of the King's navigation is suggested by the fact that he included the great abbey church of Elstow, two miles away, amongst his new cathedrals.

The King must have been travelling about his realm enjoying the hospitality of various monastic houses, observing their churches, but forgetting from time to time in just what part of the country he was staying. Newenham and Elstow were possibly upon itineraries widely separated by time.

The famous priory of Oseney outside Oxford, now vanished without trace, was to become a cathedral—and in fact did, for four years—and the large parish church of Thame fourteen miles away was also selected.

The King's choice of Peterborough abbey church was one of the few eventually confirmed. The abbey church of Westminster enjoyed a short life as a cathedral church.

Leicester Abbey, now vanished, was one of the King's selections which never materialized. Not so, however, the famous abbey church of Gloucester, burial place of King Edward II and therefore probably respected by Henry for the same reason that he preserved Peterborough where his Queen Catherine lay.

The splendid abbey church of Fountains deep in the Yorkshire countryside—the only Cistercian church on the list—was quite understandably envisaged as a cathedral. One may well wonder how it might have appeared today had its seclusion actually been destroyed with the growth around it of a cathedral city.

In Yorkshire, too, the very ordinary parish church in the important town of Richmond was selected to be a cathedral.

One of the world's largest churches, that of St. Edmundsbury, was to have been preserved as a cathedral for Suffolk, and its subsequent destruction was one of the greatest tragedies of the Suppression.

Shrewsbury abbey church, the fine nave of which remains, was to have been made the cathedral for Shropshire.

The great church of Welbeck Abbey, now represented by some fragments of its west front in the cellars of a great Victorian mansion, was to have become a cathedral. Again curiously, the fine church of Worksop Priory, three miles away, was also on the King's list. Southwell was omitted, but close by the church of Thurgarton with its towered west front was selected to be a cathedral; the west end of its nave is still in use as a parish church.

Three cathedrals were to have been established in Cornwall. The big monastic church at Bodmin, still in use as a parish church, was to have been one. At Launceston, a few pathetic fragments of what seems to have been the choir of a fine Augustinian priory church indicate all that is left of another candidate to cathedral status. Thereafter, however, the King's inventiveness gave out and he was forced to add 'with another'.

The net result of Henry VIII's attempted revision of the English diocesan plan was that two abbey churches, those of Peterborough and Gloucester, became cathedrals. Westminster abbey church had a temporary life as a cathedral but Oseney was replaced by Oxford priory church. Another Augustine church, that of Bristol, was made into a cathedral, as was also the Benedictine abbey church of Chester.

So in the end the great churches of Waltham, Dunstable, Elstow, Shrewsbury, Worksop and Thurgarton were reduced to their naves, retained for the use of the parish. Newenham, Oseney, Leicester, St. Edmundsbury and Welbeck joined the other casualties of the Reformation.

While this revisional scheme was in progress the destruction of scores of splendid churches was going on apace. The zeal was of such ferocity that it continued for many years and even after the abbey churches had disappeared the weapons of the reformers were being directed against the cathedrals—monuments, statuary, glass being destroyed without any reason other than some suspicion of their being connected with 'popery'.

The cathedral continued to survive these assaults but during them lost much of its ancient dignity and the respect it had for long enjoyed as a part of English life. And a century after the official Reformation worse disasters were to befall it.

It is strange how today we remember so little of the tragic years of the mid-seventeenth century when Englishmen fought each other under the pathetic banners of King and Parliament, facing each other across English fields, clubbing each other to death. After those battles a half-starved peasantry murdered the wounded and stripped the slain. There was not only a breakdown of government, but a relapse into savagery from that old England in which religion and chivalry had done what they could to maintain a semblance of culture. And upon the medieval cathedrals, relics of that era, the scum of the victorious faction vented their spite. Like tribesmen burning what they don't know how to use they fell upon the venerable buildings and their treasures. They smashed windows and sculpture, broke into and despoiled the tombs of the great, stabled their horses in the sanctuaries and set dogs chasing cats round the aisles of the most glorious buildings in the world.

The destruction was checked by the Restoration, but it was a long time before a growing appreciation of the value of the cathedrals as priceless architectural memorials of England's history began to release them from being regarded merely as archaic relics of a Church no longer respected in the country.

During the cultural revival of the eighteenth century, when they began to be seriously considered as national monuments, great architects of the day were called in to prevent them from falling into ruin. In some cases attempts were being made to 'restore' them into what was believed to have been their original condition. Towards the end of the century serious damage was done to some cathedrals by the architect James Wyatt who has even been dubbed 'the Destroyer' in recognition of his depredations in the course of which towers, chapels and even parts of the buildings themselves fell under the assaults of the pickaxe and tombs were taken up and shuffled away from their proper positions to be arranged as exhibits in a museum. Wyatt's indefatigable enthusiasm seems to have been tempered by little knowledge and sympathy.

During the Victorian era the cathedrals found themselves the centre of that important movement known as the 'Gothic Revival' which was based upon the view that they represented the finest achievements of English architecture and that their architecture should therefore be revived as a national style.

Architects of the greatest repute interested themselves in the maintenance of the cathedrals, carrying out their work conscientiously and only after careful study of whatever period they might be working upon. They also removed ill-considered additions made to the buildings since the Reformation.

At this period the Anglican Church was enjoying considerable popularity and some of the newly consecrated Victorian bishops were able to make use of ancient monastic churches such as those of St. Albans in Hertfordshire, Southwell in Nottinghamshire and Southwark on the south bank of the Thames opposite London which were raised to cathedral rank. The ancient diocese of Ripon, long forgotten, was revived and the bishop enthroned in the magnificent collegiate church which had replaced the ancient cathedral.

Some new cathedrals—Truro, Liverpool, Guildford—were to be built for their new dioceses, while in other cases parish churches were assigned to new bishops for the purpose. Some of these are still being enlarged in the hope of making them appear as great churches which alas they never will be.

For the 'great' church is not at all the same thing as a *large* church. The day of the great church has gone beyond recall and the most skilful architect will never be able to bring it back again.

It is an experience to visit the little cathedral of Brecon. For, without an aisle to its name, it is every inch a cathedral church. And this is not by reason of its obvious antiquity, but because of the dignity of its conception. As soon as one enters it one is conscious of the certainty that this is no architect's commission, but a great church raised by humble men for the glory of God. And it is still filled with the breath of their toil.

The twentieth-century bishop could well be proud to take his seat in the chancel of some splendid English parish church—there will be room enough for him—as his predecessor did thirteen hundred years ago, when no church could be too humble for him.

In the course of his professional career the writer has submitted designs in competition for the new cathedrals at Guildford and Coventry, finding it most difficult to treat the task as an architectural commission in view of the difficulty of appreciating the nature and purpose of a twentieth-century cathedral. It could no longer enshrine a sanctuary from which perpetual prayers would rise. From the truly practical point of view one could only think of it as an assembly hall for the performance of religious music with a throne at one end for a twentieth-century bishop. One could, of course, ignore these problems and simply try to make of it a monument worthy of one of the noblest traditions in architectural history.

A medieval cathedral cannot be brought up to date. As it is, the last fifteen centuries—even the last five—have seen the nature of the cathedral changed: from being a great empty architectural cavern it has become a seated assembly hall.

In trying to appreciate the ancient appearance of the cathedral it is important to remember that there was no furniture—benches, pews or chairs—provided as a permanent part of the equipment of a great church. There were no serried ranks of worshippers as there are today; the congregation gathered round the priest at Mass. It is doubtful whether they ever filled more than a small portion of the nave, for those more distant would never have been able to hear him. Probably at the west end there were people moving about, entering and leaving, talking perhaps. For religion in those times was an everyday affair, not merely a Sunday ceremony.

One of the advantages of the western transept—and later of the main transept itself—was that weddings, baptisms and obsequies could be taking place there, as in Continental churches today, without interfering with a Mass in progress at the nave altar. After the removal of the bishop's choir east of the great transept, the 'walking space' between the transepts with its several altars could be used by the laity, perhaps even after the canons had entered through the door in the choir screen and begun the chanting of their office.

In the England of Holy Church the cathedrals must have seemed more human than they appear today. One can easily imagine their great arcaded halls offering shelter and space for movement of people meeting their friends while barely heeding the distant sounds of worship filtering through from the bishop's church far away beyond the screens.

The writer has often wondered whether the 'Paul's Walk' of seventeenth-century London, when the citizens walked and talked and even shopped in the splendid transept of their cathedral, was such a bad thing after all. For the great building may well have felt glad to be alive!

2

The Ancestry of the Cathedral

The English cathedral has two architectural origins. One of these is a type of building which might be described as native to the British Isles. The other was imported as the country became involved in the history of European architecture. The first is of Roman origin, the second derives from Byzantium. It is in this dichotomy that we can follow the most interesting aspect of English church architecture—the constant rivalry between the two Churches of East and West over the architectural presentations of their respective places of worship.

The earliest churches in this country were founded under the aegis of the Celtic Church, a branch of Christendom which appears to have reached Ireland and Britain by the third century. The Celtic churches followed the plan of the Roman basilica in that they were axially planned. Their rectangular naves, however, usually ended in a small rectangular chancel; the building usually cited as being typical of the plan-form is the church of Escomb in County Durham. This simple plan continued in use in this country throughout the Middle Ages.

Although lacking the broad aisles characteristic of the great churches of Constantine's Rome, the little Celtic churches may be regarded as belonging to the 'basilican' type of plan the basic characteristic of which is an axial disposition aligned upon Jerusalem. This type of church would have continued into Anglo-Saxon England; possibly, under later and more direct influence from Rome, increasing in size and even adding aisles for lateral expansion.

But the cultural influence of Rome was at this time of small account when compared with that of the Byzantine Empire emanating from Constantinople, spreading across Europe to a new imperial capital at Aachen, and crossing the North Sea to this country.

Byzantine architects planned their churches not as rectangular areas set out upon an axis, but as centralized structures engineered to pile up round a tall central feature crowned by a dome. These buildings were thus designed to emphasize the monumental dimension of height and disregarded the Roman requirement of length upon an axis.

In the western parts of the Byzantine world the domed central structure became translated into the form of a tower covered with a steeple roof. It was churches designed upon these lines that were being built in England during the closing centuries of the first millennium. Although more often than not they were examples of timber construction, they were reported upon by contemporary chroniclers as having achieved an architectural style of notable repute. Some of these churches may have been amongst our earliest cathedrals, though possibly these were contemporaneous with the more conventional 'basilican' type of stone-built church.

When we accept the definition that a cathedral church is one which contains the seat of a bishop, and the fact that his *cathedra* could be moved from one place and church to another, we may appreciate that the first English cathedrals might have been no different from a contemporary parish church. In the earliest days this might have been of the Celtic type, with simply a small rectangular nave perhaps twenty feet long and twelve feet wide, and with a small square chancel at its east end. We can be sure, however, that the building would have been of notable height, for even the smallest church would have been endowed with the dignity of height.

When we learn of cathedrals specially built in the early days to serve as bishops' churches, however, we can perhaps expect something in the nature of a miniature version of the early Christian basilica of Rome, the peculiar characteristic of which is the pair of arcades separating the nave from its aisles. Indeed the early builders may have robbed ruined Roman cities for their columns as the

I. ELY

2. NORWICH

architects of Rome did in their own capital. We know from a contemporary description that the first cathedral at Canterbury was
aisled, and the foundations of what is believed to have been an
eighth-century basilica have been unearthed under York Minster.
The late seventh-century cathedral at Ripon is said to have been a
'basilica'. As late as the beginning of the tenth century the cathedral
at Wells was built upon the basilican plan, a fact which seems to
have affected the architecture of its successor.

The nature of this cathedral at Wells is strange for in 878, only a
few miles away at Athelney, Alfred the Great raised a memorial
church to the dead of Ethandune on the site where he had held
out for so long against the Danish army. And his church, said to
have been the first of its kind in the country, was of the 'four-poster'
type as established throughout the Byzantine world and in no way
resembling the basilicas of Rome.

The 'four-poster' is the type of church which has to be followed
in order to understand the history of the English cathedral. We
have lost all the timber examples, but the shells of two have been
discovered and that at Elmham is standing to a considerable height.

Comparison with the later timber churches of Essex and Scan-
dinavia suggests that they were tall structures with high steeples
carried upon posts set upon sleeper foundations and surrounded
by four short projections in the Byzantine manner, the angles being
filled in with miniature aisles covered with lean-to roofs. Originally
the walling would have been made of the off-cuts from the squaring
of the great timbers, as may be seen in the parish church of Greensted in Essex. But where Roman ruins in the vicinity provided a
supply of bricks these may have been used, while in Kent and East
Anglia where field-flints were plentiful these also could be used as
material from which to construct the light screen-walls of the
timber churches.

At South Elmham in Suffolk one can see considerable remains of
the cathedral of the Holy Cross, known today as the 'Old Minster',
to distinguish it from a later church built after the see was moved
thirty miles to the north to what is now North Elmham.

The remains now standing within the rectangular earthwork
consist of the flint outer walls of a timber church the tall posted

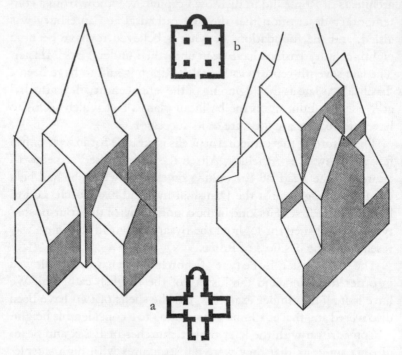

Fig. 1.   *Types of Western Byzantine church*
The central feature is a tower. In (a) its four
walls are pierced by narrow arches leading to the
small 'wings'. (b) shows the sophisticated Byzantine
plan where the tower is carried upon four stone
piers—or, in the case of timber construction, on
four posts—the whole building being in any case
enclosed within a square plan. (b) is the origin of
the cathedral plan. The tower is capped by a timber
spire or 'broach' in place of the dome which
invariably completed the Eastern Byzantine church

interior of which has vanished long ago. The walls enclose two
areas, a rectangular choir to the east and a square nave west of this.
There must have been a timber apse, probably three-sided; flint
walling now forms a large apse which was probably its outer aisle.
The original church was probably entirely of wood; the walling of
flint, which is plentiful in the neighbourhood, may have been a
reconstruction after a Danish fire-raid.

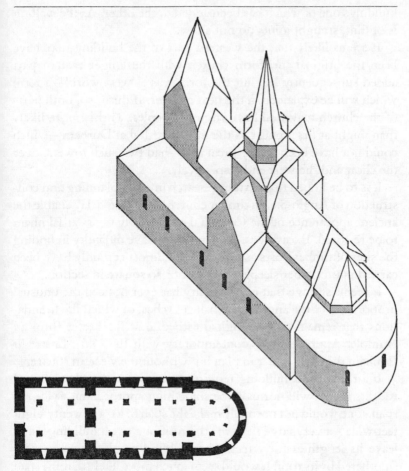

Fig. 2. *Elmham Cathedral*
Only the shell of the building remains, its span of
twenty-seven feet suggesting that it probably had a
main structure supported upon timber posts in the
Anglo-Saxon style. The sketch is a highly conjectural
reconstruction of this. The date of the building is
probably tenth century

An interesting feature of the Old Minster at South Elmham is
the presence of a cross wall. In primitive architecture, partitions are
made with timber screens, never in expensive and obstructive
masonry. Thus the two parts of the Minster are possibly separate

buildings one of which has been added to the other. As the walling is of flint, straight joints do not show.

It seems likely that the western part of the building may have been the original turriform church with the longer eastern part added subsequently leaving the former as a 'west work'—a term which will be explained in the next chapter. If this is so, both parts of the church may well have risen as steeples. This is more likely than might at first appear as the first cathedral at Durham—which could not have been of any great size—had two such towers, over the choir and the west end respectively.

It is to be hoped that further research into the planning and construction of Anglo-Saxon timber churches will some day enable the ancient appearance of the Cathedral of the Holy Cross at Elmham to be restored. Excavators, however, will have difficulty in finding the sites of timber posts as these would almost certainly have been carried upon timber sleepers two feet or so square in section.

It seems strange that no antiquary has ever noticed the unusual proportions of the ancient Kentish churches, of which the foundations that remain of the original cathedral at Rochester form an example. Approximately contemporary with the Old Minster at Elmham they are similar in plan but without the western square.

If a rectangular building requires to be covered with a pitched roof its length will normally be something approaching twice the span. One would not normally make the span of a roof twenty-eight feet wide—a very large span for the roof of a small building—and leave its length at forty feet. The building would be completely smothered by its roof. It would seem much more likely that the span must have been reduced by the provision of some internal structure, now vanished and thus probably constructed of timber, as in a barn.

The appearance of later timber churches suggests that the interior structure would have been a tall tower framed around four great posts and ending in a steeple. But it is of course perfectly arguable that the internal timberwork could have been in the nature of timber arcades so that the building retained the semblance of a 'basilica' with gables at either end. Thus there remains some ammunition to sustain an argument between the Byzantine turriform and Romanesque basilican schools of thought.

Whether or no the Kentish churches, including the first Rochester Cathedral, were planned axially or round a central nucleus, it helps to give some idea of their scale by comparing them in area to a pair of semi-detached council houses.

Anglo-Saxon stone churches were rare enough for them to be called 'white' churches to distinguish them from the normal timber-built structure of darker hue. This may account for the frequent occurrence of the place-name Whitchurch.

The church at North Elmham is of unique character. Only the lower parts of the walls remain but the building may be restored to the form of a Byzantine-type cruciform church having a long transept lying north and south, an apse to the east of this, and tiny square aisles which, in true Byzantine fashion, fill the western angles of the cross. There was probably a timber tower above the centre of the church. The building is of interest as indicating one of the various ways in which the cruciform plan could be presented.

The church was subsequently extended by the addition of a long nave with a square addition at the west end which seems to have been two-storied and may also have been roofed with a timber steeple—another example of a two-towered church. The western extension may have been made at about the time of the Conquest for the see was moved to Thetford in 1070 and to Norwich six years later.

After examining the unique church at North Elmham we can also leave the lost but once far-ranging timber-built architecture of the Anglo-Saxons and consider the development of the stone-built 'four-poster' type of church of which the prototype was that built at Athelney in 878. We shall probably find two basic types, those with a tower having its walls pierced with arches—this we might call the parochial type—and the fully fledged Byzantine church carried upon four massive piers. It is of course quite possible that these features were in fact so massive that the result was no different from the first type.

Both types of church would be surrounded by four wings making it cruciform. There might be small embryo aisles filling in the angles and making the outline of the building approximately square. That there would be an apse on the east side of the church goes without saying.

We have several eulogistic descriptions of tenth-century Anglo-Saxon cathedrals but none is sufficiently analytical and we are left with no clear impression of the architectural form of the building described.

Winchester Cathedral is described as a 'sparkling tower' with 'five compartments' which of course strongly suggests the cruciform plan.

The most notable feature of the first cathedral at Durham seems to have been its two towers, one central and one at the west end, helping to make a strong case for the popularity of the two-towered church at the turn of the millennium. Durham was of course a 'white' church.

Contemporary Latin descriptions of ancient churches are not always easy to follow and it should be remembered that *ala* does not mean an aisle but a projecting wing or transept. Anglo-Saxon churches may not have been built with aisles as we know them so they probably had no technical term to describe them. On the other hand a number of early churches were surrounded by loggias, lean-tos with the outer sides carried by posts. This was a *porticus*, and if the open side was built up with a wall and entered through doors cut in the church wall it became a 'solid portico'. Thus while *porticus* can mean an aisle it should not be confused with an *ala* or wing.

The architecture we have been considering is English vernacular, based upon the Byzantine but only very remotely so and most of it in a material quite unknown to the architects of the Byzantine world. Thus in order to proceed with a serious study of the development of monumental architecture in this country it becomes necessary to delve back into the world of classical antiquity from which all our civilization is sprung.

The great hall did not develop until Imperial Roman times. The climate of Greece made it possible for public assemblies to take place in the open air. Covered assembly halls for greater privacy were, however, eventually erected, the plan being developed from that of a rectangular courtyard surrounded on all sides by covered

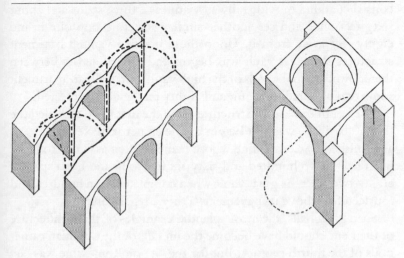

Fig. 3. *Roman and Byzantine construction*
On the left is a diagram of the pair of huge
arched constructions which between them carried
the high vault of the Basilica of Maxentius. In
the Hagia Sophia at Constantinople only the
central bay has been retained, transverse arches
being thrown across from pier to pier to form a
square base upon which to raise the central dome

stoas or porticos, the width of the structure being reduced until it
could be spanned by a timber roof. Such magnificent buildings
were known as *basilicas* or regal apartments. A splendid example
from Roman times is the Basilica of Trajan, eighty-seven feet wide
and surrounded by double stoas. (See Fig. 19.)

For the origins of Christian architecture we must go back to the
beginnings of official Christianity in the last days of Imperial Rome.
This is the period of the great bath-halls of the emperors Caracalla
and Diocletian, seen today as assembly rooms conceived on a
monumental scale and constructed with distinguished engineering
technique.

The intention behind these great apartments was to give them a
width of some eighty feet and span this with a brick ceiling or vault.
Carrying such a heavy and lively load, ordinary walls would have
stood no hope of survival. The principle adopted, therefore, was to

construct a kind of wide railway viaduct of three spans and about sixty feet wide and set another similar structure opposite it and eighty feet away from it. Upon these massive vaulted basement structures the great vault was begun and carried across between them. By filling in the ends of the high vault with walls an apartment some two hundred feet long and eighty feet wide was created.

The last of these great structures, and the first to be accorded the title of 'basilica', was that begun by the emperor Maxentius in 310 and finished by Constantine whose name is often assigned to it. Its main hall is two hundred and sixty-six feet long and has a span of eighty-two feet; the great vault when complete rose a hundred and fourteen feet above its pavement. Truly a regal building!

Such great halls, the most splendid examples of the architecture of their era, should have become the model for the Christian cathedrals of the fourth century. But for the city of Rome time was fast running out while churches were needed quickly, and it was not until the year 532, more than two centuries after the building of the great basilica of Constantine, that the architectural succession was achieved and the cathedral vision reached fulfilment in the great church of the Holy Wisdom, called today St. Sophia, in the new capital of the world.

There was another great building of the past which may not be omitted from the design of the cathedral. Rome, political capital of the Western Church, had fallen to the state of a city of ruins whence all culture had been virtually obliterated. Henceforth all new great architecture would have to be created by Greek architects. And from the ruins of the eternal city there rose an inescapable challenge to the architects of the sixth century . . . the great dome of the Pantheon.

A good deal of research has been pursued into the origins of the Byzantine dome and there is a tendency—surely biassed—amongst art historians to regard it as of oriental origin. The oriental dome, however, as found in Persia and Syria, is a tall structure developed by a primitive people who have become used to piling up stones, or sun-dried brick, into tall bee-hives serving them as huts.

The Byzantine dome is a far more sophisticated structure, derived from the barrel vault and of no great height. Its abutment is

3. PETERBOROUGH

4. NORWICH

achieved by burying its lower portion within a 'drum' and thus its external presentation is generally merely a circular roof of low pitch resting on the drum and concealing the upper curve of the dome beneath. It may probably be regarded as the adjustment of the high vault to suit a circular plan.

When the emperor Hadrian, a hundred and twenty years after the birth of Christ, planned his great temple to all the gods of Olympus, his inspiration may have been that he feared that their ancient hegemony might be already threatened. But it cannot be denied that his architect surpassed himself in their honour, for the vast dome of the Pantheon still spans its hundred and forty feet, the greatest of all the world's roofs.

Much has been written about the systems of converting the upper parts of a square plan into a circular foundation for a dome by means of various devices such as the 'squinch arch' set across the angle and the curved 'pendentive' rising from the angle of the building and worked into a curved upper level. None of these devices, however, show any particularly high degree of inventiveness and the Byzantine pendentive betrays no very great knowledge of solid geometry.

And it was in fact by means of the pendentive that the architects were able to transfer the dome of the Pantheon from its circular base and to set it above the central bay of the Roman bath-hall and thus create a new building—the Christian cathedral.

The great halls of the *thermae* had consisted of three great building bays framed around eight long piers set at right angles to the main span. The plan of the Hagia Sophia retained only the centre four of these piers, joining the opposite pairs with huge arches to frame a central square over a hundred feet across, above which rose the dome that had bade farewell to the gods of Olympus and was now to greet the God of the Christians.

Supporting the central dome of the cathedral were two great apses with their semi-dome roofs, the whole vast hall achieving a length of two hundred and thirty feet. On either side of the central square were transepts seventy feet deep set between the great piers and covered by vast hundred-foot vaults. The transepts were divided into two stories by floors carried upon vaulting rising from columns, a system acting as stiffening to the four great piers carrying the dome.

Nothing like this wonderful building was ever attempted again so that today it represents a breath-taking vision of one of the world's unique architectural achievements.

But the model for the Christian cathedral had been introduced to the architects of Christendom and its main lines thereby established.

It will be noted that the interior of the Hagia Sophia is basically cruciform though this is disguised by the fact of the transepts having been divided into two stories. Were these omitted the cruciform effect would be impressive indeed.

The great dome of the Hagia Sophia was found to be over-ambitious—especially for a country liable to experience earth tremors—and indeed it fell more than once during its early history. Thus the splendid building became at once the crowning example of the Imperial Romans' hall and at the same time the last attempt to perpetuate their splendid architecture.

But the dome as a focal feature of church design had come to stay. Limited in span to about half that of the Hagia Sophia, its base became for general purposes a square of about fifty feet for a large church.

A building has to be designed from the top downwards. Given a dome raised high above the ground, the problem becomes one of how to design supports which will safely carry such a lively load. The solution was found to be a group of four supports which were not piers, as these would be too massive and wasteful of material, but systems of four small piers set in a square and joined by a horizontal stone floor formed by a small vault. This is the tetrapylon, an Imperial Roman device used for monumental purposes as a kind of two-way triumphal arch.

Four such tetrapylons, each of which covered an area of about one quarter of the central square, were set at each of its corners. These formed the complete structural system carrying the dome. Between the tetrapylons wide vaults spanned across the four arms of the cross the ends of which were closed with light walling filled with windows. The width in each direction was something in the nature of a hundred feet.

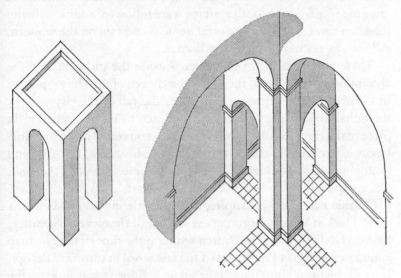

Fig. 4. *The tetrapylon*
Four piers supporting between them a groined
vault form a tetrapylon. At the angles of a
Byzantine church four of these constructions
carried the crossing arches and the dome above

Compared with the Hagia Sophia such a building could hardly
have been considered as of cathedral scale. And there was no way
of enlarging it except by building another unit beside it, in which
case its dome would suffer in dignity by reason of the presence of a
rival.

Since there was no alternative, however, this was the system
adopted, any new addition sharing two of the tetrapylons of the
original. An effort was made to increase the height of the parent
dome by raising its drum.

A single such addition on the western side of the church provided
a kind of nave to the building and gave it an axis. Alternatively the
cruciform principle could be preserved by adding to all four sides
of the original nucleus and perhaps even raising the central dome
sufficiently to enable it to be seen rising above a group of structures
gathered at its feet. (See Fig. 5.)

47

In the great church of St. John at Ephesus built a generation after the Hagia Sophia both systems were followed, additions being made on three sides of the central nucleus and two on the western. All six squares were covered by domes.

These great cruciform churches became the cathedrals of the Byzantine world. First of them was the church of the Holy Apostles in Constantinople begun in 536. After the fall of the city in 1453 the Sultan offered the Patriarch this church to be his cathedral in place of the Hagia Sophia which was to be converted into a mosque. Upon his refusal to accept the exchange, however, the splendid building was pulled down. St. John at Ephesus, finest of them all, was completely destroyed and no longer exists.

Outside the Turkish Empire, however, the five-domed church of St. Mark at Venice, begun at the middle of the eleventh century, has survived. This was the church which at the time of the Norman conquest of England represented the last word in cathedral design. In 1120 the great church of St. Front at Périgueux was built on the same plan.

It was these splendid structures which, notwithstanding their 'Orthodox' origins, were indicating the trend of cathedral design on the Continent during the years immediately preceding the great era of church building in this country.

But throughout 'Latin' Europe what was regarded as a totally unacceptable plan was being strongly opposed by the basilica-minded clergy educated in Rome. The most powerful missionaries of this branch of Christendom were the monks of the Benedictine Order, curiously powerful and energetic products of a Church which must have seemed at the time very poorly equipped to oppose the might of Imperial Byzantium.

In Burgundy the Order had established a monastic house of great wealth and power whose abbot, regarded as a kind of second Pope, may well have possessed more actual authority in Western Europe than the political Head of the Roman Church enthroned amidst the ruins of bygone splendour. It may have been due to this Abbot of Cluny that the Byzantinism of western church architecture became checked.

In 1088 the abbot rebuilt his great church upon a plan which

5. DURHAM

6. DURHAM

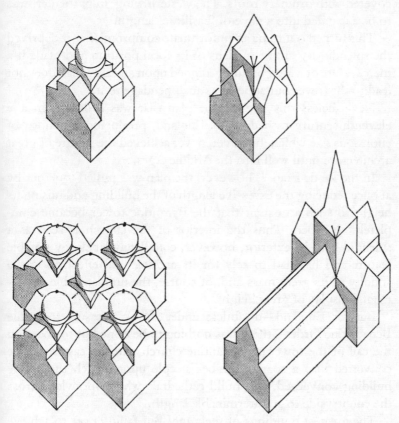

Fig. 5. *The Byzantine cathedral*
Enlargement of the Byzantine church towards
cathedral status was effected by adding similar
domed structures to the sides of an existing
nucleus. Most of these great cruciform
cathedrals have been destroyed by the Turks
but St. Mark's at Venice and St. Front at
Périgueux remain as examples. The Western
Church extended the towered nucleus by
repeating, not the central 'great bay' but a series
of the narrower bays supporting this

made it clear that, although the cruciform plan based upon a central
feature might be retained as the principal element in the elevation
of the building, its surrounding wings were to be extended and

49

covered with ordinary roofs. The western wing, in particular, was to be expanded into a nave of 'basilican' length.

This turned out to be an unfortunate compromise as it deprived the splendid Byzantine nucleus of its focal position and made it a mere feature of a long building aligned upon an axis which does not lead to the tower but appears as an appendage to it.

Nevertheless this became the plan that was followed by the eleventh-century cathedrals of England, producing buildings of enormous size which, however, never achieved the stature of great architecture until well into the Middle Ages.

In the Île de France, however, the plan was pulled together by at once reducing the excessive length of the building and raising its height to such an extent that the Byzantine tower became completely absorbed. Thus the interior of the church is seen as a splendid hall; its exterior, however, completely lacks any notable feature and has had to rely for its architectural effect upon the solidity of its great mass and, of course, the unmistakable monumental display of great height.

But for England—doubtless under strong pressure from the Benedictine Order—there was nothing to be done but to abandon the call of the towering Byzantine church with its eastern dome converted into a soaring timber steeple upon which the whole building converged, and build cathedrals which sprawled across the countryside to an interminable length.

The greatest buildings of their age! But failing ever to achieve really great architecture. Yet in the end the loveliest architecture of all blossomed from them.

Turning towards them, we leave behind us on the fringe of the Dark Ages the tall cathedrals of Anglo-Saxon England. And the tallest among them, perhaps, were those built of English oak.

3

A Realm of Great Churches

It is not always easy to realize that the great churches of England
during the twelfth century were the finest buildings in the world of
their day. Their existence was of course a direct result of the
Norman conquest and virtual sacking of Anglo-Saxon England,
and the granting of scores of English manors to dioceses in order
to augment their endowments and to assist the Conqueror's policy
of creating a powerful episcopal nobility dependent upon him.

The foundation of the huge eleventh-century cathedrals was
thus a political gesture made by the Norman conquerors of Anglo-
Saxon England. But to call the buildings themselves 'Norman' is
to make a political issue of their architecture. They were of course
raised by the Anglo-Saxon builders of this island, skilfully converting their native—and, if contemporary reports may be credited,
very fine—timber architecture into stone. Their contact with the
Continent had been across the North Sea towards the Rhineland—
seat of the Emperors—and not with Normandy. Indeed the latter
very probably could boast of no architectural tradition comparable
with that of this country.

During the eighteenth century the pre-Gothic architecture of
England was quite properly called 'Saxon'. The term was used, it
must be confessed, in a derogatory sense, as one might use 'Doric'
in comparison with Corinthian; it may be for this reason that the
Victorian antiquaries substituted for it what they may have considered a more elegant designation. One, however, most unfair to
our own Anglo-Saxon forebears.

Had the style been indeed Norman, and the English version of it a kind of colonial, we might expect to be able to visit Normandy and find there cathedrals far more splendid than those in our subjugated island. But of course this is very far from being the case.

And this of course is without taking into account our abbey losses after 1539, nor the fact that the greatest of our cathedrals, that of London itself, was completely erased after its destruction by fire in 1666, and that one of the largest, that of Coventry, a large and impressive building with a pair of western towers, was completely removed for no apparent reason after 1539.

So many of the great abbey churches are no longer able to stand beside the surviving cathedrals as evidence of the skill of the eleventh-century English builder. Gone are the great churches of the Thames valley—Barking, Chertsey, Reading, Abingdon—as though they had never been. Utterly vanished is the splendid church of Evesham and that other at Lewes which represented the power of the Abbot of Cluny. Of the mightiest of them all only a shapeless fragment recalls today that great church of all Englishmen at St. Edmundsbury, shrine of our royal saint.

Each of these great structures was designed as a complete entity and built from end to end as a single project, its main lines having been worked out before it was begun. Although novel in design, these can be fairly easily recognized as representing a straightforward development from Western Byzantine ecclesiastical architecture.

The general principle of Byzantine church construction was what might be called 'four-poster' after the four sturdy piers—or, in very small churches, pseudo-Classical columns—fixing the angles of the central square and carrying the dome covering this which in the West is replaced by a timber steeple. From the central square four tall arches led into the four arms of the cross.

From the metrological aspect the basic area comprised a central square having sides of two units' length surrounded by four areas each two units wide and one deep.

For structural reasons the angles between the arms of the Byzantine church were filled in with small square two-storied units of the nature of embryo aisles which converted the ground plan of the building into a square having sides four units long.

The important feature to notice is the small angle unit, for it is from these that the architecture of the great English church develops. It will be noted that these units had small galleries on an upper floor carried by the characteristic Byzantine vaulting, the whole serving as stiffening to the four great piers.

In the original Byzantine structural system they had also supported the high vaults of the four arms of the cross which in the West were covered with far lighter timber roofs. In both types of building the terminal walls of these wings were designed as comparatively light screen walls carrying no load and pierced with windows for light.

It is the fact that these walls were not load-bearing that made it possible to remove them at will, extend the arm of the cross the interior of which they had been protecting, continuing with similar extensions or stopping and erecting another blocking wall.

In this way developed first the multi-domed cathedrals of Byzantium and Western Europe, and thereafter the huge sprawling cathedrals of England (See Fig. 5.)

It is really not difficult to visualize the development of the great hall of the Roman *thermae* into the great church of the Christians —much more so to imagine the basilicas of Constantine developing at all. Indeed, so far from playing a part—other than a troublesome one—in the development of architecture, the basilicas were an example of what really amounted to the abandoning of a splendid architectural tradition which, had it not been for the picking up of the torch by the Greeks of Byzantium, might well have brought the history of western monumental architecture to a complete standstill.

For although it was done for the best of reasons, the founding of the early Christian basilicas in Rome forms a perfect example of how architectural history can break down through the introduction of some innovation hastily conceived, lacking any traditional basis upon which it could be developed, and thus incapable of creating any building of architectural importance surviving as an architectural style or indicating any likelihood of developing into one.

Thus the 'basilican' buildings cannot be regarded as continuing the architecture of Imperial Rome with its great tradition handed down from Hellenistic days. Yet it is most pleasant to discover that the new religion was actually producing several small but lovely buildings representing a very high degree of architectural excellence.

In addition to his large basilicas for congregational worship, Constantine built a series of memorial churches, the so-called 'martyria', raised over the holy sites of Nazareth, Bethlehem, and Jerusalem. Each was in the form of a dome, rising above a lower story, circular or octagonal on plan, projecting round its base, the dome itself being carried upon a ring of columns.

It will be seen that these little buildings were in fact aisled about, and that their aisles were of a different type from those of the basilicas in that these were roofed with timber rafters whereas the martyria were covered with domes and aisles permanently vaulted over, making them monumental structures of a true architectural character.

We like to employ the term 'aisled construction', but may fail to differentiate between the aisle arcade of a basilica which resembles that of a timber barn, and the aisle of the medieval cathedral which is a far more sophisticated piece of construction, in no way resembling the primitive device of enlarging a covered area by introducing rows of intermediate supports.

Constantine's martyria were founded upon a combination of two elements of architecture, the colonnade and the stone or brick vault. The first of these had long been a well-known architectural feature but it had never before been made to carry a wall over it and now it had in addition to this to carry a dome as well. The vault had also been in use for some time, as a longitudinal extension of the arch to carry an upper floor or, in the noblest of buildings, to act as a roof. Here it was being used for yet another purpose.

In the last chapter we explained the form of construction exhibited by the great basilica of Maxentius at Rome by likening its two flanks to railway viaducts facing each other and joined by a high vault. The 'viaducts', systems of arcades rising from buttress-like piers joined by vaults, formed the basic foundations—the 'basements'—from which sprang the high vault. We can see the same system developed, on a far smaller scale, in the little 'martyria' chapels built by Constantine.

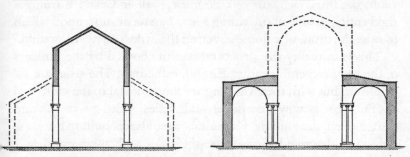

Fig. 6. *'Loggia' construction*
An aisled construction is shown on the left
in which the main building is first erected and
its aisles added after. In 'loggia' construction a
basement story is first built and an upper stage
raised upon this foundation. This was the
technique employed by Constantine in the
construction of his circular 'martyria', the
simpler aisled construction being used for
the hastily erected 'basilicas'

It is easy to see how the idea came about. A wall, carrying a roof,
is a fundamental form of construction. But a wall carried upon
independent supports, whether these be columns spanned by
lintels or piers carrying arches, is not by itself a normal architectural
feature. In those days buildings did not stand, as today, upon bare
legs!

The only situation in which such a wall might have been used
would have been in connection with the open side of a structure
such as a loggia or portico having a solid back to it. In which case
the colonnade or arcade might well have been secured to the solid
wall by means of a horizontal tie of masonry—in other words, a
vault. The engineers of Imperial Rome would have no difficulty in
meeting the thrust of the arch of the vault by 'loading' its abutments.

In the fourth century, however, to build a circular enclosure of
columns, raise a wall upon them, and cover the whole with a dome,
would have represented an architectural experiment lacking any
precedent. What the builders in fact did was to construct in effect
a circular colonnaded courtyard of small diameter, surround this
with a loggia having a solid rear wall, and cover this with a barrel

vault, the three elements of colonnade, wall and vault forming a rigid entity capable of providing a firm basement story upon which to raise the drum of a dome covering the little 'courtyard' within.

This is in reality the structural system adopted by the builders of the great eleventh-century English cathedrals. The aisles are *not* additions, but with their vaulting are fundamental to the structural design. That is why one never finds aisles added to an existing church of any magnitude. Cathedrals were always built in the same fashion as described above: first the aisles with their vaulting— never omitted—and upon this basement the main walls and the roofs.

Short arms such as the early east ends and transepts are built without aisles but as the walling becomes lengthened aisled construction is employed.

The vaulted aisles of the 'martyria' were of the barrel or tunnel variety passing round the building. But as the normal rectangular building had arches along one side it was found far more convenient to use cross vaults conforming with the arches and springing from the same level as these. These vaults met the main vault at diagonal lines called 'groins' from which this kind of cross vault is known as a 'groined vault'.

The visitor standing under one of the tall lanterns around which our cathedrals are built will be impressed by the way in which the tower seems to be carried upon very tall and slender piers. But they are not in fact as high as they appear for each is so well tied in by the gallery vaulting and the clearstory walling that only the lower twenty feet or so next the main arcade and a corresponding length, probably somewhat shorter, next that of the gallery, are actually isolated pier. The real strength of the crossing pier lies in the fact that with the bay of the aisle next to it the pier is in reality part of a tetrapylon having three arches and a length of external walling joined by the gallery vault.

Here we see the link with Byzantine construction, seeing it also extended, by the repetition of the two-storied bay, to give us the long nave of the eleventh-century cathedral.

We may see the same principle employed throughout the Gothic era, until the introduction of the 'hall' type of church in which nave

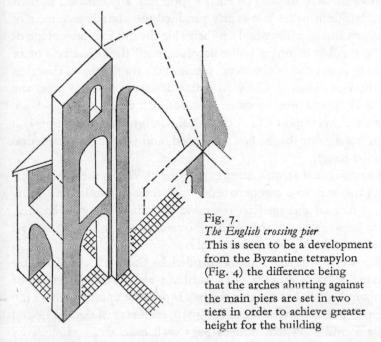

Fig. 7.
The English crossing pier
This is seen to be a development
from the Byzantine tetrapylon
(Fig. 4) the difference being
that the arches abutting against
the main piers are set in two
tiers in order to achieve greater
height for the building

and aisles are of the same height and both gallery and clearstory
have disappeared. An early example of this kind of church may be
seen at Bristol Cathedral where the choir was rebuilt on the 'hall'
principle at the very end of the thirteenth century.

To recapitulate, the vaulting of cathedral aisles was not introduced as a ceiling to them, nor even to provide 'nunneries' above
them, but simply as an abutment device to assist with the support
of what after all was a very lofty and much cut-about nave wall.
The Byzantine tetrapylon has been transformed into a single
massive pier adjoining the crossing, a lesser one on the nave side,
and two joined by a length of wall to form the fourth side. Each
bay of the nave has also become a kind of tetrapylon, part of a
'loggia' having two piers and a length of wall. In each case the
system depends upon the horizontal stone tie provided by the
vaulting.

In a later chapter we shall discuss the long 'basilicas' of Constantine's Rome and how the appearance of these buildings

developed what might be called a 'political' significance, as their long basilican naves constantly prodded the church architects of Western Europe. They had on their side the obvious advantage of being capable of unlimited expansion, until the priest be out of hearing at the end of the nave, whereas the monumental churches of the Byzantines, initially probably less commodious than the basilicas, could not be expanded without destroying the basic aesthetic effect upon which the whole design of the building had been based. But this in fact happened, and the English cathedral was the result.

Consider that tenth-century cathedral at Winchester, the cruciform tower in five compartments with their pointed roofs. How could that be enlarged to resemble an axially planned basilica, without taking away the piled silhouette of the 'gleaming tower' which was St. Alphege's cathedral?

But westwards the church expanded, by that principle of adding tetrapylon to tetrapylon, or, speaking elevationally instead of structurally, bay to bay. For the bay is the unit upon which all the great English churches were designed, each arm of the developed cross forming a succession of bays each exactly the same as its neighbour. The size of each arm could be simply stated by giving the number of its bays.

Indeed, bearing in mind that by the end of the eleventh century the elevation of the bay had practically become standardized, one can imagine that any bishop ordering the construction of a new cathedral could very well do so 'by the bay'. In the same way it might have been possible to arrive at an approximate estimate of cost.

Most books on cathedrals supply plans, but plans by themselves are misleading drawings and cannot give a true picture of the building which stands upon them unless the reader has a sound knowledge of the bay design rising in each. For the purpose of examining accommodation, however, plans give a satisfying appreciation.

Attempting an analysis of eleventh-century cathedral accommodation and taking the transepts first, we find that they are likely to be two or four bays in length. The even number would have been

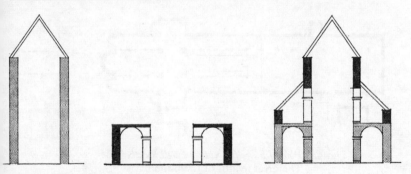

Fig. 8. *Section across English cathedral*
The aim of the cathedral builders was to achieve the
monumental dimension of height, eighty feet being the
normal target. As span was limited to the length of timbers
available, the structure by itself would have been very tall
and narrow. But by building a strong basement stage,
vaulted over in 'loggia' fashion, the upper part of the   p 55
building could be raised upon this with greater confidence

most convenient should the designers have had any idea of introducing the 'duplex' bay which has to allow for 'great' bays as well
as those of normal width. In cathedrals of primitive design with
aisle-less transepts, however—such as those of St. Albans or
Chichester—the transepts may be three bays in length.

The problem of supporting the high walling had to be considered, and at Winchester the end walls as well as those on the
east and west were assisted by galleried aisles. The long transepts at
Peterborough had eastern aisles—doubtless to accommodate altars
—but the west walls were left to stand on their own, for transept
walls, which were short, solid and not carried upon arches, provided
easier structural problems than those of the nave.

Following the basically pyramidal composition of the Byzantine
church, the eastern arm of the building usually equalled in length
that of the transept. It was, however, generally aisled and of course
invariably ended in a tall apse. The ends of the aisles would have
contained side altars and in conformity with universal custom
either had small apses contrived in their eastern walls or projecting
externally in what is inaptly called by antiquaries the 'parallel-apsed'

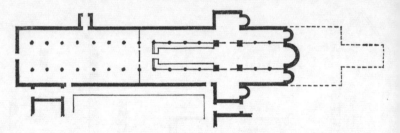

Fig. 9. *Plan of a twelfth-century English cathedral*
The great length of the building is illustrated.
The bishop's choir is seen west of the crossing
and its subsequent position further east suggested
by the indication of an extended eastern arm
provided, perhaps, during the next century.
To the south of the nave is seen the cloister of
a possible cathedral priory

plan—in a system of nomenclature which considers a plan as a two-dimensional design instead of the trace of a three-dimensional building. The extension of the aisles round the back of the apse to form the Continental type of east end—the *chevet*—will be discussed later.

The western arm of the cross would basically have been little more than a bay or so longer than the transept. In it would have been three or four bays to accommodate the bishop's choir, with a bay west of this forming the narthex or retro-choir giving access to the choir doorway at its western end, and introducing at the west end of the church an ambulatory joining the aisles in the same fashion as that sometimes provided at the east end behind the high altar.

Thus we have, basically, a bishop's church designed as a cruciform structure with four projecting arms varying from two to five bays in length and fairly equally balanced about a central lantern tower with its tall steeple.

Two features were, however, missing from this plan. One was what might be called political—the long nave of the Roman basilica. The other, more practical, was accommodation for a lay congregation. It was these two influences which resulted in the extension of the bishop's church many bays to the west and pro-

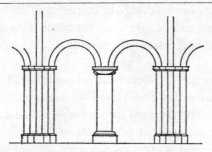

Fig. 10.   *Duplex bay design*
The 'great' bay, equal to the span
of the building and recalling its
domed origin, is indicated by sturdy
piers while between these lighter
pillars punctuate the normal bay
design

duced the extravagantly long cathedrals of eleventh-century
England.

It is of course the great naves of these churches which make
them unique in architectural history as well as placing them among
the largest churches in the world. They may be fourteen bays long.
The number is usually an even one for the reason that at the back
of the mind of the eleventh-century designer was always the memory of the square 'great bay' twice the width of the normal bay
employed for the nave walls. One constantly finds this being re-
called elevationally by the alternating of the supports of the arcade
between square and circular in the style of the 'duplex bay' design
of which the most spectacular example in this country is that in the
great cathedral at Durham. (See Fig. 10.)

Leaving the plan and turning to the elevational treatment of the
eleventh-century cathedral, one is hard put to it to discover any
appreciation of elevational design. Indeed there was little opportunity for indulging in this. The basic design of the Byzantine
church had been aimed at a pyramidal *mass*, a three-dimensional
exercise which took no account of the elevations of walling. For the
architects of eleventh-century England this creation of an architectural *pile* could no longer be attempted—the mass of the building
was now just an untidy sprawl.

Nor could elevational design be considered, for building by bays limits the design to a single unit, repeated without any hope of considering the succession of these or adding up to a designed elevation.

But although the architects had to submit to building 'by the bay' they saw to it that their lateral elevations did not appear to have been 'cut off by the yard'. Thus they appreciated the necessity for some kind of terminal punctuation—something more often than not ignored today in 'contemporary' architecture—and never left a building looking as though it had been stopped suddenly. The end of the elevation was at first thickened out by means of a 'clasping pilaster' and later by a pair of 'buttresses' which served no structural purpose but made a decent end to the run of the bays.

Where an opportunity existed for elevational treatment, such as at gable ends, the early architects were unable to get away from the bay unit and as a result designed transept ends, as at Winchester, with a centre pilaster and a pair of windows in each story, a treatment totally at variance with the rules of design but curiously attractive owing to its chance resemblance to the human face. By the beginning of the twelfth century, however, the elementary principle of centering windows upon vertical axes had been discovered and the transept ends were designed in two bays as at Norwich and Peterborough. The clumsy bulge of the apse prevented any architectural treatment being devised for the east end of the cathedral.

One of the results of designing by bays was to leave the west end of the cathedral nave an ugly shape merely representing a section through it. Nothing could have been done with such a silhouette, for any façade should have an outline that is reasonably rectangular. Of necessity the west end of the cathedral had to be regarded as an important elevation. It contained the principal entrance doorway and faced the cathedral forecourt—the parvis or Paradise. To have left the 'sawn-off' end of a cathedral nave framing such an important entrance and rising behind the forecourt of an episcopal church would have seemed unworthy of the eleventh-century architect. Except, perhaps, at Worcester where the west end of the cathedral rises above a steep river-slope.

It was necessary to regard the entrance front of the cathedral not as the *end* of a building but as an introduction to it. While the gable-end by itself might have been tolerated, the lateral portions with the aisle roofs falling away from the centre were aesthetically weak and needed something to steady them, such as the turrets flanking the west front of Rochester.

But a better solution suggested itself, possibly as a result of the enlargement of a previous church. Cathedrals were usually incapable of being extended westwards owing to the presence of the public forecourt there; and so an early turriform church would have been extended towards the east, the old building being left standing at the end of the nave, perhaps to retain its tower as a campanile. The early church probable had some kind of short transept and if everything to the east of this should be pulled down the tower and transepts would be left standing against the new west wall of the long nave, forming to this what the Germans call a 'west work'. If everything to the west of the old tower was pulled down and the walling there blocked up, the result would be a west transept to the new nave, which might or might not retain the central tower of the earlier church. (Fig. 11a.)

Be this as it may, the larger twelfth-century cathedrals were usually provided with a west transept, a cross arm which presented a rectangular front to the parvis and could be embellished to provide a splendid back-cloth towering above the entrance doorways at its foot. The façade was always completed at each end by terminal features in the form of square turrets containing staircases; in the centre the gable of the nave might be allowed to appear.

Most of the early cathedrals retain considerable remains of their west fronts, though a number have been transformed by the erection of towers above their transepts as at Chichester, Durham and Lincoln. Only at Lincoln do the gables with their elaborate arcaded decoration remain. (Plates 6 and 19.)

The treatment of the façade itself seems in some cases to have been based upon a repetition of the interior section of the church behind, with a copy of the crossing arch flanked by a pair of narrow arches the heights of which seem to represent those above the galleries. This feature is in fact much the same as the section

63

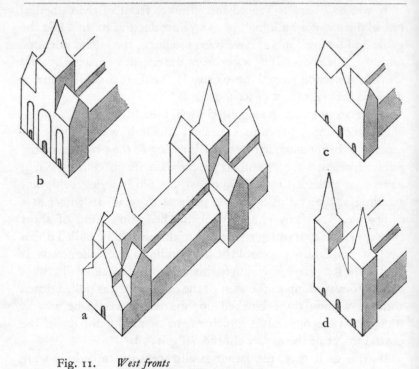

Fig. 11.   *West fronts*
(a) shows an early cathedral
extended eastwards from a simple
square structure which has been
left as a 'west work' with its
tower carrying the bells. In (b) the
western portion of the 'west
work' has been removed, leaving
the tower and retaining on the
exposed walling traces of the lofty
arches which once led to the
destroyed portion. In (c) the tower
has been removed and the roofs
of nave and wings extended over
its site to create a west transept
with a rectangular west wall
capable of being treated
architecturally to provide a west
front. In (d) the wings of the
transept have been raised to form
a pair of small towers

7. ELY

8. ST. ALBANS

through a Byzantine church and suggests the possibility that it may have originated from the retention of the east wall of an earlier church to be the west wall of the successor. Such a group of tall arches may be clearly seen at Lincoln and in ghostly form at Durham. (Fig. 11b.)

Another reason for suggesting the occasional retention of an earlier church after an eastward extension is the presence of west towers to some cathedrals. That at Ely is today the only survivor, but one existed at Winchester and it had clearly been intended to build one at Norwich had not the lantern tower been raised instead to provide a belfry. (Plate 2.)

The west front at Ely—now shorn of its northern third—was once one of the finest frontispieces in the world of its day and no longer has a rival, though at St. Edmundsbury the tower with its transepts covered a spread of nearly two hundred and fifty feet.

Such transeptal west fronts as those at Chichester, Durham and Lincoln were probably considered adequate as frontispieces to those churches lacking the funds from which to build a west tower. The problem of a bell-tower remained, however, and the west end of the church had become the traditional site for this. Hence the eventual raising of the ends of the west transept into a pair of towers which could be built at far less cost than that of a single much larger tower rising from the ground.

The large west transepts of Lincoln had to be considerably re-planned internally to enable towers to be built—in a somewhat insecure fashion which has been a source of worry to the cathedral architects ever since—and the original west front had to be extended to form a wide and tall screen masking the muddle behind.

The towers at Lincoln and Durham are clearly additions to the tops of western transepts. At Southwell, however, they seem to be all one build with the façade and to have been intended from the start to form part of it. The windows in the front below the towers are small and tower-like instead of the more normal ones seen in other early west fronts.

As the twelfth century progressed, the affluent and enterprising Augustinian Order of canons regularly adopted and developed the twin-towered west front and it is to be found in a number of their churches.

Concerned as the architects were primarily with securing the stability of their huge buildings so unlike anything else in existence, and lacking all but the most elementary experience in elevational design, the frontispieces they did in fact produce must surely have exhausted their inventiveness in the field of exterior presentation.

With the interiors of their churches, however, it was a different story. The complications inseparable from the structural design, and the numerous and varied features it required, gave the architects plenty of scope in the creation of, if not elevational, at least scenic effect.

Their interiors were undoubtedly designed to impress. As we ourselves gaze at the two-tiered vistas of fine arcades reaching away into the distance we can be sure that they must have made a tremendous impact upon an Anglo-Saxon congregation. (Plate 3.)

These interiors might have been more impressive had the arcades been in one tier—though the attempt to achieve this at Gloucester was far from satisfactory—but the double row introduced purely in order to reduce the heights of the piers, make them more stable and keep the gallery floors at a reasonable height above the pavement has produced a splendidly scenic effect.

It would seem probable that the galleries provided round our eleventh-century cathedrals never played any part in the accommodation of congregations. Nevertheless they were lit by large windows—at Peterborough, Ely and Lincoln for example—playing their part in the lighting of the cathedral, and were readily accessible by means of stairs contrived in the thickened-out angles of the building. The galleries of Westminster Abbey are used at coronations.

During the eighteenth century it was the belief that galleries were intended to be reserved for women. Hence their Georgian designation of 'nunneries'. Tickets for Georgian coronations may be seen marked 'nunneries'. It was the misreading by a Victorian antiquary of a description of the great fire at Canterbury Cathedral which caused them to be called 'triforium', which is, of course, the arcade in the story above with its triple openings giving light from the clearstory windows. The galleries seem never to have been provided with balustrades unless these were removable rails of timber. But the original cavernous arches of the galleries were to become reduced in size with more stonework to hold on to.

Some of the early gallery fronts are impressive by virtue of the simplicity of their great hollow arches, such as those at St. Albans, Norwich and Southwell where the main arcade is carried upon squat circular pillars and that of the gallery on even shorter compound piers.

In some cathedrals, however, the Byzantine practice was adopted of dividing the single arch by a slender colonette with base and cap and converting the gallery bay into a two-light opening or *bifora*— a term which is still in use by Italian architects. This is found at Ely, Chichester and Durham and, from the twelfth century, at Peterborough. It is still found at Ripon from the middle of the century but here the main arch has been reduced in width and is flanked by a pair of blind arches in a carefully considered composition.

The strange experiment at Gloucester had resulted in the gallery being reduced to the height of the roof space above the aisle vaulting; and its internal presentation being in consequence very much reduced in importance, the treatment adopted was to set in each bay a pair of biforas of the normal scale of belfry windows. This was the ordinance adopted a century later during the rebulding of Lincoln Cathedral and thereafter followed as standard practice throughout the thirteenth century. Transformed by the use of moulded pointed arches springing from dwarf clustered columns, the gallery arcade became the most charming feature of the cathedral's interior. (Plate 22.)

A feature of the Roman basilican church was the great width of its aisles which carried its side walls so far away from the centre of the church that the windows in them were hard put to it to light the centre of the building. Hence the raising of the main walls above the roofs of the aisles to create a lighting story, the clearstory, above the blind story passing between it and the main arcade.

In the Byzantine churches the place of what might have been a clearstory was taken up by the rise of the high vault. In any case their square plans were adequately lit by windows in the ends of their short arms. But with the lengthening of these arms by the eleventh-century English architects the sources of light became too remote and clearstories had to be introduced above the lean-to roofs of the galleries. Thus the old two-storied Byzantine wall had become three-storied. (Fig. 7.)

Externally the clearstory was merely a tier of windows, one to each bay. But although the outside of these windows could easily be cleaned from ladders raised upon the aisle roofs, the inside was seventy feet or so above the paving. A narrow cleaning passage was therefore contrived in the thickness of the clearstory walling and reached by spiral stairs set in the ends of the building.

In order to allow as much light as possible to pass from the window into the church the inner side of the passage was carried across each window in the form of a miniature arcade. At Winchester this arcade was broken opposite the window by leaving out a colonette there, thus widening the arch which was then raised to match the height of the window.

The combination of the large central opening with its two smaller neighbours—what Italian architects call a *trifora*—became a standard feature of the bay ordinance of the English cathedral of the eleventh and twelfth centuries. The range of these features lighting the passage which runs above the gallery arcade is of course the 'triforium' which today has been wrongly applied to the gallery itself. (Plate 3.)

Thus the vertical ordinance of the tall English nave had become established, continuing unchanged throughout the twelfth century and only modified during the era of the thirteenth-century Gothic by the reduction in scale of the gallery arcade and the greatly enhanced splendour of its architectural embellishment.

It is now possible to appreciate something of the thought which went into the design of the splendid Anglian cathedrals of the eleventh century—Ely, Norwich—and the abbey church which was to follow them at the beginning of the twelfth century . . . Peterborough the Proud. (Plates 3 and 20.)

It was not possible for this abbey church to be 'plucked down' with its brethren as the ill-used Queen Catherine had been buried within its walls. So the King permitted her to rest in peace in 'one of the goodliest monuments in Christendom'—his own comment which seems to suggest that he was not entirely without respect for the glorious buildings he was destroying.

The dignity of the nave of Peterborough, with its contemporary neighbours of Norwich and Ely, is as superlative as any of the most glorious creations of the Gothic. It was designed complete in every detail and erected without change of design, so that the perfection of the original conception is evident in the result. The transept elevations, internal and external, appear to be resting confident that they once represented the best traditions of contemporary architecture.

The medieval poet who described the great Fenland abbey as 'Peterborough the Proud' may well have been thinking of its tremendous west front, unequalled in Gothic architecture. How this design developed can only be a subject for conjecture, but it seems clear from the layout of the foundations that the church was intended to have a large west transept, probably with a western tower similar to that of Ely and as at one time hoped for at Norwich. The other element in the design is that of the triplet of recessed arched openings as seen at Lincoln. But the feature has been recessed still further to form a monumental portico and the side arches widened to absorb the whole of the ends of the transept, the ornamental gable ends which probably crowned the Lincoln front being adjusted to suit the widths of the openings below.

At Lincoln the builders had raised their west towers in desperate fashion above a transept with ends too wide for them. At Peterborough the transept was reduced in width by the portico and towers, designed—though only one was actually built—to be erected above the last bay of the nave, a great bay reduced by the portico to a normal one. A unique monument to the genius of some unknown thirteenth-century architect who had however departed too far from the architectural ordinance of his era for his splendid creation to find any imitators. For while some slight deviation can be, if approved, developed still further, all one can do with such a unique creation is to copy it, if not exactly, to a degree which leaves no doubt as to the plagiarism.

The interior of the cathedral nave presents the usual vision of immense dignity one expects from the Anglian churches of the eleventh century—though this in fact was not begun until after the century's turn. It is a most perfect church, with its long transepts provided with eastern aisles and an equally long eastern arm ending in a great apse. This last was pierced through in the fifteenth century to give access to an eastern transept passing across the east wall and allowing for a range of five altars ranged along its own east wall, the transept being two bays in width to allow for an ambulatory giving access to these.

This eastern addition is low in elevation and vaulted at aisle level with a splendid fan vault. Although built so late in the Gothic era it has a notable daintiness and is flooded with light from large windows.

As the eastern arm has always extended to a length adequate for dignity it was never rebuilt, and so the cathedral has retained its original appearance, with the choir still at the eastern end of the great nave.

When we look from a distance at a great cathedral such as Peterborough it can seem strange to us to consider that the huge structure was actually built for the purpose of containing a relatively small apartment, set in the heart of a forest of massive piers—the bishop's choir.

We have been brought up for so long on the theory that church architecture was founded upon the Roman basilica and—which is a very strange idea—that the English parish church with its nave and chancel is a direct descendant of this form, that it is difficult for the student of today to adjust his attitude towards the true derivation.

In particular it is important to appreciate that the eastern arm of the 'great' church bears no relationship whatsoever to the chancel of the parish church. We shall comment in a later chapter on the way in which the smallest cathedral can be distinguished as such from the largest and most imposing parish church by examining the relationship between their respective naves and 'chancels'. The difference of course increases with the progress of the Middle Ages and the buildings of the great eastern extensions of the thirteenth century.

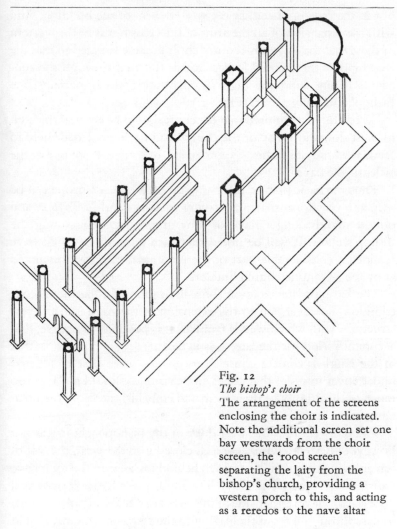

Fig. 12
The bishop's choir
The arrangement of the screens
enclosing the choir is indicated.
Note the additional screen set one
bay westwards from the choir
screen, the 'rood screen'
separating the laity from the
bishop's church, providing a
western porch to this, and acting
as a reredos to the nave altar

Returning to the Byzantine original, the crossing of the four
arms of the cross under the lantern tower is a central feature, not an
intermediate one. The whole church revolves around it.

To have set the worshippers in the eastern arm of the cross would
have forced them to turn their backs upon the central area with its
tall lantern—the principal architectural feature of the interior of
the church. Thus the episcopal choir must always have been set, if

not in the crossing itself, in the western arm of the building. And with the expansion of all the arms of the cross it was in the western of these that the eleventh-century choir became situated so that the worshippers there could look towards the altar through the sunbeams falling from the high lantern under which, perhaps, the bishop's throne was set. (Fig. 12.)

As ceremonial required that the choir should be entered through its west doorway a bay of the church had to be provided there to serve as a kind of narthex—approached, of course, from one of the aisles of the nave.

Thus the basic plan of the cathedral of Western Europe can be seen as a cruciform structure having transepts and presbytery and only a slightly longer nave of four or five bays containing the bishop's choir. It will be noted that such a building would have retained a considerable part of the pyramidal composition aimed at by the Byzantine church builders.

The Latin insistence upon some indication of a 'basilican' contribution, however, led to the extension of the nave into the vast structures with which we are familiar. It is possible, of course, that accommodation for the laity was in fact needed, and probable that in the English climate church processions were best conducted under cover in order that copes and chasubles should not lose too much of the dignity of their form and embellishment. So the great naves were built.

The retro-choir at the west door of the bishop's choir was not however interfered with. A screen closed it to the west, the 'rood-screen' which formed the reredos behind the altar in the long nave which was assigned to the laity. The rood-screen had in it two small doorways, one on either side of the nave altar, allowing processions to pass through it from the nave into the retro-choir. Only that at St. Albans remains today. (Plate 9.)

It will be appreciated that the plan of the eleventh-century cathedral was the result of fortuitous development rather than an initial calculation. Architecturally the result was a muddle, with the vast nave, clumsily cut into two, and the ritually important eastern arm a mere appendage to it. It is not surprising therefore to find that during the thirteenth century the cathedral plan was to develop along the lines of rectifying both these faults by shifting the bishop's choir east of the crossing, which at once freed the whole of the nave and provided an excuse for developing architecturally the eastern arm of the cathedral. This of course had the result of finally destroying the Byzantine dignity of the central feature which, with the cathedral divided into separate churches, was reduced to the status of a feature linking them together.

Excessive concern for the pattern created by the ground plan which led antiquaries to describe the eastern termination of the eleventh-century cathedral as being 'parallel-apsed' has created quite a false impression of the east end as it actually appeared. It is only the great apse which could have counted for anything in the view of the cathedral. We can see it at Peterborough, towering over a later building and with its windows enlarged, but still a great apse. It is not difficult to imagine it as it was when it rose direct from the ground. All great churches would have ended in this fashion except when the apse became surrounded at its base by an aisle to form a *chevet*.

Any other apses, including those at the ends of the aisles, would have had to be roofed no higher than the roofs of these and would quite likely have been mere apsidioles a third or so of the height of the great apse. This fact, and their small area, would have made them of minor value in the view. Only in the lofty Eastern Byzantine churches does one find three apses of equal height at the east end of a church.

Later fenestration apart, the interiors of the eastern arms of Peterborough and Norwich both provide an excellent impression of the eleventh-century cathedral at its most splendid. Both have the full four-bay eastern arm. Norwich has the *chevet* in addition. As these were such splendid structures they were never swept away and enlarged during the thirteenth century as were the two-bay eastern arms of many of the great eleventh-century churches.

The eastern arms of some of these cathedrals were raised on vaulted basements or crypts. The significance of these has never been explained. Attempts have been made to link them with the practice of setting the altars of churches above the tombs of martyrs and other revered persons. That this may be done can be confirmed by the writer who remembers inspecting a medieval church in Malta destroyed by bombing and finding under the site of its altar a rock-hewn sepulchre. This does not, however, seem to equate with the practice of building the whole of the eastern arm of a cathedral above a basement.

It was the practice of the Byzantines to live upon an upper floor—a *piano nobile*—unlike the Romans who were satisfied with their bungalow villas. In parenthesis it might be noted that to the present day the average Englishman objects to sleeping on the ground floor, considering it a civilized practice to go upstairs to bed.

In the Byzantine countries only animals lived on the ground floor, the living-quarters being always raised above ground level. In medieval England also, a ground floor was nothing more than the ground itself. The dormitories of a monastic house were without exception upon the upper floor, as was the bishop's chamber. It is possible, therefore, that a 'stone soller' was considered appropriate to the sanctuary of the cathedral.

Of the eleventh-century crypts remaining we have those at Canterbury, Winchester, Worcester, and the abbey church of Gloucester—the crypt is rare outside cathedral churches—elevated to cathedral rank by Henry VIII. Later crypts are those of Rochester and York. The great choir of Old St. Paul's was built upon a crypt.

The grand stair for access to the main floor of a castle became an important feature in its architecture. By raising the floor of the sanctuary of the cathedral and introducing the *perron* into English architecture, it became possible to approach the sanctuary by a wide flight of steps.

What use was made of the crypt is uncertain. In general architecture the basement was used for storage. In later days eastern walls were used as sites for altars. Often crypts, or portions of them, were employed for the quite honourable purpose of storing bones removed from the overcrowded cemeteries to make way for newcomers. Such relics of long-dead persons stored beneath the sanctuary of a cathedral could be considered to be still enjoying interment in consecrated surroundings.

Any important church had to be provided with altars at which priests might say their offices. These could be sited at the eastern ends of aisles or along the eastern walls of transepts. As in early days it was usual for an altar to be set in an apse, we see this tradition reflected in the apses flanking the great apse of the high altar and in those projecting from the transepts. We see, too, the ambulatory with its radiating apses.

As the English plan drove out the Continental and the square end superseded the apse, the minor apses also disappeared from the cathedrals. The eastern transept with its ambulatory and chapels replaced the Continental *chevet*, and the apses of the main transept were replaced by an eastern aisle which during the thirteenth century became a standard feature of all great churches.

While some early cathedrals such as Winchester and Ely had western as well as eastern aisles to their transepts, this was probably due to the desire to employ the same structural system in the transepts as in the nave and eastern arm. But it may have been a new interest in the design of gable ends that caused the late-twelfth-century designers to balance their elevation by introducing double aisles at York.

The entrance to the choir from outside was generally through a doorway, usually on the south side, near the east end of the nave wall, thence into the aisle and westwards along this into the retro-choir. With the later removal of the choir into the eastern arm of the buildings the entrance doorway was re-sited in the west wall of the main transept. The bishop sometimes had his own entrance into the eastern arm east of the transept, as at Salisbury.

One has only to watch the great west front of Ely rising up as one approaches it over the Fenland, or gaze at the tremendous wreck— big enough to contain a fair-sized dwelling-house—which is all that remains of the west front of St. Edmundsbury, to be able to appreciate the important part played in the elevational presentation of the eleventh century by the western transept.

It is a feature which in its finest manifestations is limited to this country. At this early period, England's Continental link was not so much across the Channel as over the North Sea to the Low Countries and the Rhineland of the Emperors. Dunwich with its cathedral was the great port of the age.

A number of Rhenish churches of the tenth and eleventh centuries have west towers and transepts at the west end, though not on anything approaching the English scale. The German for this feature is 'west work'.

The west work is a curious appendage if one regards it as such. Its position is completely foreign to Byzantine ideas, indeed by its presence it wrecks the Byzantine concept of a paramount central tower.

The three arches at Lincoln look very much like relics of the tower and transept arches of a destroyed west work. They may in fact be copies of these reproduced as a façade. (Plate 19.)

Medieval architecture suffered from several fundamental design defects which prevented its ever becoming a fine style in the architectural sense. Thus it was never able to produce a proper façade, partly owing to the bay-design of its lateral elevations and partly for the reason that at the end of the building it had to stop with an ugly section of the building which could never have seemed anything but the sawn-off end it in fact was.

But the western transept, illegitimate, serving no ritual purpose, and useless for accommodation, was a godsend to the architect in that it blocked off the ugly end of the building and gave him a rectangular elevation, a perfect canvas for the display of fenestration, arcading, imagery or anything he might wish to introduce.

They were certainly splendid frontispieces and their presence inspired the Gothic architects to provide proper façades to their naves. It is a sad pity that the front of Ely is today incomplete so that we cannot see at least one great eleventh-century cathedral in perfect condition. But what is left can help us to form an opinion: we can imagine the splendour of the conception and the invincible constructional skill which raised these great churches up from the ground. (Plate 1.)

4

Cathedral Design

Whenever one is trying to study the development of the details of medieval church architecture one is haunted by the mocking ghost of Thomas Cromwell whose hordes of ruffians 'plucked down' many a 'really beautiful church'—considered so by contemporary writers. And how often are such beautiful churches represented today by a pattern of white spots set in green turf. Often one must wish that their ghosts might rise, like Debussy's *Cathédrale Engloutie*, to grant us one fleeting glimpse of some of England's lost splendour. We are fortunate in knowing a certain amount about the great churches of the eleventh and twelfth centuries, but it is when we come to the splendid choirs of the thirteenth century which enshrined so much of our finest Gothic architecture, in which we might have seen the style developing stone by stone, that the loss becomes intolerable.

Enough of them is left to enable us to form some idea of the quality of their design. It is only when we try to work out the development of the detail of features that we realize how small a fragment of the whole is left, to tell us such a small portion of the story of the great architects of the Middle Ages, their art and their ability.

It is too often stated by architectural writers that some English building is a copy of one on the Continent, purely on the grounds of some imagined similarity. The writer much prefers to think that the English designer was far too busy to indulge in wandering, and indeed well content to work out for himself any problem which might be set him, and that any similarity between his and a foreign

77

design is most probably fortuitous. And when we remember that during the centuries filled with great churches this country led the world in ecclesiastical architecture we may ask what reason our designers had to copy from abroad. When we are told that some English church was copied from another in Burgundy or Provence we need not try to imagine our architects rushing about the Continent on their ponies taking notes.

At the middle of the first half of the thirteenth century the west fronts of great churches were being erected all over our own small island—yet no two resemble each other in the least. Does it not seem inconceivable that any architect worth the name would copy something built by a colleague?

What he did do, of course, was to obey the basic rule of good architecture and follow the accepted ordinance of his day as regards its basic forms. With this as a firm foundation he could develop his own design solutions. Actually, the devices at his disposal were unlimited, and so were his interpretation and use of them. And if two designers produced the same results then it was almost certainly pure chance.

It must often have been difficult for some bishop and his chapter to appreciate what their master mason was proposing to give them for a cathedral. There were no 'client-catching' drawings such as in these days so frequently take the place of good design. During the eleventh century, however, most clerics were quite able to appreciate the elements of bay design, with its eighty-foot wall divided into two arcades and a clearstory, assembled in accordance with established architectural practice so that all that was really necessary was to tell the master mason how many bays would be required for each arm of the cross. Details such as the form of compound piers and the soffits of the arches they were probably quite content to leave to the expert, who would of course be on his mettle.

There might well be occasions when some particular feature of a neighbouring church had been admired by the bishop, and pointed out to the mason with the suggestion that something like it should be included in the new cathedral. In which case a modified version of it might have been provided. For good design is developed from existing features and not despite them.

In such ways a bishop might affect the design of his new church. But there is a tendency among writers on architectural history to assign the actual design of a magnificent choir or a soaring tower to some prelate who could not possibly have been responsible for it unless he had been able to draw. Architects are familiar with the client who tells everyone that he designed his house and that the architect was not really needed. No doubt there were medieval bishops who made impressive gestures in the air while they gave their instructions to the master mason who remained politely silent and tried to gather the gist of his lordship's remarks.

Thus it would appear that the actual designer or architect of the building would have been a mason, not merely a 'banker mason' who cut stones, but one who had graduated from such a trade to be able to take upon himself the responsibility for designing and planning a whole structure.

What of course may well have happened is that the bishop might have drawn the mason's attention to something he liked, but even then would probably have added a rider that he wanted an improvement upon this, if only to take the reasonable opportunity of scoring over a neighbour.

But someone, presumably a master mason, had to prepare an actual design, something upon which he and his colleagues could work. Mere sketches, such as one sees in the famous sketch-book of Villard d'Honnecourt, are but 'doodles' and would have been of little use to the craftsman who had to convert them into masonry.

But sketches could have developed into proper drawings, in which case they would probably have been made upon softwood boards called 'ostrich' (Autriche) boards. The first designs might have been made in charcoal but eventually were probably incised with a spike into the wood.

The mason had only two drawing instruments. First came his square, an L-shaped piece of iron which he used for drawing right angles when designing or on the stone itself. The square acted as his rule and his measure for upon it were incised lines marking the inches of his foot. His other instrument was his compasses—what we now call dividers—which enabled him to experiment with proportions as today, and also to scribe circular lines, such as those of mouldings or tracery, upon his 'ostrich board'. Working upon these boards was known as tracing, and 'tracing lodges' containing 'tracing floors' were provided for masons' lodges.

The design 'plat'—perhaps the layout of a bay or the side of a tower—being still in two dimensions only, it might be thought necessary to produce a 'model' in three. For the design was elevational and had to be converted into a solid. It will be appreciated that the model could not be of a bay, which was hollow, but had to be of one of its supports, with half a bay projecting from each side of it. The writer has seen a mason making a small model in soft freestone, of one such pier, even the mouldings being indicated.

After the construction and approval of the model it had to be cut up by lines incised upon it into its individual stones. Each of these had to be studied by the mason who was assigned to make these on his 'banker' and the solid geometry of each face worked out, a task involving great skill and years of experience. Full-size details had to be approved and profiles or 'templates' cut—probably out of metal such as lead—so that stones cut by separate masons would fit together on the job. It is thought that a certain amount of Gothic detail became disseminated throughout England through the practice of masons 'borrowing' each others' templates, left unguarded in some lodge.

To recapitulate, the designing of a cathedral involved the approval of its plan, the designing of its bay elevation, the development of this into a three-dimensional model, the subdivision of this into its separate stones and the accurate detailing of these, in three dimensions and with the most careful detailing of their moulded surfaces, by the banker mason.

A word must be said here in explanation of the use of the cathedral plan as printed in guide-books. This is a device employed by the antiquary to represent the foundations which he has uncovered. It bears no resemblance to the drawing from which the building was erected, and is in fact nothing more than a map—as for instance of a holiday camp—provided to show the visitor the way about a building.

Laymen—excavators and the like—who draw plans are rarely conscious of the actual appearance of the building their plans are

9. ST. ALBANS

10. SOUTHWELL

representing. They see it as a complete design, not as merely the footprint of a three-dimensional structure. One cannot of course make much of the architectural details of the building concerned but it is a pity not to be able to form some idea as to the main features of the mass which once stood upon those footprints.

If the antiquaries' plans are to be published, whether in technical journals or in guide-books, they could at least indicate the relative heights of the various portions, perhaps even how they were roofed —a constant source of error. To differentiate between main span and the low roofs of aisles and chapels one could employ varying surface tones, in the same fashion as is seen on layered contour maps.

Plans not only represent accommodation but indicate the supports obstructing this which have to be set out in accordance with the structural system to be employed. Thus while the aisles of the early basilican churches were merely extensions of the main area achieved by the use of arcades, those of the Byzantine church were a part of the structure and in the eleventh-century churches of this country the arcade-carried main spans were not considered stable unless supported by vaulted aisles.

When designing a cathedral the early builders would first have laid out their four main spans meeting at the crossing and thereafter ranged aisles along them wherever they thought these might be needed for support.

The well-known sketch of the thirteenth-century Picard architect Villard d'Honnecourt for the plan of a Cistercian church shows clearly the initiation of a great church plan. He shows the four arms of the cross and indicates the aisles not only by their outer walls but by square vaulting bays with crosses indicating the vaulting ribs.

The dimensions are of course not shown, but it is quite possible that these could have been assumed as understood by the mason, familiar with some kind of metrological standard current at the period when the sketch was made. Designing in bays made this a very simple method of planning.

'Standard' would of course have been a loose description, as in those days no national standard was displayed, as today, in Trafalgar Square.

Although embarrassed mathematically by having five fingers on either hand and thus being saddled with a decimal system of notation, the Anglo-Saxon carpenters were of too practical a nature to carry this into their metrology. Their measure was literally a pole, and this they made for purposes of standardization sixteen feet—men's feet they were—in length. Standard poles were assessed and cut for the use of a district, or for a building job. Countrymen still measure their smallholdings by the 'rod' which is the same thing as a pole.

By cutting a cord to the length of a pole and folding it twice the yard could be obtained. Today firewood is cut into four-foot lengths and called 'cordwood', a 'cord' of such logs being sixteen feet long and four feet high.

It is interesting to note that the cord-yard itself could be folded twice to produce a foot, an operation impossible with decimalization. With the introduction of the cloth-yard the pole had to be made five and a half of these which is today's unit, the 'rod' still used in country districts.

It should be remembered that the architects of the Middle Ages had to use Roman numerals and thus could not perform even the simple operation of addition. Mathematics had to be founded upon the folded cord and the chequer-board. Arabic numerals appeared as part of the Reformation, but even then took a long time to penetrate into ordinary life, the country districts continuing to use the Roman notation well into the last century.

Since the designing of a medieval cathedral was entirely bound up with the bay system it is not surprising to find that the bay unit appears to control the whole design, both plan and elevation. In the eleventh century the bay seems to have become standardized at a pole and a quarter equalling five 'cords' of four feet, twenty feet in all. By the middle of the thirteenth century the tendency was to increase the bay to six yards or twenty-four feet.

Fixing the centre line of the building was the first task, then in all probability the lines of its main span, approximately twice the bay width. There were three systems used in setting out this span: by the span of the roof, giving a width of forty feet; by the overall width of the main building, giving a width of twenty-eight feet;

or by setting out from centre to centre of the walling, giving about thirty-four feet.

The total overall width of the building might next be fixed, probably about four bays in all giving from sixty-eight to the full eighty feet inside the building, according to whether or not the aisle walls were included.

Then the bays were marked out. In theory they were set out from centre to centre but in practice from one side of a pier-base to the next, the widths of each being added subsequently. It is as well to remember that a masonry wall has two faces to be considered when measuring is being undertaken, and that in early work they may be several feet distant from each other.

A cathedral was probably set out from west to east and actually built in the reverse direction. After the nave, the crossing piers had to be set out, each a square representing the intersection of the main walls of the building, and also the outline of the lantern tower over. Then the transepts, the bays of which were not standard as they were affected by the arches leading into them from the aisles.

Square vaulting bays for the aisles were not considered essential but the grid system of setting out the plan made it certain that each was not too far removed in plan from the square.

Together with the setting-out of the piers of the arcades their half-piers or 'responds' at either end were included in this operation. The responds of the crossing piers themselves, far taller than those of the arcades, also had to be marked out at this time. The arcade piers had to be provided with the necessary 'orders' for carrying those of the arches over, and also responds for the arches crossing the aisles and separating their vaulting bays. To balance these there was often some kind of a respond on the inner or nave side of the pier and this was generally carried right up as a half-shaft —incorrectly called a 'vaulting shaft' as a high vault for the nave was not in the scheme but used as a punctuation feature indicating the bays. Across the aisle, projecting from its wall, was a small respond to support the transverse arch coming across from the arcade pier. Outside this, on the exterior face of the aisle wall, the bay was marked by a flat 'pilaster', again a punctuation device indicating the bays on the outside of the aisle wall. It will be noted that the combination of respond and pilaster produced a kind of pier joined to its neighbour by a solid wall instead of an arch. This is a vestige of the 'tetrapylon' system of construction carrying a vaulting bay, on which the Byzantine churches were built.

Outside the building the procession of pilasters marked the run of the bays until they came to an end when the last pilaster was carried round the angle of the building to become a 'clasping pilaster', which, if broadened out, could be made to carry a spiral stair.

The setting out of the cathedral plan, while making due allowance for bays and arcades, was still a long way from the raising of its elevations, fixing the appearance of the complete building.

As the eleventh-century architect saw his elevational problem, he had to raise a structure consisting of two tall buildings crossing each other. The main walls of the building were constructed in two tiers of arcades. The lowest of these he sprung at about a bay's length above the floor with the gallery floor about half a bay above this. Thence up to the passage of the triforium was about another bay and a half or a quarter. He had to bear in mind that the gallery arches had to fit in beneath the aisle roof. The whole wall, including the clearstory, he reckoned at about eighty feet—four bays, five poles, or twenty 'cords'—in height.

Where the two 'buildings' crossed the walling had to be broken and four arches constructed connecting the massive piers at the angles of the crossing. These arches sprang from the level of the triforium passage, each of them spanning thirty feet or more and approaching eighty feet in height to the crown. They carried the central lantern and it was intended that the great arches silhouetted against the light falling from this would provide the most impressive feature of the interior of the cathedral.

The central tower had to rise above the ridges of the two roofs which it had severed and, having cleared these, was carried up for the lantern stage. It was the intention to make the lantern, which was of two bays' width on either face, exactly the same as the clearstory which it had broken. But in some cases this elevation was never achieved and light for the crossing had to be provided from windows set in the 'blind story' beside the slopes of the main roofs.

84

When completed in accordance with the standard design the top of the tower walling was close on a hundred and twenty feet above the ground. Above this rose the timber steeple, usually a masterpiece of the art of the Anglo-Saxon carpenters. They have all gone now, burnt by lightning, or taken down after their timbering had weakened beyond restoration.

From the plan to the structure which had governed it and so to the shaping of the basic mass of the cathedral, was an impressive achievement. The general volume of the interior had also been arrived at. Nevertheless, while all this work was proceeding, all the various details of the architecture were also being worked out in the lodges.

Before going on to details, however, we could take a quick look at a great abbey church, now a cathedral, the architecture of which represents that of the eleventh century at its most basic.

It is not built of stone, but of masses of bricks hauled up its hillside from the ruins of a Roman city, set in mortar and plastered internally with the same substance. In this strange fashion was built a church which is still one of the largest in the world.

As one approaches St. Albans from the south one is struck by the immense length of its cathedral lying like some great stranded ship along the ridge beside the Roman ruins. (Plate 8.)

The nave forms an immense, seemingly interminable, hall. It was extended during the Gothic era, and it is this later work which is seen first if one enters through the west doorway. If possible one should go in by the south door in the transept to be confronted immediately by the soaring cavern of the eleventh-century work spanned by the four stately arches of the crossing.

The church had originally an unusually long eastern arm of five bays and these have been considered adequate throughout its history, so that the choir was never moved out of its eleventh-century position west of the central tower. The stone rood-screen which provided a reredos for the nave altar is still in its original position. (Plate 9.)

The great interest of the cathedral lies in the minimal character of its architectural detail despite the vast scale of its conception. Brick and plaster do not provide scope for architectural detail, and everything salvageable from its predecessor—such as turned balusters from its biforas—was re-used in it.

The walling is of the usual three stories, each being perfectly plain. A slight band of brickwork surrounds the tops of the piers to act as an impost indicating the springing-line of the arches, relic of a Classical tradition which could not have been allowed to lapse. A similar projecting band marks the all-important working level of the gallery floor and another that of the clearstory passage. The soffits of the arches are almost plain but have two slight orders softening their edges; the piers are similarly recessed to match. The gallery arches are plain openings as are the windows of the clearstory. Brick pilasters pass up the wall in each bay to punctuate this tremendous but very basic architectural composition.

The only architectural features of the great church—and these of outstanding interest to the art historian—are to be found in the heart of the eleventh-century building, the transept and the blind story of the lantern, in both cases forming part of biforas lighting wall passages. They are early turned balusters from the building removed when the present great church was raised. As carpenters the Anglo-Saxons would have been familiar with the pole-lathe and probably found little difficulty in converting it for use in the turning of stone balusters such as these, which are very probably copies of wooden originals.

The eastern arm of the cathedral was rebuilt, without increasing its length, during the Gothic era, and provided with an eastern termination containing the usual ambulatory giving access to a series of eastern chapels of which the central one was a projecting Lady Chapel.

A bay and a half of the main building was reserved to be a chapel to St. Alban whose shrine was set in it. West of this is the cathedral's finest architectural feature, the splendid reredos behind the high altar, of great height and once filled with statuary but now displaying only rows of empty niches.

Externally the scene is overpowered by the huge red mass of the central tower, unique in architecture, primitive almost to savagery, more like a castle keep than a church tower. The belfry is clearly a later addition but only slightly modifies the elemental form of the story below, above which runs a gallery of biforas which is one of the most enchanting features surviving from the eleventh-century architecture of this country.

The great tower of St. Albans, built of bricks the Romans made for their city, has stood there immovable for nine centuries—an ineradicable memory for anyone who has ever seen it.

The architecture of St. Albans Cathedral is of course unique in its use of bricks plastered over and for the simplicity of the architectural style resulting from such primitive material. But this apart, despite its almost pagan austerity when set beside the glories of the Gothic, this eleventh-century English church of the first rank achieves a dignity never surpassed.

The basic aim of the early cathedral designers was to build as high as possible without fear of collapse, and it is easy to see that they were more than content to follow the simple elevational system of the two stories, each with its arcade, adding to this, for lighting purposes, the clearstory. In such cathedrals as Norwich and Ely we can see that the two-storied division was so clearly accepted as a structural system that there is practically no difference in height between the two arcades.

But the gallery arcade was bound eventually to assume a secondary importance in accordance with that rule of architecture which deprecates mere duplication as indicating uncertainty and lack of confidence. The gallery front was filled with a large shafted bifora and became developed as an ornamental story, the main purpose of which was to conceal the lean-to roof behind it. Gradually it is seen to shrink in height but its ornamental function develops aesthetically until it becomes the most beautiful feature of the cathedral interior, replacing what could have been the blind story of the basilica with a lovely arcade of moulded arches rising above low clustered pillars.

It should be noted that throughout its subsequent history the gallery arcade retains as its basic element the bifora—a pair to each bay as the height of the story shrinks—and thus it might indeed be called the 'biforium'.

With the recession of the original gallery its windows disappear from the outside of the aisle wall, those of the choir of Lincoln built by St. Hugh at the close of the twelfth century being possibly the last survivors. Thenceforth the aisle wall displays a single story only.

Now that we have reached this stage in the architectural history of the cathedral, we can begin to appreciate that early structural problems had been overcome to such an extent that more attention could be given to purely aesthetic matters.

Two-storied construction was beginning to disappear and the main arcade was being given its proper prominence. The old gallery story over, treatment of which was still essential if it was not to be left as a blind story, had become a highly architectural horizontal band providing a splendid foil to the verticality of the bays. Above this region, the developing tracery of the main fenestration could be introduced into the clearstory windows also, as these too were encroaching upon the gallery below to bring more light into the centre of the cathedral.

The redesigning of the cleaning passage became a major consideration. Hitherto it had been a narrow passage set in the heart of the wall for most of its length. It now became a series of short tunnels constructed behind the main supporting elements of the wall and between these became a narrow gallery open to the church, the trifora opening being widened and its sill lowered, so that eventually the triforium absorbed the gallery below until the two stories became aesthetically inseparable.

A series of disasters to window cleaners may have resulted in the new gallery's being provided with an ornamental balustrade, an amenity which could be included in the design of the expanded clearstory and was eventually designed in connection with the window area. This unification was helped by the systems of panelling by means of which the achievements of the carpenters were being translated into stone.

We will return for a space to the original structural problems of the Byzantines and examine the manner in which they affected aesthetics. In the last chapter we referred to the way in which the grid design of the square church resulted in the square of its crossing being set out with a side of two units of length and with the projection of the wings set out as a single unit. This last became the normal bay of the western cathedral, half the width of the great bay represented by the crossing, in turn reflected by the windows of a lantern tower such as that of St. Albans, which is clearly seen as being of two bays' width. (Plate 8.)

The great bay, relic of the domed square of the Byzantine church, remained in evidence in the western cathedral for some time. In the Byzantine church the great bays were marked by the massive piers providing the main supports, with the lesser bays between them indicated by slender columns supporting the galleries. Several of the English cathedrals mark the great bays with compound piers and the intermediate ones with circular pillars. The great bay is often indicated by making the vertical projections from the piers of the arcade—incorrectly called vaulting shafts—more prominent at the great bays. At Durham they were actually carried up across the main span by arches matching those of the crossing, a most deliberate attempt to perpetuate the great bay and one which enabled Durham nave to raise the first high vault in England.

The 'duplex bay' is remembered right through the medieval period, as though in defiance of 'basilican' uniformity. One may even see circular pillars alternating with octagonal, as in Peterborough Cathedral and in many scores of parish churches throughout the countryside.

But to see the great bay in its most majestic presentation one must visit Durham and see the River Wear sweeping round the foot of the hill from which the Prince-Bishops ruled over the northern peak of England. Nowhere in England, perhaps in the world, can one see such a splendid spectacle of medieval history as that presented by castle and cathedral towering above the city beneath.

The three towers of the great church form a group rarely met with outside this country, the western ones splendidly arcaded and the storied tower over the crossing soaring high above the roofs about it.

Within, the cathedral is overpowering in its antique majesty, the culminating achievement of Anglo-Saxon Byzantine architecture. Fine arches indicate the great bays, and these rise from elaborate compound piers. Between these the normal bays are indicated by huge circular pillars paying tribute to ancestors in Greece and

Rome but with their massive shafts incised with tremendous Anglo-Saxon motifs no other country could have produced, motifs which reach across the country by way of Norwich Cathedral to the abbey church of Romsey in distant Hampshire. (Plate 5.)

Behind the high altar is a delicately traceried and canopied Gothic reredos acting as a screen before the spreading transept known as the Chapel of the Nine Altars, the culminating achievement of the English east end, perhaps not entirely satisfactory aesthetically but certainly providing decisive terminal punctuation to one of the great churches of the world.

As we gaze down the long arcaded vistas of our eleventh-century cathedrals we are apt to take too little notice of the high clearstory with those internal arcades which gave their name to the triforium. In the vaulted Byzantine churches there was no clearstory for, apart from the fact that this story was fully occupied by the high vault, the light in the Byzantine regions was strong enough to be able to penetrate deeply into the church through windows set in the ends of the arms of the cross which were of course quite short. Above the crossing, the drum of the dome usually had small windows surrounding it.

The long basilican churches, however, were provided with clearstories of windows raised above the blind stories where the roofs of the aisles abutted against the nave above its arcades.

In the eleventh-century English cathedrals the clearstory windows were quite small and the side of the cleaning passage next to the church was opened out at each window so that a ladder could be set there to reach the glass. The inner face of the wall at this point was widened still further to let light into the building from the window, and it is this feature which characterizes the clearstory as it is seen from the church. (Fig. 25b.)

The simple device known as the bifora, an aedicular device copied from a structural one, suffered from a primary design defect in having an opening blocked at the centre by a solid obstruction. Hence the duplication of the shaft of the bifora to convert it to a trifora, a device found as part of the standard ordinance of the bay design of the eleventh- and twelfth-century cathedral and continued in expanded form through the Gothic era.

We can see the established three-storied bay design splendidly presented at Norwich Cathedral, which was begun exactly thirty years after the Conquest after the see of Elmham had been transferred to its final site. At Ely, begun thirteen years later, the same noble proportions obtain, but there is a difference in that the gallery arches have each been filled with a large bifora, its internal arches carried upon a slender shaft.

Norwich Cathedral is a perfect example of a great English cathedral and has been so since 1096, after the bishop had ceased his wandering round the old Kingdom of East Anglia from its great port of Dunwich, through lonely Elmham and flinty Thetford, to settle down in Broadland. Although today linked with a busy industrial city, the cathedral has retained its Close, above which a splendid twelfth-century tower, richly ornamented with arcading, still carries one of the few cathedral spires left in England.

It seems there was to have been a bell-tower as at Ely, and in the west front of the cathedral one can still detect the piers built in preparation for it. But it was never built and the great church is the poorer for it.

Walking round the cathedral one can find all the architectural details of the twelfth century, the transepts in particular being perfect illustrations of this splendid period in English architectural history. At the east end is the great apse with the lesser apsidioles of its *chevet*, modified by the addition of the large windows and flying buttresses of Gothic days. (Plate 2.)

The interior is one of the breath-taking spectacles from the days when England led the world in building great churches. The primitive yet undoubtedly stately two-storied arcading holds the eye, the triforium over only slightly disturbed by the brilliant cones of the later high vault. The original lantern still lights the crossing, one of the few left from its period which have remained standing against the drift of the great arcades pressing upon it. Looking up into the lantern we are taken back eight centuries and can begin to appreciate the architectural splendour of the twelfth century and try to imagine how England might have appeared when it was covered with magnificent churches. (Plate 4.)

Looking up into that lantern we can feel carried back to proud

Byzantium, or Anatolia, or Syria—Jerusalem even—but never to ancient Rome of the Caesars.

The serenity of the great apse of Norwich—one of the very few left to us from the eleventh century—has not in any way been lessened by the introduction of very large clearstory windows.

The great cathedral entirely lacks the carved capitals and other sculptured ornament of its Gothic successors—the Anglo-Saxon carvers, so skilful in transferring their art to the embellishment of architectural features such as doorways, were not yet to be allowed to take over a whole cathedral. But the splendour of its design and the purity of its architectural detail alone suffice to set Norwich Cathedral amongst the noblest buildings in architectural history.

And as a contrast to the grandeur of the great church is the tracer-ied Gothic of the cloister beside it where one can rest and enjoy the sculptured detail of its elaborate vault. But the glory of Norwich is its great nave, where the two-tiered arcades stalk beside each other down the length of the church.

What happened in the naves of most of the vanished abbey churches has been for ever hidden from us, but from what is left it seems probable that few of them designed their stories to be of equal height, the gallery arcade being usually about three quarters of the height of that below it. This was the case at Peterborough, begun in 1118. In the huge church at St. Albans the gallery with its cavernous arcades clearly takes second place to the tall arcade below. The same may be said of ponderous Durham where the gallery story is lightened by the use of the bifora. (These galleries, by the way, not being intended for use, did not always contribute to the lighting of the cathedral.) The proportion of about three to four is followed at Chichester begun in 1091, and Southwell with its gaping gallery arcade strangely open to its nave, which dates from about 1108. (Plate 10.)

In elevational design, the factor which affects proportion most ba-sically is structural requirements, the main lines of the elevation, its solids and openings, having to take these requirements into account. The resultant assemblage of structural features may, however, be improved in appearance by adding architectural punctuation.

Since the system of elevational design has to be controlled by the system of building in bays, the form of punctuation most commonly encountered is vertical. The cathedral was deliberately set out in bays without any intention of attempting to join these together to form a continuous elevation, and aesthetic stability was achieved by indicating the run of the bays by means of vertical punctuation. Externally this was done by the pilasters, internally by the so-called 'vaulting shafts' which carried the lines of the main supports right up the wall to its summit. Vertical punctuation does not appear in Classical architecture. It appears for the first time in the Western Byzantine churches and it was largely due to its use that Gothic architecture was able to extricate itself from the restless horizontality of basilican architecture and the stolid compactness of the Byzantine. In parenthesis it might be suggested that the English use of the 'vaulting shaft' might well have derived from a similar use of timber poles in earlier timber buildings.

Horizontal punctuation has a practical origin. The early builders had no system of levelling by instruments. They could prepare a level foundation by a method suggested in the next chapter, but after this had been established the rest of the rising building was kept level by the use of 'story rods'.

The use of the story rod will be explained more fully in the next chapter, but it should be noted that its requirement of horizontal 'tablements' at certain fixed levels is the origin of the 'string-course' which provides the horizontal punctuation of the elevation and adds greatly to its aesthetic stability, not only by creating visible levels but also by tying together the isolated vertical elements of the elevation. String-courses not only appear at story heights but also join the sills of windows and the springing levels of arches of all descriptions.

In buildings built by the bay a very important form of punctuation is the terminal, for without this refinement the elevation comes to a sudden stop and appears as though it had been abandoned incomplete. This fundamental defect is seen everywhere today in buildings constructed round a steel frame, no provision being made for the aesthetic requirement of terminal punctuation: the elevation simply ends at a stanchion as though waiting for more bays to be added when funds permit.

The lateral elevation of the medieval cathedral would have looked equally amateurish had the builders adopted such an inept practice. The procession of pilasters is always terminated by the broad clasping pilaster covering the angle and making it clear that the elevation is finished there. When the projecting pseudo-buttresses of the thirteenth century were introduced, they were not only employed at the angles—where they could not have been of the slightest use—but were set in pairs so as to provide a strong item of terminal punctuation, which eventually became combined with the clasping pilaster and expanded to form a stair-turret capped with a little spire.

West fronts, such as that at Lincoln, were always provided with terminal features of considerable presence and the principle is exploited to the full at Wells where the ends of a wide western transept are carried up as towers.

On the whole it seems possible that the Byzantine architects, concerned as they were with the presentation of mass—and this moreover concentrated in a vertical direction—may not have been interested in elevational architecture. This of course is true of architecture today, with the difference, however, that the modern 'functional' building is often seen as a mere prism, displaying no signs of even three-dimensional design, silhouette or massing. Thus buildings of this sort lack any qualities whatever which might enable one to regard them as demonstrations of architectural skill.

The Byzantine elevation was probably restricted to the presentation of an entrance front with a central doorway possibly flanked by two others. And lacking the imperative lift of the tall gables of the West, a single doorway might have seemed inadequate to create a strong centre line about which an elevation could be woven.

We have already observed that the transept ends of the eleventh-century cathedrals were set out like any other piece of church walling—a pair of bays adding up to a single great bay such as could have been seen in a wall of the lantern tower. The external effect was that of a gable end split down the middle, a breach of one of the most elementary rules of architectural design which requires a centre line to be covered by an opening and never by a solid.

The west front with its centre doorway, however, could never

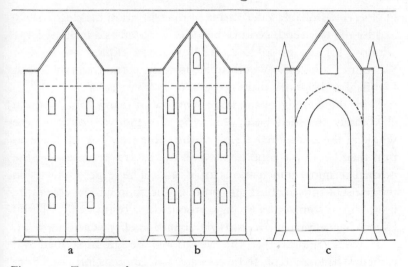

Fig. 13.   *Transept ends*
The development of the medieval elevation. In (a) this
is merely a repetition of the bay design of the building,
a pair of normal bays set in the great bay representing
the width of the building. During the architectural
boom of the twelfth century it began to be appreciated
that a central opening was aesthetically more welcome
than a central obstruction. Bay design was therefore
abandoned in transept ends and the elevation redesigned vertically so as to divide it into three. (b)
The principle of a central opening once accepted, the
Gothic architects continued the practice and used large
windows centrally placed (c)

have been treated in this fashion, for there the most elementary rule
of bay design would have insisted upon the windows above it
being aligned upon its centre line. This requirement, transferred to
the two-bay transept end, resulted in the latter being redesigned
with three bays of much less than the normal width. By this means
was evolved the design which is illustrated so attractively at Peterborough and Norwich; with its adjoining walling it has created
one of the most delightful forms of twelfth-century interior.

Such was the breakdown of the system of bay design for transept
ends, which thenceforth were considered as plain wall surfaces
with a centre line as demanding as that of the west front. The group

of lancets—probably a derivative of the triforas of the clearstory—had by the thirteenth century become accepted as a form of large window for use in gable ends. Very large triplets are seen at Salisbury Cathedral. A quintuplet is seen in the transept end at Lichfield and at York there is the famous 'five sisters'.

With the coming of the large window of many lights with an elaborately traceried head, this type of window took over the whole of the elevational design of the gable end. The gable elevation then became a window flanked by features representing the normal terminal punctuations of a wall. The large windows in the transept ends enabled the centre of the church to receive more light and in some cases brought about the closing of the central lantern by vaulting and its conversion into a belfry or ringing floor.

It would appear that the elevational design of a medieval cathedral had inevitably to be concentrated upon its interior. From the start of things the real problem the builders had faced had been how to create a stately prayer-hall of monumental height. This had been achieved, but at the cost of absorbing the whole of their designing skill.

Externally the same tremendous effect had from the start been rendered impossible of achievement owing to the unavoidable presence of the appendages formed by the aisles, without which an elevation such as that of King's College, Cambridge, could have been bestowed upon a medieval cathedral.

But during the Gothic era the aisles had become so absorbed into that basic system of designing by bays that the architects had planted an architectural forest of tall shapes concealing those areas which might have been developed as an elevation.

II. WINCHESTER

12. GLOUCESTER

5

Cathedral Building

When we enter one of these great buildings of eight hundred years ago—almost thirty generations—and marvel at the immensity of their conception and the grandeur of the achievement we may think not only of the inspiration which brought them to pass ... but also of the men, our own ancestors, who were thus so sublimely inspired.

Think of them particularly in the winters of their years. Living in shelters of poles and mud thatched with heather. Wrapped in clothing of some coarse material and hooded to keep out the winds howling at them while they perched upon some wall-top. One wonders how were they shod ... possibly often with straw bound round with rags from clothing worn out a generation or more before.

Think of them climbing the scaffolding a hundred feet in the air, while the months pass into years as they lug stone after stone up and up to help the walls rise while the spirit of the tower-top beckons them upwards still and the carpenters are waiting to begin their difficult task of assembling huge beams to form a tall steeple.

Surely the work of the builder of the eleventh century was verging upon the superhuman. Called from a world of hovels, none more than a single story in height, he found himself having to raise a pair of walls eighty feet high and cover them with a roof.

We have considered some of the basic elements of the design of the cathedral. But the most difficult aspect of the design was not the aesthetics of its presentation, but the operation of getting it built at all.

97

A great cathedral of the eleventh century occupied an area of ground some hundred and fifty yards long and half this in width. Levelling a site of this size in those days must have been limited to the removal of obstructions. In the absence of machinery a site must be chosen having a perimeter which was basically level, because all levelling of the building had to be done by sighting or, as it is called today, 'boning'.

There were no levelling instruments. Where there was a visible horizon, as in parts of East Anglia, levelling could be effected by sighting towards it. But the ancient method of levelling was to use the property of water which causes it to remain level. As the modern caravanner levels his home by placing a saucer of water on its floor and adjusting his jacks until the water no longer runs over the edge, so might the eleventh-century builder set a large cauldron of water on his site and adjust it until its rim was level. Once a level has been established it is not difficult to project it in all directions by sighting. And once a basic level has been carried all round the building by the method which will be described later, all subsequent upper levels can be fixed by measurement from this.

In medieval contracts the builder was charged to build true 'by level and by line'. By 'line' is meant the plumb-line by which, as today, he kept the wall-faces vertical. Levelling instruments were limited to a development from a combination of the plumb-line and the square, with the latter made into a T the upright limb of which incorporated a plumb-line. But levelling in the courses was probably done, as today, by fixing the height of certain points in the wall, such as angles or bay divisions, and then sighting between these by eye.

In levelling, the important thing was to start right. It will be noticed that all medieval buildings are set upon a plinth. This is not an aesthetic device but a structural one, upon which the whole of the structure depends. In a building the size of a cathedral, it must have taken a long time to get the whole of the plinth, including that of the isolated supports, truly level.

The line of the plinth was consolidated by a row of stone slabs or 'planks' known as the 'tablement', from which all subsequent vertical measurements were taken. These were taken by means of story rods, lengths of timber set vertically and having the vertical dimensions marked on them. As the foot of the rods had to be rested upon the tablement from which dimensions were being taken, this was always projected from the wall-face to provide a lodgement for the rod. This is the reason for the plinth. In simple buildings the plinth is plain, but in most buildings its outer angle is chamfered away so as to make it less crude, though there is always a flat ledge upon which to rest the story rod.

As there were no tape-measures in the Middle Ages, heights were all measured with story rods. In a tall building such as a cathedral it would have been inconvenient to use story rods eighty feet long, so during its erection each of its three stories was provided with a story rod, a single rod for each story which was moved about the building as it rose, the height of the story being kept constant through there being only one rod for each story. The story rod is still used today but for checking the levels of secondary items within the story.

In actual fact, there must have been two story rods in use for each story of the building, one for each face of the wall. For such features as the sills of windows would be at different heights externally and internally. It is absolutely vital in masonry work that the horizontal courses are designed to fit such features. In between them, however, the courses can be worked out to suit the sizes of stones available.

The levels of a large building are most important. Such a level, for instance, as the height of the springing of the main arcade would run at a constant height for the complete circuit of the building. All this was kept true by constant use of the story rod.

For each story rod a new tablement was required, completing a story and serving as a datum for the next. These are the 'string-courses', projecting bands of stone at story level, changing their section in each century and often becoming mouldings charged with ornamental carving and indeed fine architectural features of the building. (Fig. 14.)

Within our eleventh-century cathedrals we can see string-courses at the level of the gallery and at that of the triforium passage. There

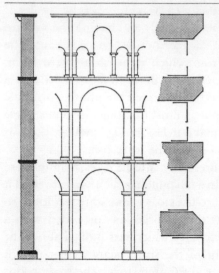

Fig. 14.
Tablements
In medieval building practice
the stories of a tall building
were separated by 'tablements',
layers of dressed stone
protruding at story level in
order that wooden rods called
'story rods' could be rested
upon them and the height of
each story kept constant and
level. Architects call the projections of these tablements
'string courses'. A simple
twelfth-century section is indicated. During the Gothic era
they became moulded and often
carved with running ornament

was usually another crowning the top of the wall where all was
being made level for the raising of the roof.

The positions of these internal tablements at the edges of the
floors of the gallery and triforium were dictated by clear con-
venience. Externally, however, it might not have been necessary to
indicate, for example, the level of the gallery floor, on the outer wall
of the aisles. So the tablements for such situations might be set at
the all-important level of the springing of the arches of the aisle
windows, a line which might also need to be introduced into the
elevation for aesthetic reasons. Such springing-line string-courses
could be taken over the window arch as a 'hood-mould' for keeping
water running down the wall-face away from the window glass:
the whole arrangement an example of a combination of structural
requirements resulting in architecture.

A little knowledge of the systems adopted in past times for
designing and building the great cathedral structures makes it far
easier to understand how structural necessities often governed
design and in some cases actually created it.

We have explained the reason for the three stories of the eleventh-
century cathedral: the two lower ones for creating overall height
without straining the structure of isolated supports made too high

for safety, and the third story for light. The heights of the two lower stories, about thirty feet apiece, with the upper about twenty, gave a total height of about eighty feet. It will be noted that this reduced the height of isolated supports to about twenty feet; and that the use of Byzantine aisled construction kept the heights of the great piers of the crossing, apparently sixty feet high, in fact no more than those around it.

The particular aspect of 'ordered' architecture which characterizes Western Byzantine architecture—and was in the end to develop into Gothic—created a special system of masonry planning in order to establish from the foundations the exact positions of those orders which were to join as arches overhead. Thus in piers and responds, what was laid out on the ground was not the mass of its *silhouette* (to the evident delight of the excavator of today who measures and plots them on his plan). (See Fig. 16.)

The importance of keeping the heights of piers within reasonable limits lay in the nature of eleventh-century walling which aimed at creating neat or even elaborate visible faces rather than constructing strong walls. This was due to the basic principle of masonry technique which built wall-faces and filled in the 'core' with what was left over from the stone-cutting. It was not until this practice changed completely and walls were built 'through' from face to face, that supports were able to be reduced in size and yet at the same time raised in height, thus making it possible to develop the sensation of a soaring slenderness which characterizes Gothic architecture.

Yet notwithstanding the unscientific nature of their masonry construction the tall buildings of the eleventh century have all stood remarkably steadfast down the centuries. The main trouble has come from lateral pressure against the crossing piers, due to ignorance of building statics rather than masonry defects. After all, they were buildings of a scale quite outside experience.

One can see, in fact, that a great many structural factors had to be taken into consideration when setting out a cathedral, and that aesthetic requirements could not always be given due consideration when the great problem of stability was constantly supervening.

The setting-out of all the innumerable portions of the plan and elevations of the cathedral formed a large part of the mason's duties. Thus he had to be the cathedral surveyor as well as its designer and builder. This is what enables one to appreciate the difference between the master mason—who today would be called the building contractor—and the 'banker masons' who cut the stones in the lodges and the 'setting masons' who laid them in the walling.

Early walling was formed of field stone, the corner stones— quoins—and those framing openings being made of mason- wrought or 'dressed' stone. Such walls, although built in masonry fashion with two true faces and a core between them, were still rubble walls and not true masonry. For this is constructed of facing stones which have been wrought with a smooth face which matches that of the 'dressings'. All architecture of monumental class has been constructed of true masonry.

Prehistoric stone building was megalithic, using very large boulders of moorstone heaped without art into walls several feet in thickness. Masonry is stone which is laid horizontally in courses.

The history of monumental building in stone appears to have begun with the Dynastic Egyptians and to have been either handed on by them to the Hellenic builders or, more probably, discovered by them independently. From the Hellenic period it becomes part of the ancestry of our architecture.

Every stone which has been worked by a mason to be laid in the regular courses of a wall has a face, normally rectangular, a bed upon which it can be laid, and another bed above upon which another course can be set. The sides of the stone are trimmed so that it can be fitted neatly to its neighbours in the course. The sixth side of the stone is left rough and is known as its 'tail'.

Masonry walls are always built in the same fashion. The thickness —that is the distance between the two wall-faces—is decided upon and the two wall-faces laid out along these lines. In the case of a compound pier the silhouette of the plan is marked out and stone cut to fit. It should be noted that it is the elevational presentation of the wall or pier which is the desideratum, neither is primarily considered by the mason as a solid mass of stonework. In a wall, the shapes of the jambs of the openings are of primary interest to

the mason. He works to a plan, not of a building, but of that particular solid element of it on which he is engaged. The tails are
hidden within the wall and its 'core' just filled in, to be hidden
from view.

Masonry depends for its stability upon the use of mortar which
forms a soft bed upon which each stone is laid and which takes up
any minor irregularities of each stone in contact with another. The
quarrying of limestone and its burning in tall kilns to make quick-
lime formed an important element in the organization of the building of a cathedral.

In Hellenic days the structures, however large, had walls of
masonry which were of no great strength and were used as screen
walls carrying no load, the Hellenic temples being founded upon a
quite different structural system than that which we use today.
Derived from the tent with its pole-supported roof, the temple was
founded upon columns built up in drums of solid stone laid so as to
imitate living rock. This posted framework carried the heavy
timber roof with its covering of stone slabs, the walling within
being formed of a masonry of large stones laid without mortar and
with a hollow interior.

It is the columns of the Hellenic temple which represent that
other style of stone building which follows the principle of trying
to reproduce a building as though it were carved from the living
rock. Stone, by the way, is always laid on its natural bed.

The Gothic builders transformed their masonry technique into
something resembling that of Classical times. Although they
avoided using stones of the size of the drums of the ancient temples,
they built up each course of masonry as though they were creating
a solid layer of rock. No longer was there a rough core of pieces of
stone thrown in between the carefully laid facings. The wall was
built solidly from face to face. In this way the circumference of
pillars could be greatly reduced and at the same time they could be
raised so as to seem slender. Areas of walling between windows
could also be greatly reduced so that the windows themselves could
be widened.

Building stone, unlike moorstone or field stone which is simply
gathered, has to be cut from a quarry. A stone quarry has to be

Cathedral Building

prospected for in the same way as a mine of metal. Outcrops of suitable stone are sought for and explored.

The quarry site selected, the first task is to expose a vertical plane to see if the stone is capable of being worked to a quarry face. Then soil and rubbish are moved from before this to find if the depth of the stone is sufficient for it to be worth quarrying. Ancient quarries could not be very deep as the stone had to be dragged up an incline from the quarry face.

The 'overburden' of soil and rubble stone had to be cleared away from above the stone bed. As the stone was quarried away the overburden was thrown back onto its site, which accounts for the insignificance of the quarry sites today. The great quarries of Barnack in Northamptonshire out of which grew the greatest buildings in the world of their day are nowadays known merely as 'the hills and holes'.

After the top of the stone bed had been exposed this had to be explored for cracks in the surface, which could be developed by prodding with 'jumpers' and straining by wedges until the stone could be prised away from the quarry face onto the bottom of the quarry. The stone was dragged away in large lumps to be broken up into portable pieces before being transported to the building site by pack ponies or drawn on sleds.

The building of a cathedral was dependent upon a supply of building stone. True 'freestone' is limestone, easy to cut when 'green' but eventually acquiring, under the influence of weathering, a hard 'callus' which protects it from deterioration. But this is true only if it be laid upon its natural bed; if 'face bedded' it will flake away and perish.

The south-east of England, the region which might have first come under the attention of the post-Conquest church-builders, is practically stone-less—though a small area of lovely stone was later discovered in the Horsham area—and had to rely upon material imported from the quarries of Caen in Normandy carried across by sea and up the quiet rivers to Canterbury, Rochester and the like.

But the Anglo-Saxons were aware of the great belt of workable limestone which reached across England from Somerset, through

104

Wiltshire, Gloucestershire and Northamptonshire to the Wash. The quarries at Doulting in Somerset were being worked in the eighth century, while at the other end of the belt the quarries of Barnack were opened, the waterways of the region providing the necessary transport.

From the Somerset end of the stone belt developed the quarries of Bath and Ham Hill, and a notable school of masoncraft developed round the ancient religious centre of Glastonbury which, among other structures, produced Wells Cathedral. North-east of this the Cotswold region gave us Gloucester Cathedral.

The masons were apt to gather where the supplies of their material were most plentiful; and what schools of architecture there were must have been started in the quarry areas. Thus if we could get back to the days of the great Anglian cathedrals we should probably find that they stemmed from the masoncraft of Barnack.

As Glastonbury had remained during the Dark Ages an outpost of the Christian Faith in south-west England, so had the same service been performed in the north-east by Lindisfarne. A belt of limestone passed down the eastern side of the country from New-castle to Nottingham, and it was this source of material which was tapped during the eleventh century to build the great cathedral at Durham. A century later Hugh of Avalon used the southern end of the same belt to rebuild the great cathedral of Lincoln. It was the masoncraft of this stone belt which thenceforth developed the glorious thirteenth-century Gothic of the Yorkshire abbeys and produced the cathedrals of York and Ripon. Finally the Ham Hill culture burst into splendid prominence during the fourteenth century to create the towered landscape of Somerset.

Amongst quarries famous in their day one must mention those of Chilmark in Somerset which produced Salisbury Cathedral. The Clerk of Works of the cathedral told me that these quarries—which are subterranean—have dates cut in their walls recording the years during which stone was taken from the faces there.

Exeter Cathedral was built from the quarries of Beer on the Dorset coast and a little further east of these are the quarries on the Isle of Purbeck which supplied all England with lovely grey marble-like conglomerate—today sometimes artificially coloured (it is said with boot-blacking) to make it show up against the freestone.

Few indeed are the quarries open today, and these are for the most part producing road metal to carry the twentieth-century motor car across the countryside of England. Amidst their roar it is impossible to imagine a countryside ringing with the sound of axe and bolster and the tracks blocked with laden sleds and the rivers choked with stone-filled barges on the way to the sites of great churches.

The Midlands and the West of England had no freestone but were able to build Lichfield and Chester Cathedrals out of the red sandstones of Cheshire and south Lancashire.

Among the medieval schools of masoncraft no longer represented today is the Cotswold School which produced Gloucester and the vanished abbeys of the Vale of Evesham. Oxford Cathedral is perhaps a product of the Cotswold masons.

During the Middle Ages the mason was the most valued of the country's craftsmen. In company with his fellow tradesmen— smith, carpenter and so forth—he possessed great skill with the tools of his trade. But in addition he had to have a remarkable knowledge of solid geometry and, if a master mason, had to design and organize the construction of buildings of a gigantic scale.

In prehistoric days the stones gathered from the fields were dressed with hammers, as is the granite of Dartmoor to this day. Field stone used for walling is also hammer-dressed by 'nobblers'. But the traditional stone-cutter's tool, still used today around the Mediterranean, is the stone-axe. This has a very large and heavy head with a long blunt cutting edge and is often double-headed to improve its balance. In skilled hands it will quickly trim the five faces of a building stone. This was the tool which during the twelfth century fashioned the greatest buildings in the world.

About the year 1200, however, while King John and his quarrelsome barons were pursuing their squabbling courses about the countryside and allowing the English building trade to continue unhindered its experiments in improving its technique, the masons were discovering a new tool with the aid of which they could smooth away the irregularities in the face of the stone left from the assaults of the cumbersome stone-axe.

This was a form of chisel, a heavy broad-bladed tool called a 'bolster', which was held against the stone and driven across its face by blows from a wooden mallet or 'mell'. In order to use this tool, the block of stone to be dressed was lifted from the ground and set upon a block of stone or a section of tree-stump known as a 'banker'.

When newly introduced, the bolster was used with great care, the slight grooves left from its passage always appearing vertically on the stone and each tap from the mell being so carefully regulated that the distance apart of the grooves remained constant.

This type of face is characteristic of the thirteenth century and displays a very different aspect from the rough diagonal grooves left by the earlier stone-axe.

After the end of the thirteenth century the banker masons become more slapdash in their work, abandoned the careful practice of making their bolster-strokes vertical and just ran the bolster diagonally over the stone without troubling to make the strokes at all regular.

There are very few banker masons left in this country and very little stone left for them to work upon. But where one can always find them is in the cathedral workshops of Lincoln, Salisbury and so forth, maintaining their age-old struggle to keep the great buildings standing.

It was the banker masons who set out and worked the exceedingly complicated architectural detail of the Gothic era. Capitals, mouldings, arches and vaulting ribs with their complicated intersections of mouldings, all had to be set out with superlative skill in three dimensions, in 'circular' work and in 'circular circular' work which is spherical geometry of an extremely complicated kind. And all this from a lump of round stone.

Where the carver has to be called in to carve the sculptured detail of a capital, corbel, vaulting boss or perhaps some running ornament, the banker mason leaves a projecting lump of rough stone 'boasted for carving' and the carver takes the stone to his own bench where he is able to indulge his own artistic freedom.

Nowadays our cathedral carvers are often students from colleges of art, who loyally imitate the style of the period upon which they are working.

It is interesting to note the change in the appearance of walling during the course of the centuries. In the eleventh century, when the stones were either slung on pack ponies or drawn on sledges, and on arrival at site had to be hauled up—or possibly carried—to the high scaffolding, they were kept small. They were set into the wall like the headers in brickwork and show on the face an almost square shape about eight inches deep in the course.

With the coming of the thirteenth century and the great change in architectural design and detailing, the stones became about twice as large and were set in proper courses along the wall showing lengths of almost twice the depth of the course. The result looked much more like masonry and less like the Roman walling in which more attention was given to the strength of the wall-face and less to its appearance.

The same development, by the way, occurs in English brick-work, the Tudor work being mostly headers; stretchers did not really come into general use until the seventeenth century when the bricklayers were fairly sure that they would not fall out.

After the thirteenth century, when transport and hauling machinery was improving, the stones became much bigger, several times their height in length and the courses themselves deeper. The difference in the appearance of the three main masonry styles, the 'header' arrangement of the eleventh and twelfth centuries, the dolls'-house perfection of the thirteenth century, and the heavy, almost industrial, appearance of the later work, is easy to recognize.

So much for the wall-face. Archaeologists who excavate the sites of ruined abbeys will probably notice the difference in the technique of the actual wall construction through those periods.

In the eleventh century the designers had to be sure to get the architectural features, in particular those which carried the work above, correctly set out. Thus the plan of any section of a wall or pier was the plan of its faces. These were all that mattered. The rest of the wall was filled in. With the large masses of the early buildings and the small size of their openings this technique sufficed. But by the thirteenth century the new technique of building a wall of solid rock, the core laid as conscientiously as the faces, enabled the supporting areas of the cathedral to be greatly reduced so that the dainty Gothic forms could replace Byzantine massiveness. And in the same way the spaces between supports could be greatly enlarged to provide room for the large Gothic window.

The steeple of Chichester Cathedral collapsed in 1861, as horrified onlookers watched the core of the eleventh-century crossing piers cascading out of the riven facings. But it has been proved by careful boring into the thirteenth-century crossing piers of Salisbury Cathedral that these are solid stone from face to face, showing that the masons had achieved the Gothic aim of building as though out of the living rock.

The original aim of masonry had been to build faces with each stone having a 'tail' to be buried in the core of the wall rather like a 'header' in brickwork. But with the coming of the thin parapet walling, which was necessary after eaves had been abandoned in favour of lead roofing, the masons were required to cut stones which had faces showing on both sides. Such stones, often laid so that the height of the course was more than the thickness of the walling, were known as 'perpend' stone, today called ashlar.

In ordinary walling ashlar was not employed as masonry but applied as a facing to a wall built of field stone or rubble. It became very useful when an old building was being re-faced in a new architectural style, the whole of the new design being simply stuck onto the old in ashlar. Half-finished alterations can be seen at Ripon Cathedral. At Exeter the twelfth-century cathedral has been completely re-cased by the present stonework; the old cathedral was exposed after a German bomb had blown this away.

From the fifteenth century onwards ashlar often replaced masonry in order to save expensive mason-work, rubble walling being built and then faced. An ashlar casing can often be detected at the angles of a building where its edges, perhaps eight inches or so thick, show in place of proper quoins.

Above the dusty or muddy floor of the site rose the walls of the cathedral. It is often difficult to realize how different the situation in the Middle Ages was in respect of matters which we today take for granted. There was, for example, no such thing as a floor as we know it. There was just the surface of the ground, quite impossible to clean and thus in a condition impossible to conceive today. It was this fact which prompted the Byzantine civilization to abandon ground floors to animals and storage and withdraw above this to an upper floor.

Only stone floors were suited to the manners of the age. Upper floors were the surfaces of stone vaults—the 'stone soller'. But ground floors were a serious problem because only in certain parts of England—Yorkshire and Somerset for example—could paving stone be found. So paving the huge churches was not one of the least of the problems facing the builders, especially as cathedral floors were always being disturbed for the purpose of interment.

At the end of the twelfth century pottery tiles came into use, the material developing a fine art of its own, both in individual tiles and in groups forming large designs. The Benedictine abbey of Chertsey on the Thames founded a notable pottery for producing these interesting tiles, with patterns ranging from heraldry and architectural design motifs to pure grotesques. The areas covered by these tiles were generally limited to parts of the church, especially before altars, where interments would be discouraged.

While the plan of a new cathedral would have been set out complete from end to end before building began, work might not necessarily have progressed evenly—as at Salisbury, for example—throughout the whole building. The long nave, for example, was not an essential part of the bishop's church, and so it is possible that the eastern arm and the crossing and transepts, and the eastern part of the nave where the choir was situated, might have been constructed first.

And even this might have been carried up only as far as the gallery floor, the story which corresponded to the foundation stage of the church. It should be borne in mind that for every foot the cathedral rose the work became slower and the cost higher. Thus funds might permit of the completion of the aisle walling and the erection of the gallery arcade with a temporary roof covering nave and aisles, until more funds accumulated and work on the elaborate clearstory with its passages and the lantern tower could be completed.

At Salisbury the church was raised evenly to the gallery floor, the eastern chapels roofed over and the building brought into use. The work however was not stopped, but the character of its architecture displayed a striking change from the austerity of the overall design when building continued with the gallery arcade.

At Rochester the manner in which the building was stopped at the gallery floor is even more clearly indicated, as the mason who continued with the gallery front paid no attention at all to the provision made by his predecessor for carrying up half-shafts as punctuation for the bays of the nave. Possibly he was averse from what he may have considered too Byzantine a style for a cathedral situated so near to the Channel coast.

Rochester Cathedral may always have suffered from being, as it were, the poor relation of its mighty neighbour at Canterbury. It is completely overshadowed by the great tower of the king's castle and squeezed between it and a similar but smaller keep built by one of its early bishops. Thus its site has always been congested and it lacked the free situation of the great Anglian churches which were its contemporaries.

The indications of indecision evidenced by its nave have been noted above and this was unfortunately followed by the erection of a clearstory of parochial class and a flat timber roof of extremely mediocre design. Fortunately, however, its eastern arm was sufficiently meagre for this to be replaced by a large thirteenth-century choir. Nevertheless part of the old eastern arm was allowed to remain *in situ*, and this caused the new choir to reproduce that same atmosphere of congestion which seems to have been the lot of the Medway cathedral.

As an example of the architecture of its period, however, the choir of Rochester is far from lacking in charm, and is moreover of unusual interest in the peculiar nature of its arrangements: the congestion seems to have pursued the cathedral right into its interior.

After extricating itself from the remains of the earlier eastern arm the new choir expands in true episcopal style. Basically it is aisle-less, but the eastern transept has eastern aisles for altars. The main walls make up for their aisle-less state by being designed with false arcades framing deep openings and thus creating the effect of aisled construction. As no blind story was needed the triforium of the clearstory is brought down over what might have been its site. The choir is vaulted with a French type of vault known as a 'sexpartite' or 'ploughshare' vault owing to the constriction of the intermediate vault cones to a shape resembling ploughshares.

The choir is raised upon a fine crypt and approached through a choir screen set above a perron, or platform with steps. The 'duplex bay' system of alternating compound piers and circular pillars is noticeable in the nave. While Rochester choir may be unspectacular in comparison with some of the great contemporary structures, it forms a charming example of Gothic architecture such as might have been seen in scores of churches once belonging to the smaller monastic houses of this country, now vanished for ever.

The writer once enjoyed a conversation with a Maltese master mason which threw a good deal of light upon the way in which a medieval cathedral was designed. A church was being built, a large circular edifice covered with a flat dome carried upon eight piers. There was no architect. The whole great structure was being entirely designed and erected by the master mason—who rather disarmingly described himself as its 'genius' (probably a naïve translation of the Italian word for engineer). The piers were being worked out in three dimensions as models cut in soft freestone, perhaps one-twentieth of full size, fashioned so accurately that even the mouldings were shown.

Congratulating the mason upon his pier detail, the writer asked how the dome was to be constructed and how its abutments—it was to be all of solid stone—were to be stabilized. It was in the reply to this query that the man supplied a complete explanation of the system of structural design employed in the medieval cathedral.

The drum upon which the dome rested, the 'genius' explained, would have to be higher externally than internally. This indicated that the man was quite familiar with the principle of a weighted abutment. But when he was asked how much the difference was to

13. OXFORD

14. GLOUCESTER

be, he thought for a moment, smiled knowingly, and replied 'quite a bit'. In this reply he not only demonstrated his confidence in divine support for the abutment of his dome, but also included what we should today call 'the factor of safety'.

Salisbury Cathedral was begun in 1220 and five years later had been completed to the gallery floor with the eastern chapels roofed and available for worship. The hollows of the vault cones had to be protected from rain which would have filled them up and during a frost might have burst the building asunder, so the aisles were covered with a temporary thatch. The centering for the main arches had been struck and the building was beginning to take up the strain.

It would take a volume as large as the present one to describe the indications of the continual troubles which beset the builders of Salisbury as their cathedral rose. Yet in spite of everything they eventually brought the amazing structure up to over four hundred feet from the ground.

The first part to give trouble was the crossing, where the drift of the arcades began to topple the crossing piers, then only at gallery height. Undismayed, however, the builders kept on with their task and just straightened the piers with each course until they had got them plumb. It will be appreciated that all arcaded structures have a tendency to drift and that the system is so elastic that usually everything settles down more or less as built. But at the crossing the angle of the aisle walling prevents any give at that point so that drift is bound to be concentrated upon the crossing piers. Hence the collapse of so many eleventh-century crossings, which was avoided by the later builders with their stronger system of wall-building.

The cathedral rose and the walls were finished. The centering of the great arches of the crossing was struck. Then a new drift began, this time caused by the settling of the crossing arches and consequent pressure upon the lightly built arcades of the gallery. The transepts began to feel the strain and their clearstories to drift away from the crossing, the great piers of which again began to lean, this time in the opposite direction. The result is that the great tall piers may be seen today in the form of bows bending into the crossing.

Having waited to see whether the cathedral would fall down and found that it had come to rest, the builders proceeded with the lantern tower by building an arcaded blind story to receive the main roofs, and by constructing above this the usual lantern, probably replicas of the bays of the clearstory. This lantern they proceeded to cover with a high vault, ignoring the fact that no abutments for it existed, nor any top weight other than the timber steeple.

The vaulting of the lantern spread. Flying buttresses were later added to try to check this but in the end the vault had to be taken down and the high vaults of nave and choir joined by a new vault which concealed the lantern from below. Eventually, of course, the wrecked lantern with its steeple was taken down—the blind story below still shows the signs of its dissolution—and the tremendous tower and steeple raised upon the tortured piers of the crossing which the builders obviously believed would stand any load they cared to put upon them.

The cathedral remained unmoved by its tribulations. The southwest crossing pier sank slightly under the enormous load so Christopher Wren plumbed the spire—but found its four hundred feet less than two feet out of plumb. Concerned for the safety of the split angles of the crossing tower, however, he bound them with bands of iron which were made for him by the anchor-makers of Portsmouth Dockyard.

So the cathedral abides. Beneath the mighty steeple the prayers still rise. And from its summit our history watches over us, in the shapes of many poor men who hauled its stones four hundred feet in the air.

6

Details of the Architecture

When examining an architectural style of such eminence as the Gothic it is of interest to discover what particular aspect is illustrated by that style alone, and then try to follow the way in which this element developed from preceding styles.

Starting from first principles, there are two basic forms of architecture. There is the trabeated in which openings are spanned by a beam first of wood and then of stone. And there is the arcuated in which they are covered with arches formed of pieces of stone or brick known as 'voussoirs'. Gothic is one of the arcuated styles and its fortunes are bound up with the development of its arches.

There is a third style which has hitherto been little considered by architectural historians as its material is ephemeral and most of its structures have disappeared. This is a style which towards the end of the first millennium was regarded as architecture of the highest order, the timber building of Anglo-Saxon England. As more and more consideration is given to the form of these buildings as they might have been, we shall learn more about the origins of our English Gothic. For the time being, however, we must bear in mind that it existed and cannot be ignored, especially in view of the fact that one of its basic elements, the curved 'cruck', is so very Gothic in appearance.

For the time being, however, we shall confine our study to permanent architecture of masonry. An arch has to be built by setting the voussoirs upon a temporary wooden 'centering' which is struck after the mortar of the arch has set. The centering has to be virtually the full width of the arch from wall-face to wall-face.

Assuming an arch to be properly supported at either end to prevent its thrust from overturning its 'abutments', the part of the arch masonry which does its work by resisting the forces trying to crush it is what architectural historians call the 'archivolt' but in common parlance is the 'soffit', the underside of the arch which is laid upon the centering.

The history of the arch is the history of the development of the form of its soffit. The silhouette of the arch is of small significance.

In the trabeated architecture of Classical days the underside of the lintel was basically flat, though it could be ornamented by shallow panelling which did not alter the form of the soffit. When the Romans began to use the arch its soffit followed the same general scheme as the lintel.

The Classical beam spanned from column to column, the Roman arch from pier to pier of massive masonry designed to withstand its tendency to spread and collapse. The column began to find itself relegated to an ornamental role, carrying only very light arches forming part of the scheme of interior decoration.

The Byzantines followed this up by giving the column a definite part to play in helping to support the fronts of galleries carried upon vaults across an opening between two main piers.

Thus was introduced into architecture a new device—the secondary support. While the roof of the structure was supported upon piers, interior features could be carried on columns.

The secondary arcades being of lesser width, wall-face to wall-face, than the main arches, the face of the inner feature was set back from that of the main supports on the sides of which half-columns or 'responds' were provided to carry the ends of the lesser arcade. Thus a complete 'inner order' of supports with their arches over, subsidiary to the main structural order of the building, became accepted as a normal feature of architecture.

The gallery arcades of great Byzantine churches could be five bays long as at the Hagia Sophia, or four as at St. Mark's. They could be fewer still in the smaller churches—a trifora perhaps, or even a bifora having a single central column. This final ordinance resulted in the 'duplex bay' formed of a great bay enclosing two smaller ones, such as we see so splendidly displayed at Durham.

It is in its aedicular form, as the bifora window seen in the belfries
of Byzantine campaniles, that the most interesting aspect of the
secondary order appears, for it is from this valuable feature that
so much of Gothic architectural detail develops. (Fig. 24.)

One of the earliest of the great eleventh-century buildings of
this country is Winchester Cathedral. A study of the transepts,
which remain free from later remodellings, gives a perfect illustration of Western Byzantine, very humble in its ordinance yet
absolutely confident in the nature of its presentation.

Each arch of the upper of the two stories is filled with a bifora,
the feature with its tympanum set back behind the wall-face. The
bifora has a central shaft and two responding half-shafts. In the
main arcade below, the bifora is of course absent. But the responds
are there and between them passes a single arch instead of two small
ones, this arch forming an inner, narrower arch, beneath the broad
main one. Thus the flat soffit in the tradition of Classical architecture
has vanished and been replaced by an arch built 'in orders'.

This is a very important innovation, a creation of the Western
Byzantine architects which laid the foundations of the Gothic style.

The transepts at Winchester provide the only example of an
inner order used at this early date in an English cathedral; but at the
priory church of Blyth in Nottinghamshire, a relic of the days of
the great monastic churches and now used as a parish church, the
same primitive ordinance can be seen.

That the device was found acceptable there can be no doubt. It
probably enabled a great deal of centering to be saved, for each
order could act as centering for that over it. At Ely Cathedral a
third order has been introduced.

One cannot but be impressed by the confidence with which such
an innovation as the inner order is used at Winchester. Actually
there are many instances in parish churches of tower and chancel
arches being built thus. One might have supposed that the ordered
arch came first and the ordered pier was designed to carry it. But
at the ancient Wessex cathedral the two fit so neatly together as to
suggest that the complete device may have had a history behind it.

This is where we may detect the influence of Anglo-Saxon timber
architecture. It seems very probable from the evidence supplied

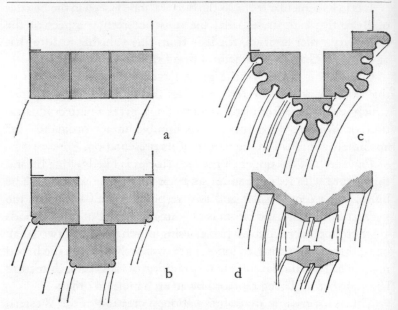

Fig. 15. *The 'ordered' arch*
The Classical arch with its flat soffit is
indicated in (a). In (b) the inner ring of
stones has been turned first and the outer
rings, one to each wall-face, are supported
upon it. This is the 'ordered' arch which
characterizes the English Byzantine style
and forms the basis for the Gothic arch
when the Gothic moulding (c) is
introduced to disguise the structural
orders. An extension of the 'order'
principle into the arches of windows
enabled bar tracery to be introduced (d)

by twelfth-century timber building that the basic structural element
of a timber church was a group of four great posts perhaps two feet
square, and that these were joined by curved struts meeting in the
form of arches. These braces would have been of lesser scantling
than the great posts and carried down alongside them in the form of
smaller posts attached to them, the combination of post and strut
forming an inner order in relation to the main constructional
element provided by the great posts. The post with its surrounding

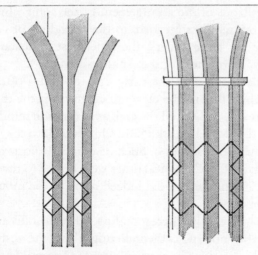

Fig. 16.   *The 'ordered' pillar*
This may have been developed as a
result of the application of timber braces
to a timber post. This may indeed
represent the true origin of the
'ordered' system of construction and have
been transferred from timber to
masonry. The ordered pillar is a
concomitant to the ordered arch, but
which came first may still be a
matter for speculation

members is of course a timber prototype of the masonry compound pier, and this in due course becomes the clustered pillar of Gothic days. Each of course is based upon the Byzantine pier and is in no way descended from the Classical column.

There is strong evidence that the ordered arch of the Winchester type was frowned on by contemporary architects. The flat soffit had enjoyed far too long a tradition for it to be lightly abandoned. St. Albans and Norwich showed an interest, however, in that they softened the edges of their soffits by introducing small orders beginning to intrude into the flat surface.

Peterborough shows the inner order already broken up into arch mouldings, a development well on the way to the Gothic arch. Ely has two inner orders simply embellished with edge roll

another acceptance of the arrangement of the soffit which was to convert it from its Classical form to the splendour of Gothic. At Hereford we see three orders, the innermost enriched with the splendid zigzag ornament of the Anglo-Saxons.

One of the variants of the early ordered arch—often seen in parochial architecture of the eleventh century—is the carrying up of a half-shaft respond round the arch as a large roll moulding. It is this which is developed in cathedral architecture into the triple rolls of Durham and Peterborough. Such determined efforts as these to destroy the flat soffit of Classical times were bound to revolutionize architectural ordinance and did indeed result in the moulded arch of the Gothic.

The half-shaft and its corresponding half-roll soffit are a crude device probably not of 'cathedral' origin but the result of less sophisticated operations in parish churches. The real beginning of the Gothic moulding may be seen in the edge roll formed by cutting 'quirks' on either side of the 'arris' or edge of the stone and the arris itself worked round into a roll. The half-shaft could have been cut with the mason's stone-axe but the edge roll represented carving and until the introduction of the bolster would have had to be worked with the chisel of a carver. During the twelfth century the centre roll and its derivatives disappear and the edge rolls become standard practice, the number of inner orders being increased so as to destroy for good all memory of the Classical soffit. (Fig. 15.)

Late in the twelfth century one can see the progress of this development in the choir at Canterbury and at the close of the century it can be seen in the east choir of Chichester at a stage closely resembling the Gothic form, though the arches displaying it are still semicircular.

Chichester Cathedral is one of the most primitive of the pre-Conquest great churches. Badly off for building materials, the bleak chalk downs about it produced nothing better than flint. In 1082 the original cathedral at Selsey was abandoned to the waves and a new one begun in the ruins of the Roman city at Chichester.

The main arcade of the cathedral is so primitive in its construction that it does not even have properly designed compound piers, the supports of the arcades being merely sections of walling with their ends faced with masonry to form jambs for the arches over. Nevertheless there seems to have been an attempt to provide a west front by building a west transept, the wings of which were later raised to form a pair of towers.

A unique feature of the cathedral is the fact that its nave has five aisles, the eleventh-century aisle walls having been pierced with arches during the thirteenth century and the nave widened to beyond the projection of the west transept.

The eastern arm of the cathedral was not enlarged during the thirteenth century for at the end of the twelfth the eleventh-century *chevet* was removed and the building extended by two charming bays to form a chapel for the local saint, Richard of Chichester. This chapel, with its slender pillars each ringed by four Purbeck marble shafts, is an interesting example of the development of the Corinthianesque style which reached here from the Île de France, probably through Canterbury, but made small progress in this country.

The late-twelfth-century alterations to the cathedral included an attempt to improve the appearance of the rather primitive nave with the aid of Purbeck marble shafts.

The lantern tower was rebuilt during the thirteenth century and one of the rare cathedral stone spires added. In 1861 the crossing piers failed and the whole structure fell into the church. It was rebuilt to the same design.

Instead of a belfry story added to its lantern tower the cathedral was provided with a sturdy bell-tower standing in isolation beside it. The same situation existed at Salisbury where a similar tower was built. This tower, however, was pulled down at the end of the eighteenth century by the destroyer Wyatt; in hot summers its foundations show in ghostly fashion through the turf.

In the very Continental choir of Canterbury the inner order has clearly been accepted but it is most uncomfortably balanced upon the Corinthianesque pillar. At Chichester the same pillar has been provided with extra shafts to carry the inner order. We see here a substitute for the clustered pillar which was the real answer to the ordered arch and which grew out of the compound pier, not the Corinthianesque column with shafts added.

What can clearly be descried at Chichester, however, is the

development of the ordered arch by means of mouldings until the separate orders have almost vanished among them. This is the real beginning of the Gothic, and is irrespective of the shape of the arch, which at Chichester is still Byzantine.

For the shape of the arch does not make the Gothic. Most of the grim arcades of the twelfth-century Cisterian churches have pointed arches, their soffits unimaginatively flat. But the richly moulded arcades of the lovely twelfth-century choir of St. Hugh at Lincoln have arches which are very little raised above the semi-circular, certainly far from approaching that acutely pointed form hitherto regarded as a primary feature of early Gothic architecture.

Once the principle of the ordered arch had been introduced into this country and joined to its supporting ordered pier, its aedicular form was bound to appear.

There was considerable aesthetic appeal in the ordered arch springing along its jambs, direct from the ground. The multiplicity of nooks and crannies gave plenty of scope for the inventiveness of the carver. Where an arch was to be seen mainly from one side it was possible to adjust the soffit so that this side had more orders than the other. This technique may be seen employed to the full in the large arches of west fronts, as at Lincoln.

But it is in its aedicular form as a surround to doorways that it is most splendidly displayed, every inch of the doorcase enriched with all the skill of the Anglo-Saxon carver.

The necessity for planning from the roof down is what landed the early builders into difficulties the result of which can be seen to this day. In particular one sees examples of the erection of a Corinthian pillar and then the dilemma of how it was going to carry the various arches above. The ordered pier avoided such complications.

Reduced to basic terms, the fact was that the Corinthian column had never been designed to carry an arch. It spread itself pleasantly against a lintel, but presented with the square downthrust of a pair of arches the volutes stuck out unhappily and looked strange. Brunelleschi was to discover this one day in the future and turn to strange methods to solve the problem.

The arch belonged to the pier and the ordered arch to the compound variety of this. If the twelfth-century designers thought otherwise they could go to Gloucester and see the sad muddle they had got into there with their huge round pillars—having to design soffits with pairs of large half-rolls to try to fill in part of the gap at the top of the pillar. Even the designers of the great Anglian churches, employing circular pillars out of deference to the great bays of Byzantium, found they had to do strange things with capitals.

The only solution to the problem of the arcade and its supports was acceptance of the compound pier. Once this came into use architecture was able to progress; the piers were designed from the top downwards with orders to support those of the arcades, and with others to carry the transverse arches of the aisle vaulting. Often, to balance this, an order carried a half-shaft passing right up the face of the nave wall so as to provide bay punctuation. It is these shafts which are often mistakenly assumed to be preparations for a high vault.

The column, or its successor the pier, was an independent structural feature incomplete without its cap and base. Even when converted to the task of carrying an arch, the pier seldom rose from its springing line without this being marked by some kind of horizontal feature preserving the level. This band was known as an 'impost', and is a prominent feature of any arcuated style. The crude plastered brick arches of St. Albans had their rough imposts formed in the same material.

The proper finish to a column is its capital. But no sort of capital had been invented which would provide a finish to a Byzantine pier. The compound pier, however, with its half-shafts, angle-rolls and nook-shafts, was able to include with each of these a cap at springing level, joining their upper mouldings with a continuous band indicating the impost.

The Byzantine cap which became adopted in the West was a derivative of the Classical capital known as the Doric, the nature of which will be discussed later. Reduced in width to that of a shaft, it becomes the universal Western Byzantine cap seen in most of the compound piers of the eleventh and twelfth centuries in this country. This is the 'cubiform' type of cap which might be called the Doric of Anglo-Saxon architecture.

Any attempt to design a single capital to fit a large circular or compound pier was quite useless, as can be seen at Peterborough or in the remarkably naïve experiment at Gloucester, which has simply resulted in what is in effect a very clumsy impost moulding put to shame by a similar feature, charmingly designed and embellished, at Hereford. This is a remarkably confident piece of design, perhaps the most successful treatment of the circular pillar in English architecture. The round pillars of Durham have octagonal versions of the cubiform cap expanded to form very unsatisfactory capitals. It is clear that no English designer ever really discovered or even developed a satisfactory finish to the circular masonry pillar which under the influence of 'basilicanism' had been virtually forced upon the English architects. In spite of its adoption by the Cisterian colonists of the mid-twelfth century the circular pillar could never have survived, and we see the progressive Benedictine Order continuing to employ the far more convenient compound pier of the Anglian cathedrals.

We have noted the interesting compromise between the Corinthianesque pillar and the compound pier effected in the east choir of Chichester which might almost be said to be the first of the clustered pillars of the Gothic. But this experiment is in reality a group of five independent shafts and not a true cluster such as that which was being developed from the compound pier.

The break-through occurred with dramatic suddenness at Wells, where the compound pier appears completely transformed into a Gothic clustered pillar. It was achieved by applying the principle of the Gothic arch moulding to the orders of the pillar, covering each order and filling each nook with a shaft and then cutting a pair of quirks into each of these so that the single roll became triple. By this simple device eight Byzantine shafts had become twenty-four Gothic ribs. The Gothic had arrived, and in a fashion which demonstrated that the style was not a product of sophisticated thought but of simple craftsmanship on the banker.

The eight caps at Wells are in essence Corinthianesque but the foliage is native and not Hellenistic, the ancient conventions being interpreted, as befits islanders, with the confidence born of freedom.

To return again to the Chichester pillars, the development from such a plan was bound to be to gather the five components into a single unit, even though this meant sacrificing the central column with its capital, so that the pillar could become resolved as a cluster of four shafts.

It will be seen that the significant change in the nature of the arch soffit from a flat surface to a wedge-shaped section was bound to influence the plan of the supporting pier by converting it from a square set in line with the arcade and turning it at an angle of forty-five degrees with this. This abaxial pillar is the concomitant of the moulded arch and thus is one of the basic elements of the Gothic. The compound 'Western Byzantine' pier of the eleventh century was the first stage of this deviation, and the shafted column seen at Chichester might be called the twelfth-century 'Romanesque' or 'basilican' version.

We have seen how the first came to fruition at Wells. From it a great family of clustered pillars was born to fill our cathedrals, culminating, perhaps, in the pillars at Exeter.

Development from the Chichester type is not so clear to follow owing to the losses after 1539, but one cathedral at least, Salisbury, gives us a splendid illustration of at least one of its derivatives. Here the central core became skilfully expanded into a form of column never before seen in architecture and which thenceforth becomes a typical Gothic pillar. It is a cluster not of shafts but of circular columns and only a fraction of the circumference of each is showing. The purpose of this curious arrangement is to provide re-entrants into which Purbeck shafts can be inserted.

The Salisbury pillars are themselves structural innovations in that they go a step further than the solid-core pillar that was being actually built of drums of hard stone in the fashion of the Classical column. Thus they are in fact of 'Romanesque' rather than Byzantine origin. The building of pillars in drums, while difficult to achieve in the case of large buildings, was a great help in parish church architecture, but where heavy structures were concerned depended for its success upon the existence of much harder stone than the ordinary freestone upon which medieval architecture had been based. Thus in normal practice, although the smaller pillars of parish churches could be built in drums of freestone, cathedrals had to continue to build their much larger supports of freestone used in the traditional manner. Accordingly we find Lichfield, Worcester and other cathedrals building slightly more restrained forms of the Wells pillar, with clusters of shafts, some of which are of Purbeck 'marble', attached to the body of the pillar while others are formed with it.

There can be no doubt that the fine stone of Purbeck, lovingly called Purbeck marble, played a large part in the development of English Gothic. When polished it has a lovely dove-grey colour and mingles charmingly with the freestone. The Victorian blacking which makes the shafts stand out like drain-pipes is a shocking desecration. Some years ago the Clerk of Works at Salisbury cleaned away some of the blacking and was enchanted with the result.

Had it not been for the necessity of devising some such scheme for incorporating the Purbeck shafting the craze for which was infecting all contemporary designers, the Gothic pillar might never have been invented. But where there were no such shafts the core of the Salisbury pillar was just turned round forty-five degrees so that its four protuberances could adopt the normal abaxial setting. In future this 'quadritruncate' type of pillar was to become standard in all parish church architecture and it can also be found intermingling with the shafted compound pillar to create many delightful examples of wholly Gothic features stalking through our cathedrals.

With all this experimenting with the design of pillars the problem of the capital remained to be solved. The cubiform cap had disappeared during the twelfth century; the Corinthianesque cap was flourishing but could only be used as a finish to a slender shaft and in any case required the attentions of highly skilled carvers.

In all architecture, the capital is the most important feature of the ordinance. It crowns the column and indicates the level from which the arch springs.

It is well known in its Doric guises, as displayed by the Parthenon at Athens, the swelling *echinus* rising from the sturdy shaft of the column supporting the plain square *abacus*.

Far too crude for Roman taste, it was never used by them in its archaic Bronze Age form. But the Byzantines, who after all were largely Greeks, revived it in curious fashion, combining the two portions into a single very crude capital resembling one half of an ordinary domestic cushion which has been split into two. These clumsy 'cushion' capitals continued to perform the function of spreading the top of a circular pillar so that it could carry the springing of an arch.

But such over-extended angles as those of the cushion capital were prone to break off in the course of buildings' settlements to which the regions of Attica and Anatolia are prone by reason of their earthquakes. If the angles of a cushion capital happen to be deliberately broken off almost back to the face of its shaft the result is a 'cubiform' cap which has four flat faces semicircular in shape owing to vestiges of the 'cushion' surviving at its angles.

Although deprivation of its spreading function made the cubiform capital of little value for carrying arches in its aedicular form, it was invaluable for serving as a cap to the slender shafts that softened the edges of piers and filled their re-entrants with 'nook-shafts'.

The cubiform cap could not be satisfactorily expanded to form a proper capital, though attempts were made in some cathedrals such as Ely and Peterborough to perform this with somewhat doubtful success.

With the intrusive 'basilican' element which characterizes the twelfth century came the introduction of the Corinthian capital, the splendid crowning feature of the giant columns of the Hellenistic era but employed by the Byzantines as a secondary feature mainly for the purposes of ornament.

This capital has, instead of the convex *echinus* of the Doric, a concave 'bell' embellished with fern leaves and fronds. During the twelfth century there appeared in this country curious presentations of the Byzantine cushion capital with its *echinus* scalloped and even ornamented with little 'volutes' or crockets at the angles. Very commonly used in parish churches they only appear in one cathedral, that of Exeter, the early work of which has been encased within the present building. A variety of these scalloped capitals is the 'coniferous' which has its bell carved into a series of cones, another curious type of capital peculiar to twelfth-century England and not used in cathedrals. The motif, however, may be encountered upon impost mouldings at Hereford and Carlisle.

These experiments with curious types of capitals were all due to one persistent problem—how to design a Gothic capital. The cap, cubiform or Corinthianesque, was well established and understood, but only one has to examine the results of the strained attempts to convert the former into the capital of a large column—as at Peterborough, for example—to realize that the situation had become desperate.

Notwithstanding the use of the modified form of the Byzantine cushion capital at Exeter, such uncouth features seem to have become the hallmark of the parish churches of the twelfth century, to which they have undoubtedly lent a great deal of rustic charm. But the cathedral capital was, inevitably, to develop from the Corinthian. This feature will be described more fully later, but its main features are a tall concave 'bell' set between the moulded 'abacus' which it supports and a narrow moulded band called an 'astragal' connecting it with the shaft.

The cathedral which must have set the fashion for the architecture of the early thirteenth century was that of Salisbury begun in 1220 on a new site. There are indications that the bishop who inaugurated its erection was a man holding somewhat outdated Cistercian views on austerity. Carving is scarce in the cathedral and there is no trace of Corinthianism. But what we see in the capitals of the columns is the Corinthian capital without its carving but with the hollow bell and the upper and lower mouldings run, in true Gothic fashion, round the top of the pillars to provide it with a capital. (Fig. 17.)

This employment of the basic elements of a Corinthian cap without its ornament was a very skilful piece of design, one, moreover, which was to set its mark upon Gothic architecture.

It must be remembered that for every cathedral built, scores of parish churches were being erected, and that these too required

15. WELLS

16. LICHFIELD

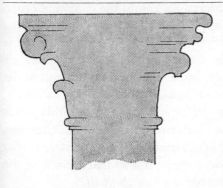

Fig. 17.

The Gothic moulded cap
The Corinthianesque cap continued to be popular during the twelfth century and Anglicized forms of it with modified foliage appear through Gothic architecture. But carvers were not always available, so the Gothic banker masons converted its silhouette into systems of mouldings in the design of which they had long been proficient

architectural direction. Purbeck shafts were not for them, nor could they often find carvers to produce Corinthian capitals. But the architectural style of Salisbury, lovely in its austerity, provided a simple form of Gothic which could be used anywhere. So the rustic Gothic pillar became based upon the 'quadritruncate' type, a band of moulding which was in fact a Corinthian capital without its ornament.

In the cathedrals the pillars were generally speaking shafted, either with or without attached Purbeck shafts. The moulded capital surrounding the whole top of the pillar was used but its bell was more often than not filled with carving.

The capital continues its traditional role right through the Gothic era, greatly changed from its Classical ancestor, however, in its guise of a strong horizontal feature rather more of an impost than a capital. But towards the end of the Gothic era, when architects were striving to augment the effect of verticality which had ever been their aim, they began to extricate themselves from the tyranny of the springing line, anachronistic relic of Classical architecture. The great pillars of Canterbury are only here and there caught at the springing line by a small cap or impost moulding and elsewhere are permitted to shoot up unchecked from pavement to high vault.

To recapitulate the history of the pillar through English medieval architecture: this originates in the Byzantine pier and develops, under the influence of the ordered arch, into the compound pier. The 'Romanesque' column appears in the circular pillars of the twelfth-century parish churches with their modified Byzantine cushion capitals aiming at the Corinthianesque. These pillars are of course built of small stones, but a more serious attempt at the Classical type of column is seen in the hard-stone pillars of Salisbury, of the 'quadritruncate' type which develops into the Gothic parish church pillar but plays only a small part in cathedral architecture. With the increased verticality of the later Gothic the clustered pillar begins to lose some of its independent caps so that the rest of the pillar shall rise unbroken from paving to high vault.

We have begun to deal with the origin of the capital in its Doric form and the modifications of this basic shape into the cushion capital and the breaking down of that into the ubiquitous cubiform cap. The real capital of architectural history, however, is the Corinthian. In its original form—possibly salvaged from destroyed temples—it formed the only architectural feature of the Roman basilican churches. Derived from the original Greek, its disadvantage in an arcuated world was that it had been designed to carry flat soffits, was inconveniently designed to take an arch, and was hopelessly unsuitable to support an ordered one. One only has to visit the interior of a great thirteenth-century church in the Île de France to be able to appreciate the difficulties which attend attempts to assimilate two completely different styles. Not only do the orders of the arch fail completely to achieve aesthetic union with the columns, but when it comes to additional features such as vaulting shafts the whole assemblage is seen to be most uncomfortably balanced upon the unsuitable capitals of the columns from which they are supposed to be springing.

In its aedicular form as a cap to a small shaft the Corinthian Order performed a signal service for the twelfth-century architecture of this country, and it is doubtless the ancestor of the carved cap—and its assemblage into a complete capital crowning the whole pillar—which is one of the delights of Gothic architecture. But its most lasting effect was upon the ordinary Gothic capital of the English parish church, and in a most extraordinary manner which is difficult both to contemplate and describe.

Details of the Architecture

The Corinthian capital is joined to the shaft of its column at a narrow band of moulding known as the 'astragal'. The upper member of the capital is its 'abacus', a moulded band which as it happens turns out at the angles to accommodate the characteristic voluted angles of the feature. Between astragal and abacus is the 'bell' of the capital, a bell with its mouth upwards. Around this bell are arranged bands of leaves which in the Classical capital are those of the acanthus fern but in the English version might be clover leaves or some stylized foliage.

But the characteristic features of the capital are the four uncoiling fern fronds, the 'volutes', which rise to support the outthrust angles of the abacus. It is the uncoiling frond, like that of English bracken, which eventually becomes stylized by the Gothic carvers as the 'crocket' to be ranged around arches and up the sides of gables and pinnacles.

If one draws the *silhouette* of a Corinthian capital one finds this to be rising from the small astragal moulding in the shape of the upturned bell to end, not in the abacus but in the uncoiling frond of the volute. Above this pronounced feature of the silhouette is the moulded abacus itself. This is the Gothic capital, encountered everywhere in the parish church arcade. In general appearance it is nothing like its noble progenitor: only its silhouette reveals its descent from this. (Fig. 17.)

Here is Gothic at its most revealing, an illustration of the paramount importance of the moulding. Who but the Gothic designers could have made a circular moulded capital out of a Corinthian silhouette?

The capital we have been discussing is the moulded capital, the true capital of the Gothic ordinance, in parish church architecture set upon the 'quadritruncate' pillar and in the cathedral following the convolutions of the clustered pillar.

The queer capitals developed from the Byzantine cushions had a long vogue during the twelfth century in parish churches, but by the end of that period had vanished utterly together with all other relics of Classicism. Apart from the curious attempts to spread the cubiform cap into a capital these were the only true examples of that architectural feature.

The moulded cap which by spreading round the circumference of the clustered pillar became a kind of capital was the Gothic form of capital which was rather more like an elaborate impost moulding. It should be noted that in its purely moulded form as at Salisbury the Gothic cap has no carving. This has been stripped from its bell, the only survivor being the curious moulding below the abacus recalling the Corinthian volute.

But a culture which during the twelfth century had been enjoying the effects created by Corinthianesque caps was not likely to be satisfied with plain caps unadorned with carving. Thus the carved bell soon came back again, but in an entirely different form, the bell often being convex—almost Byzantine—instead of the true bell of the Corinthian. In carved caps, by the way, the vestigial 'volute' moulding disappears, absorbed into the carving. So here is a second class of Gothic capital, the moulded capital with its bell, usually convex, richly carved. Generally speaking, the carved bell begins to have Corinthian proportions, tall and concave, later bells being lower and convex. On the whole the carving tends to develop from stylism towards naturalism, the former being attempts to imitate Classical models dimly understood, the latter a reversion to the craft of the Anglo-Saxon carver.

It should be appreciated that while the strange features discoverable in twelfth-century parish churches were true capitals, the eleventh-century crowning members of the great piers were not capitals but were developed impost mouldings placed there to indicate the springing line and perhaps in some cases to provide lodgement for story rods during erection. The imposts at St. Albans are plain square bands—all that was really necessary. But during the eleventh and twelfth centuries the standard impost moulding had a square upper edge and its lower edge chamfered off. This was part of the ordinance and is never absent. It marks all springing lines, passing round the pier to do so. Any cubiform caps which may happen to be crowning ornamental shafts come below it. Any isolated caps are finished with it. It passes round the arches of windows as a hood-mould to keep stormwater running down the wall face above from reaching the glazing. It serves as a string-course either at springing lines or at story levels. It is, of course, a 'tablement' and with its chamfer reflects that of the plinth below.

As has been explained earlier, the string-course served an important function in the constructional setting-out of the building. Thus it continues into the thirteenth century, but in a more sophisticated form. The flat top goes, the moulding becoming either a narrow roll or two of these with a hollow between, often filled with the curious pyramidal pile of petals known to antiquaries as 'dogtooth'. The same rounding-off is seen on the abacus of the moulded capital.

After the thirteenth century the round 'bull-nose' moulding changes again, the lower quadrant being set back behind the upper in what may perhaps have suggested a roll of parchment. Towards the end of the Gothic era the moulding becomes very characteristic; much larger, it has a wide splay above and a hollow beneath ending in a kind of miniature astragal—it may be a kind of aedicular rendering of the moulded capital and indeed is used a great deal for small caps.

As a result of the twelfth century the builders learnt a great deal about building for climate. Their timber buildings must have been beautifully designed to keep them safe from the cold and damp of the winters they had to endure. Now the builders were learning weatherproofing features available to the masonry builder. The hood-mould over windows is an example; it was also used over the arches or main arcades where it provided a pleasant aesthetic device.

But what they learnt at the end of the twelfth century in particular was the principle of the 'drip'. The old impost moulding had led the condensation water down its chamfer. The bull-nose was more likely to shed it, and if it is undercut to provide a 'drip' as is seen on the modern window-sill water cannot pass up into the hollow and thus must drop off. The undercut 'abacus' or string-course is typical of the early thirteenth century.

Since the buttress had not yet been invented as a structural device its sloping 'set-offs' were not yet evident, but at Salisbury the buttress-like projections have sets of water-shedding mouldings apparently put there for ornament.

No support is complete without a visible base. During the

eleventh and twelfth centuries piers and walls were both set upon their 'tablements'—plinths. Shafts with caps, however, had to have bases to balance these in proper Classical fashion. In all Classical architecture there is only one type of base, known as the 'Attic' base. It has two roll mouldings with a hollow between. In the eleventh-century churches a form of Attic base was used in which all three mouldings were indicated but had little vigour.

During the thirteenth century the Attic base was brought in—probably an aspect of 'Corinthianizing'—with great vigour. The shafts, and even the large circular pillars themselves, are provided with a splendid array of base mouldings. But the Attic base is not suited to this country and the deep hollow was always filled with water condensing upon the masonry and running down it into the 'water-holding bases', as antiquaries call them. Thus as the century progressed the fine old base became a series of three rolls.

Again it must be emphasized that the base is a part of the column, or, in Gothic architecture, a part of its diminutive the shaft. A pier does not have a base, for it is similar to a piece of walling and has a plinth. Only its shafts, if it has any, have bases.

As we have seen, the plinth was not a foundation—not even an aesthetic foundation. It is a constructional necessity. But, once provided, there was nothing to say that it could not succumb to that fundamental system which was the basis of Gothic architecture —the system of mouldings. Thus it did in fact become an important aesthetic feature, giving the building as it were a visible foundation.

The sills of the main windows of the aisles, representing an important level, were often joined by a string-course. This, too, was frequently expanded as a band of mouldings which, combined with a moulded plinth below, actually gave the building that most splendid of aesthetic foundations, a podium.

If we may pass from the podium up to the wall-top, we see there the eaves carried on the inevitable corbel-table, a 'tablement' supported by projecting corbels, often grotesques.

During the thirteenth century the corbel comes very much into prominence. The structural vaults above the cathedral aisles had been carried by the main piers and by responds set against the aisle walls. The high vaults had no such provision made for them. Some of the early churches had half-round shafts rising from the main piers. Intended merely for punctuation, these could now be made to serve as vaulting shafts. Generally speaking, however, the erection of a new high vault meant the provision of vaulting shafts from which to spring it. And such shafts had to be carried upon corbels, often set low down between the arches of the arcade.

At first a kind of shaft-less cap, the corbel expanded downwards into a fine architectural feature, achieving its zenith in Exeter Cathedral, where it is enriched with splendid naturalistic carving.

The study of carving is a subject for the attention of the art historian rather than the architect, and most of the features so far considered have been in essence structural and their ornament only a secondary matter. But there is one ornamental feature in architecture which, although purely decorative as regards its purpose, derives its form from some structural architectural source. This is the type of feature known as the aedicule.

The aedicule, literally a building in miniature, is a structural feature reproduced on a much reduced scale for decorative purposes. One can easily understand how this device came about. All architecture has at some time or other been drawn up on parchment or on a board to a small scale, prior to its enlargement in the building itself. One can see that the draughtsman could have been struck by the potentialities of his sketches for decorative purposes.

Byzantine architecture is based upon the square pier carrying the great arch and in many cases the Classical column carrying a pair of lesser arches set between them—the 'duplex bay'. Reduced to the scale of a belfry window this composition becomes the Byzantine bifora which is found throughout eleventh-century English architecture, particularly in the fronts of cathedral galleries as at Peterborough. We shall later observe the vital part it plays in the architecture of the Gothic.

Almost the only contribution of the Roman 'basilican' style of church architecture was the arcade, in the Byzantine church unknown. This horizontal—and therefore non-monumental—motif becomes in its aedicular form the applied wall-arcade appearing everywhere in all periods of English cathedral architecture, especially as a dado. It is also used for horizontal punctuation, for joining bay features together, and for the decoration of wall surfaces such as those of early towers or the great west front of Ely.

The dado is a feature which must have developed from early days. In an altered form it has continued in use almost to the present day. It undoubtedly owes its origin to the poor condition of the interior of early buildings, caused by damp rising from the ground meeting that driving against the outside of the building and accumulating in the lower parts of the walling. There was probably some provision, comparable with the matchboarding of Victorian days, to conceal these conditions and make the building appear more decent internally.

In a timber building the need must have been indeed great. The lower part of a wall built of field stone in weak mortar must also have been an unpleasant object to lean against. Dados, perhaps of good masonry, were probably first used to create a better impression of the lower part of the wall next to the user of the building.

By the eleventh century the arcaded dado has an established position around the interior of the cathedral. Its design changes with the periods through which it passes. During the thirteenth century its arches become trefoiled, something a real arcade could hardly have achieved. In St. Hugh's choir at Lincoln Cathedral the interlacing motif popular during the twelfth century is restored by applying one arcade upon another.

The Gothic depends greatly for its external effect upon its skyline, broken into interesting silhouettes by turrets and pinnacles.

By definition the turret is a small tower. It is usually a stair-turret situated at the angle of a building. Architecturally speaking its form may well be aedicular, so that the turrets of the twelfth century could well represent smaller versions of those which crowned the lantern. Often they are octagonal, a form which might well be that of a vanished steeple. Some are circular, like the splendid examples terminating the west front at Ely. At Salisbury the turrets are capped with aedicular clustered pillars, a typically Gothic approach. Most are finished with some kind of stone spirelet, though those at Ely, which are very elaborately fashioned, might have ended in timber steeples.

With the coming of the structural buttress supporting the thrust

136

of the high vault by way of the flying arch, the buttresses had to be raised high above the aisle roof and heavily weighted to take the strain without toppling. The finish of the early buttress was usually a tall gable of stone, a feature prominent on the exterior of Lincoln.

But the characteristic terminal feature of Gothic architecture is the pinnacle which appears on the gables and 'set-offs' of buttresses and piercing the skyline above the tops of towers. The Gothic pinnacle is altogether an interesting feature and seems to embody more of medieval architecture than might have been imagined.

It would seem obvious that it is an aedicular representation of a steeple. And when we examine its exact form we find that it is a steeple rising from a miniature square tower having its side walls finished in gables. And, moreover, that these gables are not purely elevational but are the ends of roofs set in cruciform fashion with the actual pinnacle rising above their intersection. This is a very remarkable discovery, for we have only one type of gabled tower remaining, that at Sompting in Sussex, and this has a 'helm' spire rising from its gables. Nowhere have we a tower-top roofed in cruciform fashion. Yet it would appear that at some time they were so common as to become, in aedicular form, that most ubiquitous of Gothic features, the pinnacle.

It would seem very probable that there were Anglo-Saxon timber churches—or even later stone ones—which had no central tower but were simply squares roofed with two roofs crossing each other and with a small steeple, like the French *flèche* which is the Continental substitute for the English lantern tower, perched upon the intersection. (Fig. 18b.)

The gables of an early church would certainly have been excessively tall, and its area possibly so small that the central steeple would have taken up quite a large amount of this. Thus the whole church might have looked like a rather large and squat pinnacle.

There seems to be no other way of explaining the form of the pinnacle which in Gothic architecture appears without any ancestor yet to a very clear ordinance.

It is interesting to note that the gables of the Gothic pinnacle are often ornamented with tracery in the form of a two-light window

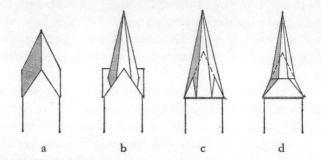

a   b   c   d

Fig. 18.   *The spire*
The spire, and its diminutive the pinnacle, are
found only in medieval architecture. Comparable to
the Eastern Byzantine dome, the spire forms a
roof to the central area of the Western church.
(a) shows the Rhenish 'helm' roof of which an
example remains at Sompting in Sussex. The
spire in (b) is based upon the cruciform roof,
rare but still to be seen at Hinton Friary in
Somerset. It is from this form that the Gothic
pinnacle is derived. The remaining two spires are
founded upon the pyramidal cap, that in (c) being
the form upon which the masonry spires of
Northamptonshire are based, and in which the
angles of the cap are exposed. The spire in (d) is of
lighter form and is that adopted by the timber
spires of Sussex.
    Later medieval spires were founded lower
down the tower walls which were carried up as
parapets around them, the angles between spire
and tower being covered over with lead roofs

and that the whole design, without the pinnacle itself, appears,
again without any obvious origin, up the sides of stone spires such
as those of Lichfield Cathedral, looking like dormer windows,
although these did not come into architecture until centuries later.
In view of the fact that the steeple is certainly derived from timber
antecedents, may not its stone embellishments also be derived from
the lost architecture of the Anglo-Saxons?

    The crockets which ornament the slopes of pinnacles may have
a dual origin. They seem curiously like the carved heads which
ornament the stave-churches of Norway and appear on the Bayeux

Tapestry. And they may have a Classical ancestor in the Corinthian volute.

Amongst our list of aedicules, may the niche worked into arcading be a miniature of the apse? When found completely furnished, it can be flanked with miniature buttresses, capped with a gablet, and completed with tiny pinnacles. These are all architectural features reduced to ornamental scale.

Although architectural ornament at times may become involved with detail which is purely sculptural and thus becomes the sphere of the art historian, by far the greater part of the ornament in our cathedrals is of architectural origin, in some cases the result of aesthetic use being made of structural necessity, in other cases pure aesthetic invention. All this architectural ornament will have been derived from two building styles, one timber and one masonry. The latter is fairly easy to recognize, and what is left may well be descended from Anglo-Saxon architecture.

Probably the best picture-book of their work left to us today is the splendid west front of Ely Cathedral. Its building took all but the last decade or two of the twelfth century to complete. The front itself was probably begun with the century and an examination of it shows each architectural story changing with the advance of the decades. (Plate 1.)

Most interesting is the lowest arcade, clearly a copy in stone of a stone arcade which has itself been copied in wood. The verticals are timber baulks with edge-rolls worked on them—the same may also be seen worked in brick on the face of the tower of St. Albans— the arches are horizontal timbers with arches cut in the underside.

The arcade above has a range of biforas the inner arches of which are similar to those described, but the enclosing arches are properly constructed stone ones. These two arcaded stories seem to occupy the 'vaulted basement' of the building, above which the design becomes more sophisticated.

The whole front is most elaborately ornamented with carving. Some of it is simply chip-carving and much of it possibly ornament copied from the clothing of the well-dressed Byzantine gentleman, a source of much of the running ornament of the orders of contemporary doorways.

An interesting feature is the presence of long slender shafts like fir-poles running up the sides of the angle turrets, apparently ancestors of those which cover the west front of Wells Cathedral. What they once represented is a mystery, but that they are copies of timber poles can hardly be disputed.

In the course of their descriptive eulogies concerning the excellence of the Anglo-Saxon timber churches the contemporary chroniclers made much of the elaboration of the carved ornament. In antiquity, builders in wood were very probably enthusiastic carvers for the material is soft enough to surrender easily to whittling with a knife. The writer has noticed that in Malta, an island producing a soft freestone easily worked, even the small children are born sculptors.

So while we examine the architectural origins of Gothic, the ordered arch and pillar, and the invention and elaboration of the Gothic moulding to soften the aesthetic crudities of this structural device, we have to give all credit to the Gothic carver. Perhaps he, too, was a born sculptor, living on the fringe of some quarry amongst the debris of which he played as a child. And as he grew up he would begin to turn out capitals, corbels, gargoyles—ready to drive his chisel into anything which would help to contribute to the richness of Gothic ornament, a riot of carving unlike anything to be found in any other historical style.

7

Basilican

The course of true history seldom runs smoothly. We rarely find the story to be one of leisurely development as each phase succeeds its predecessor with this melting easily into the new until it becomes totally absorbed.

More often the tale is one of conflict, of opposing influences—forces of the Right and Left—taking turns to occupy the stage, defying each other until one achieves some temporary ascendancy which it in turn loses, possibly to some third influence which has secretly been developing until such time as it becomes strong enough to defeat both factions.

In the history of English architecture one such battle was the Victorian struggle between the Gothic and Classical Revivalists, both of which were in the end defeated by a revival of the Renaissance.

But the conflict which plagued our eleventh-century architects and at the same time enabled them to develop Gothic architecture was that of the Byzantines against the Basilicans. It is a fascinating struggle to watch and both its scars and its honours are clearly seen depicted in the fabric of our cathedrals.

The origins of the dispute were in reality dogmatic and political. That the Byzantines were the better architects there can be no doubt. The trouble was that they belonged to the wrong Church and that in consequence of this their architecture was regarded with disfavour and persistently denied the stamp of authority. Byzantine architecture was placed as it were upon the Index.

It all goes back to the basilicas of Constantine. The word

Basilican

'basilica'—which is simply Greek for a regal building—has been an obsession of English ecclesiologists for at least a century. Thus a church must be a basilica. St. Peter's at Rome, built on the site of, but not in the smallest degree resembling, Constantine's original structure, is called today a basilica—incidentally illustrating in this fashion the abiding nature of the Orthodox Greek.

Even the English parish church, say the antiquaries, is derived from a copy of the basilica. This can only be for the reason that the larger English churches, like the basilicas of Constantine, have, for purely structural reasons, aisles. Cathedrals, even more so, are said to have begun as basilicas, though how the central tower possessed by every one of them comes into the picture is not explained.

The whole fantasy stems from the most interesting sources, easy to discover when one studies the circumstances surrounding the early days of the official development of the Christian Church.

For hardly was the Church of Rome founded, and its hastily erected basilicas completed, when the city, already abandoned as an Imperial capital, was sacked. Politically it could, and did, remain the headquarters of the Western Church, but culturally and architecturally it became a ghost town.

Meanwhile the great metropolis on the Bosphorus had flourished. Moreover, founded as a Christian State, it was in process of developing an entirely novel and splendid architectural style which was being founded primarily upon the church as a basic building type.

The Greek-speaking 'Orthodox' Church was carrying on what had long been an established tradition, the idea that all culture was basically Greek. The liturgical language of even the Roman ritual was for some time Greek. Thus the early Popes were suffering from the disadvantages of having to use the speech of a rival Church in buildings of no great architectural merit when compared with those beginning to appear in the Byzantine lands.

Consequently from the start there was instilled into the Western Church a prejudice against anything 'Orthodox' which expanded during the Middle Ages and is maintained to this day. Scholars have ignored its architecture, the dome which is its pride being called by art historians 'oriental' and every effort being made to sustain the fallacy that it is Persian, Moslem and so forth whereas it is of course the Pantheon at Rome itself which still displays the grandfather of them all.

The effect upon architecture of this attitude towards the Byzantine is found to be a sustained campaign to correct any tendency towards cruciformity in church plans and as far as possible to force them to appear 'basilican' by encouraging the building of long pillared naves.

In the history of major architecture the early Christian basilica has no place at all. Were it not for its religious significance as one of the earliest known types of church, it would have been ignored by the architectural historian.

At the time of its first appearance it must have surprised the citizens of Rome, capital of a world enriched by a host of magnificent building complexes concerned with the worship of the great gods of Olympus whose rule had been acknowledged ever since civilization had reached the world of contemporary culture.

Constantine's decision made in the year 330 to retire these splendid personages and to concentrate the state religion upon the worship of a single deity must be compared for its effect upon contemporary architecture with the suppression of the English abbeys in 1539. By a stroke of the pen all the glorious achievements of centuries of effort were consigned to the scrap heap. Vast and splendid buildings were closed to worship and abandoned. Obsolete, they became quarries for the building of humbler structures. And a great era of architecture was brought to an end.

The problem then presented itself as to what kind of building to provide for the ceremonial connected with the new religion. The new form of sacrificial ritual had to be performed under cover instead of in the open air, and it required a building of very large area to accommodate a vast congregation. The only contemporary building of adequate size, however, was the great hall of the public baths, huge structures of monumental scale taking many years to build.

It thus became necessary to devise a type of building having a large floor area but capable of speedy erection. The result was the introduction of a structure designed on the same principle as a

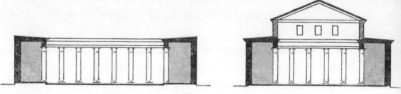

Fig. 19.   *The basilica*
On the left is a section through a Greek agora
surrounded by colonnades. By reducing the width
of the area until it could be spanned by a roof
the covered basilica is achieved

barn, a rectangular hall with its timber roof carried upon walls which were themselves carried upon rows of columns so that lateral aisles could be planned to almost treble the accommodation of the nave. The columns were sometimes salvaged from destroyed temples. Above the colonnades or arcades was a raised clearstory to help with the lighting of the wide building which at St. Peter's actually had five aisles in all.

In order to endow these poor structures with the title to dignity they were given the same name—*basilica*—as the monumental hall built by Maxentius with its vast span covered at a great height by an impressive vault. And notwithstanding their architectural un-impressiveness they were to exert a quite disproportionate influence upon future church architecture.

To say as much is not to approve the constant attempts which have been made by architectural historians to give the basilicas an undeserved status in architectural history by attempting to establish a recognizable style called 'Early Christian' to cover the period of the basilicas erected at the time of Constantine and subsequently. For the fact remains that they were hurriedly erected, could never have represented serious architectural excellence, and in any case such a noble designation would have been more suitably applied to the great halls of the Imperial baths with their high-flung vaults spanning huge bays—perhaps the finest apartments the world has ever seen.

Representing as they did a regression in the history of great architecture, the basilicas could never have achieved a place among

17. WELLS

18. HEREFORD

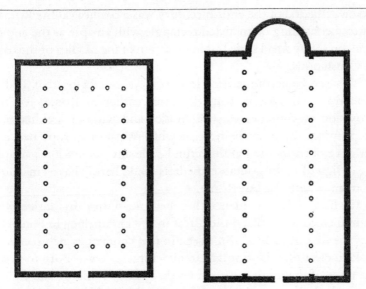

Fig. 20.   *Basilica plans*
On the left is the Classical basilica with its
surrounding loggias. The Christian architects
omitted the terminal loggias and raised a building
flanked by aisles and emphasizing the orientation
upon Jerusalem, completing the vista with an apse

the great buildings of the world. To begin with, they lacked that
essential element of height which characterizes a monumental
building.

What distinction the basilica possessed was confined to the
horizontal field. The long internal colonnade or arcade, meagre
though it was in scale when compared with that of contemporary
monumental building, was nevertheless an attractive and indeed
original feature. The 'blind story', the blank strip of wall above the
colonnade against which the aisle roof abutted, could be developed
as an architectural frieze. This proved to be the only feature of
basilican architecture that was to survive into future design.

The Roman church was from the start committed to the basilican
plan. From excavations conducted in 1930 by Sir Charles Peers in
the crypt at York Minster, and from surviving descriptions of an
early cathedral at Canterbury, it would appear that the Anglo-

Saxon cathedral of the eighth century was a basilica on the Roman pattern consisting of an aisled rectangle with an apse at the end of it, all on a very small scale but in imitation of the basilica of the days of Constantine.

This can be accounted for in two ways, one being that at that time the need was, as four centuries earlier in Rome, for the provision of churches at short notice and without architectural preparation, the other being that while Western Europe had not yet developed its own architectural style any inspiration towards the design of metropolitan cathedrals could hardly have emanated from anywhere else but Rome.

We have written evidence that the 'four-poster' Byzantine-type church erected by Alfred the Great in 878 at Athelney in Somerset was the first of its kind to be seen in this country, which seems to make it clear that the English architectural style was born towards the close of the ninth century and that prior to this we can expect any cathedrals, one at Ripon, for instance, to have been built as long 'basilicas'.

That the basilican type of church in its English form, with massive piers instead of Classical columns, survived throughout the later Anglo-Saxon period is illustrated by such churches as that of Brixworth in Northamptonshire. It is noticeable that in this case there was a supply of Roman bricks available and one is tempted to suggest that the site of a Roman city or station with its promise of an unlimited supply of building materials might have produced a kind of primitive 'school' of bricklayers—or, as they were called in later years, 'red' masons—who would perhaps have acquired an exceptional knowledge of architectural matters. And this would help to account for the extraordinary fact that large and permanently built Roman cities disappeared almost completely, their materials removed almost to the last brick.

Builders living by a Roman town would have been able to study its most sophisticated architecture and with the same materials might very well have evolved their own form of 'Romanesque'. They would of course have no knowledge of the main Byzantine style spreading across the Continent, and the construction of a tall 'four-poster' such as that at Athelney would never have occurred

Basilican

to them. And as no cathedrals were needed anywhere in the
vicinity of a church such as that at Brixworth its architectural style
must be regarded as an isolated phenomenon.

We are always apt to regard our Continental link as the seaway
of the Channel. But the Anglo-Saxons came from across the North
Sea. The Continental capital to which they were linked was not
Paris but Aachen on the Rhine, seat of the Emperors of the West
and link to the Imperial capital of Constantinople. Dunwich and
Orford were great ports of the Anglo-Saxons, the former having a
cathedral. Although it was set in a countryside completely lacking
in building stone, on the western side of the Kingdom of East
Anglia were the quarries of Barnack near Peterborough whence its
cathedral and those of Ely and Norwich grew up as illustrations of
a style of architecture which might be called the Anglian and which
spread across the country to be employed in a series of huge
buildings.

But it would seem that the basic influence behind all this church
architecture was Byzantine, deriving from Constantinople and
reaching England across Lombardy, up the Rhône valley and down
the Rhine.

Although its architecture seems to have been carried along this
route, however, the actual inspiration behind this great church-
building boom had been the colonizing propensities of the Benedictine Order taking its instructions from Rome. And in Burgundy,
along the 'Byzantine' route, lay the abbey of Cluny, whose abbot
had raised his house to such a degree of importance that he was
regarded by some as a kind of second Pope. The Cluniac Order had
in fact broken away from the Benedictine and was founding its own
houses each with a church specially designed to be the finest possible, in other words an architectural exemplar, to be followed by
all Western church builders.

The head house of the Cluniacs in England was at Lewes in
Sussex and was so deliberately and completely razed at the Suppression that not a stone of it remains above ground. Despite its somewhat remote situation, however, it may well have exercised a considerable influence upon English cathedral architecture now alas
no longer discoverable.

We can however be fairly certain that Cluniac architecture would have tended towards favouring the Romanesque or 'basilican' style with circular pillars instead of the compound pier and with arches having flat soffits instead of ordered ones.

The basilican influence had already been demonstrated very effectively with the attachment of the long cathedral nave to the tall Byzantine towered nucleus, thus destroying the primary aim of the former to achieve a soaring effect to which the rest of the building would contribute.

By the time great architecture had reached this country the Byzantine inspiration of *hypsosis*—the striving after the monumental element of height in architecture—had become hopelessly bedevilled by the Roman desire for large congregations. Under the limiting influence of roof-span this aim had to be achieved by concentration upon inordinate length, which again encouraged 'basilicanism'. Thus we see the inspirations of the two styles represented by height for the Byzantines and length for the Romans.

At first there was some attempt by the English cathedral builders to resolve the problem of association by designing their cathedral as a series of tall Byzantine bays which though assembled to form a single unit were carefully punctuated by vertical shafts in order to preserve their individuality. This was of course fundamentally bad design and open to pressure from the 'basilicans'.

Thus we see the punctuation disappearing in order that the arcades could sweep down the building without a break in the continuity. We also see the three-storied bay being replaced by a series of horizontal treatments, the main arcade and the fine arcaded band which replaced the open gallery of the Anglian church. The horizontal story formed by the triforium of the clearstory was left to become absorbed by the high vault.

Wells Cathedral in Somerset, one of the first to break away from the established Anglian ordinance, may be said to represent a Gothic basilica. (Plate 15.)

Wells is like a fairy tale. The bishop lives in a real palace in a setting out of Froissart with swans gliding along the waters of his moat. Hard by are the walls of the Close, entered through towered gateways giving onto a spread of English turf behind which rise

Basilican

the glorious towers of Wells. The greensward laps the sculptured west front, one of the noblest frontispieces in architecture.

The interior of the cathedral may not have either the grandeur of the immense halls of the Anglian churches or the towering splendour of Canterbury, but the naïve appeal of the immature Gothic of Wells cannot be denied. Ranges of clustered pillars with their richly moulded arches reach away to the curious stone saltires built to restrain the crossing piers from collapsing inwards as did those of so many of the early cathedrals. The short eastern arm is typical of the early days of choir development and the Lady Chapel beyond it, octagonal on plan and ingeniously worked into an English eastern transept, is Gothic at its most enchanting.

Wells is perhaps the daintiest of English cathedrals.

Its surroundings are unmatched by those of any other. North of it rises one of the stateliest of Gothic chapter houses reached by a steep stair which seems as though it were really intended to be a stage-setting for some medieval play. From the stair-head a Gothic bridge crosses the Close to give access to the medieval courtyard around which are gathered the little houses of the vicars choral who still continue to sing their offices in the lovely choir of Wells.

On the south side of the cathedral one may discover and enjoy the walks of a peaceful cloister set in the heart of an enchanting monument to English history.

By the time the Cluniac Order arrived in this country, most of our great abbey churches and cathedrals had been completed and their architecture established. But the mid-twelfth-century coloniz-ation of the English countryside by another Burgundian Order, that of the Cistercians, is bound to have had a considerable effect on the general development for two reasons. The first was that the Order was a new one, its ideas on church building untrammelled by existing architectural ordinance. But the most interesting feature of the Cistercian Order in terms of architecture was that its churches were designed to a standard plan by a mother house and built complete upon the site to be developed before the draft of monks with its new abbot took over the new house. Such organization as this might not make for superlative architecture but it had at least the advantage of establishing a well-considered ordinance and discouraging expensive experiments in 'contemporary' architecture. The design would have included the basic elements of the elevations, subject to deviations imposed by local problems such as materials.

Unfortunately, however, the Cistercian Order eschewed all manifestations of pomp and affluence, and the architecture which resulted was not of the highest quality. Austerity, combined with the discipline involved as a result of the building organization, militated against the development of notable architecture. The Cistercian Order colonized the countryside rather than the settled areas already occupied by the more worldly Benedictines, and thus it seems very probable that the familiar parish church architecture of the twelfth century with its circular pillars and plain arches is fundamentally of Cistercian origin. The pillars themselves are very interesting, emphatically 'basilican' with their English Byzantine cushion capitals—the only type possible for such pillars—naïvely Corinthianized with their scalloped or coniferous bells and their tentative volutes.

The early Cistercian abbey churches have for the most part vanished but those that remain seem to suggest adherence to the same somewhat parochial ordinance, the clue to which is the squat circular pillar, the flat soffit and of course, the simple horizontal design paying no attention to the Byzantine unit of the bay. Exeter is probably the only cathedral originally built to this ordinance which seems to have been followed more in the backward parts of England such as the south-west.

The Cistercian churches, little concerned with excessive height, had no galleries, a rejection which must have played its part in the subsequent development of the Gothic ordinance.

To obtain some idea of twelfth-century Cistercian architecture one should visit the splendid church of Fountains Abbey in Yorkshire or the more normal one of Buildwas Abbey in Shropshire, from either of which one can perceive the sombre effect of the uncompromising Cistercian style. The arches are pointed and the soffits flat in accordance with the basilican mood. Even the arches fail to give the smallest impression of Gothic sentiment.

The bishop who founded Salisbury Cathedral and at the same

time a Cistercian church nearby in which he wished to be buried left unmistakeable evidence of his architectural taste in the austerity of the former. In it there is no trace of the system of design by bays which had by the time of the building of Salisbury been transferred without difficulty from the Anglian cathedral to such Gothic buildings as those of Lichfield and, above all, Lincoln, without any difficulty and with charming results.

One might call the nave of Salisbury, like that at Wells with which it seems to have had a neighbourly affinity, a Gothic basilica. Possibly the rather primitive gallery arcade at Wells and the frankly unfortunate one at Salisbury may have been due to Cistercian inexperience of this feature so attractively handled everywhere else. The muddle at Salisbury is particularly surprising in view of the fact that at the west end of the nave is a charming arcade, built as part of the 'basement story', which one might have hoped would have acted as a model for the later gallery arcade.

One may speculate whether it was a series of architectural solecisms, such as the failure to design an attractive gallery arcade at Salisbury, that may have helped the Cistercians on their way from abandoning the dreariness of their early architecture towards setting their mind to outshine the lordly Benedictines and in the end create the superlative Gothic of Rievaulx and other abbeys in Yorkshire.

The early Cistercian churches and their protégé at Salisbury saw the end of the basilican type of interior. In particular the archaic circular pillar gave up the struggle against the lovely clustered pillar of the Gothic.

But during the conflict which occupied perhaps a century or more of English church-building a number of cathedrals and abbey churches were built which have left us with evidence of the strength—and general inefficiency—of the basilican movement.

In its insistence upon the long nave the Roman party had won without difficulty, even though the architecture of this had remained unmistakably Byzantine. But when it came to trying to introduce basilican architecture the results were unhappy, in some cases even ludicrous.

The crowning example of the folly of trying to plant in a country an architectural style from a country far removed from it geographically and completely unconnected with it historically may be seen at Gloucester Cathedral.

Until the Suppression, Gloucester Cathedral was the church of a very rich and powerful Benedictine abbey. When the present church was planned in 1089 it was planned on sophisticated lines with its eastern arm raised upon an undercroft—unusual for a church not of episcopal rank—and with provision made for a Continental-type *chevet*, with the usual three apsidioles, surrounding a great apse three-sided in the English fashion. The choir was of the normal two-storied type but with West-country circular pillars instead of the more usual compound piers of the Anglian school.

In the nave, however, an experimental type of structure was erected, quite clearly an attempt to create an English basilica. The two stories were combined in one, the pillars over thirty feet high and of immense thickness to compensate for the lack of medial support from aisle vaulting. (Plate 12.)

The result has a certain primitive dignity but is sadly destitute of any kind of architectural elegance which the two-storied Anglian elevations never lacked. The basilican experiment was repeated in the two sister abbeys of Tewkesbury and Pershore but not elsewhere and did not affect the development of English architecture by way of the established ordinance. The narrow story above the main arcades, however, which displayed a pair of biforas in each bay, may or may not have affected the subsequent Gothic form of this story.

The eastern arm of Gloucester Cathedral was never rebuilt in the normal thirteenth-century fashion and the choir remains in its original position at the east end of the nave.

In the fourteenth century, however, the eastern arm of the cathedral was dramatically remodelled, the apse being removed and two tall bays built in its place. The style of the work was in imitation of that which was being developed by the carpenters in the course of their screen-making and transferred into stone by the masons. The tracery of windows was being disciplined away from its arboreal fantasies towards rectilinear designs capable of being assimilated with the encroaching panelling.

At Gloucester the masons not only carried their panel systems over the face of the new walling but actually extended it in the form of tracery completely across the face of the old structure, openings as well as solid supports, so that the sanctuary became completely transformed from a primitive eleventh-century building to a splendid Gothic achievement, the whole covered with an intricate lierne vault. (Plate 14.)

At the end of the building is an immense panelled window, possibly the largest in the world, nearly forty feet wide and over seventy feet high. In order to lessen the risk of its being blown in it is canted outwards to form a shallow bay.

East of the sanctuary and in the same magnificent style is a long lady chapel, while above the crossing rises a tall tower of two stories, its elevations panelled in Western style.

As a one-time Benedictine abbey the cathedral is associated with various monastic buildings gathered round a magnificent cloister, the finest surviving in this country, elaborately panelled in stone and the design carried up into the cones of what is believed to be the first of the English fan vaults.

The east end of Gloucester Cathedral is one of the most splendid of the Gothic presbyteries. The nave, however, is perhaps of interest only as an example of misdirected effort.

For great architecture, like any creation of civilized effort, has to be based upon rules of procedure. Every period, or style, has for its basis an ordinance, a broadly conceived design plan agreed upon by all contemporary architects who know that it has been developed through past centuries and will itself suffer modification in the years to come.

Architecture must develop stage by stage, and should not break out into some startling innovation which is unlikely to be accepted and followed by the profession as a whole, or even a notable section of its members.

Where design is concerned, any individual experiment by an architect sabotages the work of the profession and frustrates rather than assists the logical and approved development of architecture.

The interesting experiment at Gloucester—followed loyally by its two sister abbeys but by no other—was undertaken with the best of motives as an attempt to 'Romanize' the Byzantine architecture of the English abbey church. But it appeared that such a transformation needed to be introduced stage by stage, as considered development, and not thrust upon the English designers, without preparation, if they were to be enabled to study, understand, and perhaps appreciate, the novelty of the intention.

We have commented elsewhere upon the enterprise of the Augustinian Order in their experiments with every aspect of architecture. As far as design is concerned, nowhere is this more clearly illustrated than at Oxford Cathedral, before the Suppression an Augustinian priory. The bay design of the interior is so unusual that a description is difficult to attempt.

Almost a century after the Gloucester experiment the canons tried to rebuild their church as a basilica lined with tall Corinthian-esque pillars, in the Roman style with just a clearstory over. The problem was to erect an arcade of this height, and upon such comparatively slender pillars, without the traditional vaulted aisle to support them. This was of course done, with lower arches spanning between the tall pillars to carry the usual gallery, but set back so as to allow the pillars to run up unbroken on the nave side to form what in Renaissance architecture is called a 'giant order' passing through two stories. Beneath the tall arches the gallery front fills the upper part of the arch and exhibits a small bifora; it is kept sufficiently far back to allow perspective to emphasize the illusion that one is entering a Roman basilica. (Plate 13.)

Unfortunately for us today, however, in 1525 the priory was seized by Cardinal Wolsey and suppressed by him in order that it might be converted into a college of priests. To reduce the priory church to a size more suited to a college chapel he destroyed half the nave, at one and the same time ruining the basilican effect, and depriving us of the chance of appreciating whether the Augustinian architect's brilliant experiment with perspective really achieved its aim.

But at Oxford Cathedral the Augustinian architects have given us one of the finest high vaults in the country above the eastern arm of the church. Again its complications are such as to defy description. It begins at the floor of the clearstory triforium, where the little arches leading to the passage are elaborately ornamented and the window reveals are brought into an elaborate, panelled treatment which sweeps up over the soffits of their heads. This vault above the window-head is thrust out into the church to meet the main high vault which is cunningly supported by fine transverse arches rising from the main supports and diving behind the vault, from which point the cone of the main vault sweeps upwards into the most elaborate of lierne designs. But the most remarkable feature of the vault is that stone pendants, suspended like similar features seen in the elaborate timber roofs of the period, carry the cones downwards to end in lanterns of exquisite workmanship.

These pendants are in fact the keystones of the vault, their weight locking the whole marvellous construction together. Later fan vaults made use of the same device, but their designs are quite ordinary when compared with the fantastic complications of the Oxford vaulting, undoubtedly one of the English mason's finest achievements as far as surviving examples go.

Added in the manner of the Augustinians to the north side of their choir is the lady chapel, and against this yet another chapel, making the choir at Oxford Cathedral five aisles wide. This lateral expansion of the eastern arm is typical of the churches of the regular canons.

The lantern tower was rebuilt in the thirteenth century with pairs of Gothic biforas, a typical treatment of the period followed at Chichester. Instead of its original timber steeple it was given a stone one, a humble structure which may be the oldest surviving stone steeple in the country.

During the thirteenth century, a period at which every church tower was capped with some kind of a timber spire, the masons of the north-eastern end of the limestone belt were copying these in masonry. It is probable that by a study of these one could arrive at a better idea of the appearance of their timber prototypes. The dormer windows, for example, are essentially features of a raftered roof. At the other end of the stone belt the masons of Somerset did not begin their splendid series of towers until the timber steeple had been replaced by the flat lead roof with its pinnacled parapet.

Both attempts to build major churches in England to represent the Roman basilica were failures. At Gloucester the Byzantine gallery was omitted but at the cost of having to make the pillars so massive that the result was almost ludicrous. At Oxford the properly proportioned Corinthianesque pillar was used but only with the support of the Byzantine gallery.

Henceforth the efforts of the basilican school had to be restricted to architectural detail, a field in which they were well able to challenge their rivals.

The Byzantine style had been evolved, and had succeeded, by virtue of its feats of engineering, the legacy of Imperial Rome rather than of the Hellenic Greeks. The mathematical ability of the Greeks, however, had enabled them to develop their engineering technique in the direction of covering spans with the most economical use of materials and at the same time raise their buildings to a monumental height without risk of collapse. But while the intelligence of the Greeks enabled them to perform such practical tasks as these, their traditional contribution to Western culture had been in the realm of art. The whole of the aesthetic aspect of the architecture of Imperial Rome had been taken over from the Hellenes.

Aesthetically speaking, the Byzantine style succeeded by virtue of its appreciation of the value of three-dimensional design which controlled the visible mass of the structure. In a way the original Byzantine achievement was a kind of foretaste of our Industrial Revolution—great advances in building technique accompanied by a neglect of architecture as an art form. For the architectural details of Byzantine buildings are poorly conceived with most of the embellishments provided by means of the applied arts, in particular that curious form of architectural painting, the mosaic.

The Byzantines were builders in brick rather than in stone, and it may have been for this reason that they seem to have lacked the sculptural ability of the Hellenistic world. Generally speaking their columns were roughly turned and lacked fluting, and their capitals were more often than not simply barbaric. And considering that they were Greek-inspired it is most curious that they abandoned the Classical Orders of architecture which had been the standby of the architect since the beginnings of Western civilization.

The great buildings of Imperial Rome had been feats of engineering, and doubtless highly respected as such. But a veneer of civilization—seemingly missing from our 'contemporary' buildings today—was insisted upon. This was represented by the application of the Orders. There was no need for them to be used in the endless colonnades of old, but they had to be presented in certain places in the design, generally as Corinthian columns with portions of their entablature.

It is this cachet of the 'Corinthian' which became the sign manual of the basilican style of architecture, which completely controlled the design of the capital in twelfth-century English architecture, which in a quite remarkable fashion formed the basis for the capital in parish-church Gothic architecture, and which in eighteenth-century England became regarded as the hallmark of general culture.

It is no longer regarded as necessary to teach architectural students the Orders of Architecture. It is perhaps only a quarter of a century since it was decided to kick away the ladder, up which architects have been faithfully climbing during long centuries. But now we have encountered the snake and have slid down it with catastrophic speed until we have abandoned not only the Orders of civilization but the whole principle of architectural ordinance.

The grim old Bronze Age temples of the days of Pericles adhered strictly to their ordinance so that architecture had a basic theme running through it and all could be assured—'this is architecture.' But the Doric was too stern a style to be able to assist the lighter aspects of a blossoming civilization. Curiously enough, though, its Roman rephrasing provided the basic ordinance not only for the great Renaissance but for all modern architecture until this flew to pieces in recent years.

It was colonial Hellas which conceived the second Order, that of the Ionians, derived from timber forms and more suited to colonnades than the stern solidity of the Doric. This was the Order which governed the architecture of the lovely cities of antiquity and produced the greatest temples—Ephesus, Didyma—of the Hellenic civilization.

But the Ionic Order, designed for colonnades, failed the architects when it was asked to turn the angle of a peristyle, its volutes having to be twisted together to form a weak angle just where a strong silhouette was needed. In a re-entrant angle it failed completely. So it ruled over a splendid architectural empire and retired from the scene. For what was needed was a capital which would look equally well in any part of a colonnade, or even stand alone.

It is said to have been a little child of Corinth who by her death unwittingly gave the world the solution, and the English language an expression denoting the superlative. For on her grave her sculptor father had set a basket containing her toys with a slate above to keep out the rain. Round the basket he had planted the acanthus fern of Greece. And as the fronds of the fern opened their volutes to enfold the basket the sculptor saw before him the design for a capital—the capital of Corinth.

It has passed through many forms. Many races, including our own, have tried to imitate it—often from hearsay—to the best of their ability. Research has been made into its true character and it has been revived in all its splendour. Now again it is forgotten. But only for a time. For the Corinthian capital has ruled over our civilization for too long and cannot be replaced by any other form.

The basilicas of Constantine employed the Corinthian capital—often salvaged from destroyed temples—in their arcades. It was their only architectural feature. Thus it became the sign manual of the basilican element in twelfth-century England and easily succeeded in ousting the crude cubiform Byzantine cap. Its convexity made it much daintier, and the sculptors at first were careful to retain this element when adding their carved ornament of trefoiled foliage. The volutes, however, those uncurling fronds of bracken, were in the end either abandoned or else spread about over the capital as part of their foliage. In the end, of course, as was noted in the last chapter, they became a Gothic moulding.

The twelfth-century conflict between the Byzantines and the 'basilicans' resolved itself in the end as a compromise. The towered central feature of the former culture remained, first subjected to, and in the end overcoming, the basilican appendage of the long nave. So in the end it was the strength of the Byzantine conception that enabled it to conquer. Aesthetically, the battle was won from the beginning by the great superiority of the Corinthian capital, from which we may probably derive most of Gothic architectural sculpture.

Throughout the Middle Ages in Europe the rivalry between the Byzantine and Romanesque styles continued, the former spreading easily all over the Balkans and Russia while Western Europe combined the two to enjoy the lovely era of the Gothic cathedrals.

But the tremendous revival of Classical architecture, right in the heart of Papal Italy, during the fifteenth century, reintroduced the ancient struggle. The early Renaissance palace, it is true, was with its *piano nobile* and its biforas nothing but pure Byzantine architecture with an overlay of Classical detail. But the Classically minded amongst the Italian architects were busily Romanizing all elevations and even Hellenizing their windows as they created their new Roman style.

When it came to the rebuilding of churches, however, they could not but admit that the basilica was a poor substitute for the Hagia Sophia. And with one accord they brought to Rome the soaring domes of Byzantium.

They knew good architecture when they saw it before them, and could easily understand the spirit of *hypsosis* which had raised those domes and supported them upon churches which were gathered around their skirts to form a great architectural mass.

All the famous architects of the day competed for the honour of rebuilding St. Peter's. And all submitted designs based on the dome as the central feature of a church gathered about it. The detail was Renaissance in the sense that it was derived from Classical sources, Hellenic and Roman. But the building itself was pure Byzantine in conception.

So it appeared as though the struggle was again joined and that the 'basilicans' were going to have to be content with Roman detail applied to what was in reality an 'Orthodox' form of church.

But Michelangelo was not allowed to build his great church as he had designed it. One can to this day imagine his chagrin when he was ordered to set it out upon an axis and provide it with a long nave, just as his predecessors had been forced to do four centuries earlier. It is of course called 'basilica'.

Amazing to relate, another famous architect, Sir Christopher Wren, suffered the same experience two centuries later when asked to design St. Paul's. He too submitted a plan for a church gathered around a central dome. And once again the ecclesiastical authorities —reformed though they might be—insisted upon the same adjustment as that which had ruined the conception at Rome. So in the end the traditional compromise resulted: a dome-crowned Byzantine exterior and a Roman interior set out upon an axis. So we went back into the eleventh century with our tower become a dome.

Despite the architectural superiority of the Byzantines, the humble basilica of the Romans has won through. There can be no doubt of the successful conversion of the English away from the Byzantine conception of expressing religious architecture in terms of monumental height and towards the basilican attitude that a church should be axially planned and as long as possible. Partly this is the acceptance of the practical requirement of accommodation —Sir Henry Wootton's First Condition—as more important than the Third Condition of aesthetic beauty. Partly, also, it is the feeling that after all it is the interior of a building which really counts and that the exterior must be left to look after itself. Which is of course exactly the present attitude.

Thus the Englishman abroad will not be impressed by the soaring interior of St. Mark's at Venice when he compares this with the vista he left behind at Peterborough or Ely.

In the long English cathedral spaciousness is not present but the impression of dignity derives from the remoteness of the high altar. The Englishman is not used to great buildings, only to long ones.

He would however agree that the most striking external feature of his longest cathedral will be its central tower, a development from the Byzantine conception unknown to the basilica.

19. LINCOLN

20. PETERBOROUGH

8

The Sanctuaries

The English cathedral may be said to have three main divisions which in order of seniority are the central crossing with its tower, relic of the Byzantine churches, then the long 'basilican' nave, and finally the eastern arm which has usually been rebuilt during the Gothic era.

The Byzantine churches had no definite eastern arm. The Hagia Sophia has none. An apse, symbol of reverence, was regarded as an essential setting for the altar. If the church was cruciform the apse was attached to the eastern arm but this would in no sense become a chancel as in later medieval churches. The Byzantine church was an entity, a great hall.

The apse as originally provided took the form of a large alcove projecting as an excrescence from the east wall. Later however the desire for some means of passage behind the altar led to the incorporation of the apse as an extension of the main span so that the side aisles could be carried round this to form an ambulatory. The loss of the altars at the ends of the aisles was made up for by protruding a pair of apsidioles from the ambulatory while a third was added centrally between them. The two lateral ones, being aligned towards the ordinal points, were sometimes provided by the more conscientious designers with attached apsidioles set due east in which to place the side altars. This may be seen at Norwich and at Canterbury where the parent chapel is square. Gloucester has the semi-hexagonal Anglo-Saxon type of apsidiole.

The curved walling of the great apse is carried upon piers or pillars and the general form of the aisled construction is carried round it, the whole resembling half a round church such as was built by the Knights Templar in recognition of the martyria built by Constantine in the Holy Land, and which would probably have become familiar to the Crusading armies.

This form of periapsidal east end is called by English antiquaries a *chevet* due to a misunderstanding of the French use of the word to describe any type of east end which on the Continent always includes an apse.

A striking peculiarity of English church architecture is its speedy abandonment of the apsidal east end traditionally established by common consent of both Western and Eastern Churches. This may have been for two reasons, one political and one architectural. It should not be forgotten that the Mother Church of this country was the Celtic Church, which is believed to have reached Ireland by way of North Africa and Spain, losing on its way any kind of official architecture it might have acquired from time to time on its travels. A Celtic church appears to have been simply a building, four-square with a gable at either end. It did eventually acquire a chancel or sanctuary but this was simply an even smaller four-square building added to the east end reached by a tiny arch. The apse was lost somewhere on the journey from Rome.

The existence of circular walling at the east end of an early church does not suggest an extensive use of the feature. Such churches are all in the south-east corner of England where Continental influence would have been most likely to occur. They are of too wide a span to have been roofed without some interior support and probably represent ambulatories added to timber apses now destroyed without trace.

The timber construction employed by the Anglo-Saxons would not have lent itself conveniently to the building of an apse owing to the difficulty of using curved timbers on plan. Thus it is almost certain that the semi-hexagonal apses met with in cathedrals such as Gloucester or Lichfield—and perhaps at Canterbury itself—represent the true English form of the feature, which as at Gloucester even forms the nucleus of a *chevet*.

But by settling for a square east end the English cathedral builders were in no way deprived of the possibility of providing

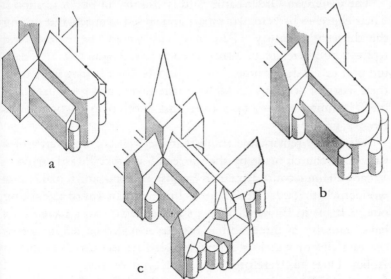

Fig. 21.   *English chevets*
(a) shows the ordinary apsidal ending,
which in (b) has its aisles carried round the
apse to form an ambulatory. This is the
Continental chevet copied in this country at
a number of cathedrals, notably at Norwich,
and at Gloucester where the apse is polygonal.
(c) shows the fully developed English chevet
with a long eastern transept with the apse
and ambulatory projecting from this.
Remains of this may be seen at Canterbury
and Lincoln, in both cases mutilated by the
loss of their eastern portions. Small apsidal
chapels are introduced wherever access
can be achieved

an ambulatory. It was a simple matter to carry the aisled construction across behind the east wall. And as the length of wall concerned was so short they could even dispense with the aisled construction and provide a low transept, double-aisled, with three pillars down its centre carrying a vaulting system which was more in the nature of a high vault. The western aisle formed the ambulatory, and leading out of this were the chapels formed in the eastern aisle, the whole forming an English version of the French *chevet*.

The Cistercian Order came to this country in basilican mood. Their churches had circular pillars and ended in apses. But during the thirteenth century when they had become better disposed towards good architecture they seem to have begun to take a leading part in the development of English Gothic. It may have been their pastoral occupations which made them such good Englishmen, helping them to take over and develop in particular the English east end.

It is a very remarkable thing that the well-known sketch of a Cistercian church made by the thirteenth-century Picard architect Villard d'Honnecourt depicts an English east end, and it makes one wonder whether it is a design for a church or a survey of an existing one, perhaps in England. It is a small church with a nave of six bays, transepts of three, and an eastern arm two bays long across the east end of which is a double-aisled transept such as that at Abbey Dore in Herefordshire, prototype of that at Hereford Cathedral. What is interesting is the way in which the vaulting is shown, making it clear that this was no mere added refinement but an integral part of the design.

The low eastern transept depicted by d'Honnecourt and remaining at Abbey Dore was covered by a pitched roof running north and south. At Hereford it was extended crosswise by adding another bay at each end making five in all. Although only at aisle-height this structure provided an interesting terminal feature contrasting delightfully with the pompous *chevets* of Continental type. (Plate 18.) Raised to the full height of the church it becomes the Chapel of the Nine Altars at Cistercian Fountains, repeated to form an imposing façade across the east end of Durham Cathedral.

The Cistercian colonization of the West of England is well illustrated by the architecture of Hereford Cathedral. The Anglo-Saxon cathedral of the Marches had been burnt by the Welsh and was rebuilding in 1079. Its eastern arm with its sturdy compound piers is pure Anglian but the arcades of the nave provide the most finished examples of the kind of style introduced by the Cistercians a little before the middle of the twelfth century. The well-proportioned circular pillars are finished with pleasant coniferous cappings and are stabilized aesthetically by means of attractive coupled shafts; the whole presentation is refreshingly original. Unfortunately the nave has been badly treated, having lost two of its nine bays—incidentally the usual Cistercian number—owing to an unwise attempt to build a western bell-tower over them which brought them to ruin. The remains were cleared away by the enthusiastic Wyatt who also rebuilt the upper part of the rest of the nave, so that what might have represented one of the best of the twelfth-century Cistercian-type naves has lost much of its interest.

The north transept of the cathedral shows an interesting attempt to vary the normal Gothic ordinance by springing its arches at an angle instead of from the vertical, an experiment repeated with equally unattractive results in the gallery arcades of that other crypto-Cistercian cathedral at Salisbury.

The most attractive feature of Hereford Cathedral is undoubtedly its eastern transept, a low building six bays in length passing across the east wall of the sanctuary and divided into two aisles. The westernmost of these is the ambulatory with before it a row of chapels of which the centre pair have been joined and extended to form a lady chapel. The transept is clearly a development from the eastern feature of nearby Abbey Dore, the only Cistercian choir remaining in use and one of the most charming of all Gothic memorials.

The central tower of Hereford is a fine sturdy structure of the panelled Western type designed to serve as the base of a timber steeple, removed by Wyatt. The latter part of the eighteenth century and the beginning of the next seem to have been an era of steeple destruction. This may have been partly for practical reasons but it may also be that the taste of the age was for a pinnacled tower-top.

Always to the fore where innovations were concerned was the Augustinian Order, the choir of whose priory church at Southwark, on the south bank of the Thames opposite London, was preserved at the Suppression to serve as a parish church. Raised to cathedral rank in 1904 it has been provided with a new nave.

Its splendid choir is typical of thirteenth-century rebuildings of eastern arms and is five bays long, an unusual length for a monastic church not of the first rank. It is a charming example of the Gothic and is finished with a high vault. Behind its east wall is an eastern chapel of three bays' width instead of the usual two, which enables the chapels to be of twice their normal length. The pillars supporting its high vault are unusually slender giving the interior a notable impression of daintiness typical of thirteenth-century Gothic.

After Westminster Abbey, Southwark Cathedral is London's most important Gothic church. A surprising feature of its choir is its magnificent reredos similar to those at Winchester and St. Albans. Although long despoiled of its statuary it is a remarkable survival from pre-Reformation days and an unexpected treasure to find in a comparatively unimportant priory church.

The increasing number of votive chapels, in transepts and at the east end behind the high altar, suggested the propriety of providing a special one for the worship of the Virgin Mary. Although the Augustinians persisted in placing this alongside the choir, as at Oxford Cathedral, the more usual position was at the extreme east end of the building.

We have seen this planned at Hereford. At Wells the lady chapel is an octagon, cunningly woven into the low transept. At St. Albans the chapel projects to a considerable length while the late example at Gloucester is a complete building linked to the ambulatory by a vestibule. At Lichfield it forms the east end of the church, having been raised to the full height of the building; presented externally this makes the eastern arm of the cathedral one of the most impressive amongst English cathedrals.

In the third quarter of the twelfth century the eastern arm of the cathedral of St. Osmund at Old Sarum had been extended and provided with a square east end with the usual low transept beyond it—a very early example of the English form of ambulatory. Late in the century the two centre chapels were replaced by a single wide chapel with miniature aisles extending to the eastward. When the new cathedral was planned in 1220 the east end of the old one was repeated but with the lateral gables abolished and the whole roofed parallel with the axis of the cathedral, showing five gables to the east. This is called a lady chapel but as the cathedral is dedicated to the Virgin it may be that it was intended as a memorial chapel to St. Osmund.

At the east end of Canterbury Cathedral an enormous chapel was built as a memorial to St. Thomas Becket. This was to have been finished with a remarkable building in the shape of a circular chapel rising to form a tower, a structure which thus presented would have provided a splendid monument to one of the most venerated of Englishmen.

It may well have become apparent to the cathedral builders of medieval England that an assemblage of assorted shapes at the east end of a great church did not represent good design. They may also have become aware that the cathedral elevation, instead of rising eastwards towards a splendid terminal feature, was actually sliding away to end in a huddle of appendages.

As good designers they sought ways of absorbing the extraneous structures within the main building. At Exeter the ambulatory part of the east transept has become absorbed. If the lady chapel projected, as at Lichfield, it did so as part of the main building. For that was the true answer—to carry the Celtic east gable right to the end of the building as at York Minster and fill it with light from a vast traceried window.

In this fashion we watch the cathedral growing along the passing centuries, extending ever eastwards. When looking at one of these great buildings it is difficult to appreciate that the portion of it actually forming the bishop's church is but a small part of the whole structure. Within all this mass of masonry there is just the walled-in choir with its splendid seating, the presbytery east of this, and the sanctuary before the actual high altar of the cathedral. All around this area are aisles and transepts and chapels, and westwards of it is the great bare nave which is the church provided for the public.

In early days the bishop's part of the cathedral was even less impressive owing to the short length of the eastern arm of the building. A mere two bays—the width of the crossing itself—was a common length; Canterbury had no more. Only the great Anglian cathedrals of Norwich, Peterborough and Ely, had eastern arms four bays—two great bays—in length.

Thus the total length of the bishop's church of the eleventh century may have been some three great bays, perhaps under a hundred feet, in length, with its westernmost third occupied by the seating, with the presbytery in the centre under the lantern, and with the sanctuary with the high altar before the great apse as the eastern third.

Dignity apart, greater space was needed to separate the seating from the altar, accommodate the bishop's throne and provide room for manoeuvre during the ceremonial connected with the celebration of the Mass on important occasions, perhaps with royalty present.

With the increasing panoply of the medieval nobility it became desirable that the bishop's church—which it should be remembered was completely enclosed—should assume the proportions of a great hall. A noble apartment was required, the sides of which were to be composed of fine architecture in the shape of screenwork amongst which could be sited the monuments and chantry chapels of past holders of the see.

The expansion of the old eleventh-century eastern arm began to take shape towards the end of the twelfth century. The ambulatory with its chapels formed the first extensions. Later a new factor entered upon the scene with the rising popularity of native saints and the desire to make pilgrimages to their tombs bringing offerings, which in the case of noble visitors might prove valuable contributions to the episcopal treasury.

The usual site for the shrine was behind the high altar and it was here that an extension to the eastern arm of a cathedral might be planned.

The insular patriotism of the medieval Englishman is indicated by his devotion to English saints. Chief of these was of course the Anglo-Saxon king St. Edmund in whose honour the greatest church in Christendom was raised. Another much venerated Englishman was St. Thomas of Canterbury. The lovely 'Angel' choir at Lincoln was added in the middle of the thirteenth century in honour of its bishop St. Hugh, part of whose splendid *chevet* was destroyed to make way for it, the new east end being a towering gable filled with a spacious window. The eleventh-century eastern arm of St. Albans Cathedral was replaced by a long choir the eastern end of which became the chapel of St. Alban. St. Chad was similarly housed at Lichfield; two charming bays were added to the eastern arm of his cathedral to form a chapel to St. Richard of Chichester. One of the greatest of the thirteenth-century cathedral choirs, that of Ely, nine bays in length, had at its eastern end the chapel of St. Ethelreda, while at York a choir of similar proportions had the chapel of St. William set in its three easternmost bays. But the longest choir of all, the twelve splendid bays of Old St. Paul's, had no saint's chapel; it was merely the place of sepulture for the great men of the English metropolis.

Whatever the apparent reason, however, the accumulation of the various factors outlined above resulted in the removal of all the two-bay eastern arms of the eleventh-century cathedrals and their replacement by a splendid structure in the Gothic of the first half of the thirteenth century.

While the great Anglian cathedrals were spreading the use of the massive compound pier through the country, the more backward parts of England were adopting the circular 'Romanesque' pillar of Hereford and Exeter. Another cathedral to be built with a basilican nave of this description was that of Carlisle. Its nave was of the simple two-storied type with plain arcades similar to those of Southwell Cathedral. After the Civil War, however, with the cathedral badly damaged, the nave was pulled down save for its two easternmost bays, the crossing and south transept also surviving from the eleventh-century church.

Carlisle Cathedral was one of those which had transferred its choir bodily during the thirteenth century into a completely rebuilt eastern arm. It is this part of the cathedral which is its great glory. Begun in the middle of the century, the work was checked by a fire and the choir was not completed until more than a century later. The most notable feature of this fine Gothic choir is its east window, one of the largest in Gothic England.

A natural concomitant of the rebuilding of the eastern arms of cathedrals was the eventual removal of the eleventh-century bishop's choir completely into the eastern arm, especially if the rebuilt arm had no saint to enshrine as at Carlisle. Southwell Minster is another example of a great church enlarged with the express purpose of moving the whole of the choir into it, confining what in this case was a collegiate church into the part of the building east of the crossing. This factor of Gothic cathedral replanning will however be discussed later, for the intention was formulated at an early date well before the general movement which took place during the thirteenth century.

Above their village city of Southwell the three towers of its cathedral indicate the ecclesiastical importance of the place. It seems much more like the dying remains of an ancient cathedral city than the newly constituted city it has become since 1884.

In fact it holds a curious position amongst English cities for during the Middle Ages it was a kind of pro-cathedral city, its great collegiate church serving that purpose for the southern half of the great diocese of York.

Its importance is indicated by the west front of its cathedral, very plain but possessing a pair of towers which seem to have been intended as a part of the original design, and not the raised transepts which may sometimes be encountered. The clumsy pyramidal roofs are modern and seem quite unnecessarily unattractive.

Within, the nave is of surprising interest as an example of a three-storied Anglian nave having instead of the normal compound piers squat round pillars both for the main arcade and that of the gallery over, those of the gallery being curiously stumpy. There is no triforium, only plain single-light windows giving but little light.

Southwell followed the usual thirteenth-century practice of building a new choir in place of the old short eastern arm. Today it represents a fine example of the choir of a monastic church such as might have been found in many places over the English countryside before 1539. It is only two stories in height, the triforium arcade having been extended downwards to absorb the blind story. The main arcade is tall and graceful with clustered pillars leading up-wards to a simple vault. (Plate 21.) The choir is entered through a good stone screen crossing the eastern arch of the tower.

Two of the architectural treasures of Southwell are of very different styles. First there is the great north porch, a splendid example of twelfth-century architectural elaboration. Above all, there is the thirteenth-century chapter house, full of naturalistic sculpture agreed by all to comprise the most perfect example of this typically Gothic form of art to be met with in this country.

The Sanctuaries

It will be appreciated that the huge cathedrals of eleventh-century England developed not from planning but out of muddle, displaying long naves never envisaged by the designers of the centralized churches of what might perhaps be called the Byzantium-Aachen axis.

The most important part of the building, the bishop's choir, lacked any architectural separation from this either internally or externally.

With the exception of a few of the great Anglian cathedrals the eastern arms of the early cathedral were so short that they had to be rebuilt in order to enable them to stand up architecturally to the huge naves. And after this had been done it might have seemed the obvious thing to move the choir out of the nave into the eastern arm.

If such a move were contemplated during the twelfth century, however, there would have been considerable anxiety concerning the loss to the choir of the crossing with its lantern over, for centuries past the very heart of the Byzantine church.

For this reason any early removal of the bishop's choir east of the crossing was always preceded by the rebuilding of the eastern arm with a second transept, making it a complete cruciform church. It should be noted that this was a complete confirmation of the validity of the Byzantine church plan and a snub to the 'basilicans'. Internally, however, the lantern was not included in the new choir, possibly because its appearance externally would have competed with the adjoining central feature, and possibly because its down-draughts might have been less than welcome to the bishop who had to sit under them. (Fig. 22.)

The first of the great choirs was that of Canterbury, completed in 1126. The choir itself occupies five bays east of the central tower after which comes the wide bay of the eastern transept. Two more bays lead to the apse—which may have been semi-hexagonal in the Anglo-Saxon fashion—with its periapsidal *chevet*, the middle part of which was pulled down in 1179 to make way for the building of the great eastern chapel to St. Thomas Becket.

In 1192 Bishop Hugh of Avalon, later St. Hugh of Lincoln, began to extend his cathedral with a new eastern arm. His choir was

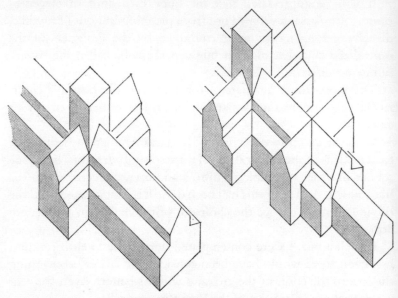

Fig. 22. *English choirs*
On the left may be seen the rebuilding
of the eastern arm of the early
cathedral as a long aisled hall. On a
grander scale the bishop's choir was
provided with choir transepts
recalling the earlier choirs sited west of
the main crossing. At the east end a
projecting lady chapel added to the
already considerable length of the
building

five bays long and the eastern bay was extended laterally to form
an eastern transept. Out of this led a semi-hexagonal apse with
chapels in the form of a *chevet* as could have been seen at Canterbury.
St. Hugh's choir and transepts remain and are lovely examples of
early Gothic, but his *chevet* was pulled down in the second half of
the thirteenth century in order that the lovely 'Angel Choir' could
be built as his memorial.

Thus by the end of the twelfth century the plan of the English
cathedral had been completely reorganized, with the bishop's
church represented by a cruciform building with his choir in its

western arm, the whole comprising an entirely new structure situated east of the central tower. What one might call new churches were built in this position at Rochester and at Worcester. At the former cathedral it would seem as though thenceforth the bishop lost interest in the nave of his cathedral which, with its half-finished design and plain timber roof, seems more like the remains of an old parish church than a cathedral nave.

The new cathedral at Salisbury, planned in 1220 as the latest in cathedral design, gives the bishop his own cruciform church east of the crossing and the great transepts.

The transept is a peculiarly English feature of medieval architecture. For some reason not yet fully explained it remains as an essential part of the English parish church right up to the Reformation. We have seen at Hereford and at Wells the English form of *chevet* expanded laterally as part of the array of chapels there, and of course the huge eastern transept at Durham. Such developments, however, seem to have represented attempts to bestow dignity upon the east end of the cathedral, in *chevet* fashion, rather than to recapture the Byzantine cruciform plan for the bishop's choir.

On the other hand, long after the Byzantine conception had been forgotten the choir of York Minster was provided with tall transepts, reduced in projection until they ranged with the aisle walling but with tall windows like huge dormers lighting the centre of the choir like the transepts of old. A century earlier at Exeter, however, the choir transepts had become mere projecting chapels no higher than the aisles.

The cathedral at Bath, swan song of the abbey builders of the Middle Ages, is a building of unique interest. The huge eleventh-century abbey church having become dilapidated beyond repair, the monks pulled down its nave completely, using its eastern arm while they built a new church on the site of the old nave.

This new church was built in the form of a monastic choir as it had been developed through the centuries, as a complete church with transepts and, now, its own central tower at the crossing. It was a return to Byzantine days, with the difference that the crossing was not square, as would have been the case had the transepts been the arms of a Byzantine church, but the meeting-place of choir transepts only the width of a normal bay. The bays of Bath Abbey are of course somewhat wider than those of the eleventh century but are still narrower than the main span of the building, so that the tower is noticeably rectangular on plan instead of the usual square. Bath Cathedral is all of one building, and that of the very end of the Gothic era. It was not finished when the abbey was suppressed in 1539, remaining roofless until 1610, the bishop using his other cathedral at nearby Wells.

Still called Bath Abbey, it is also known, by reason of its huge windows, as the Lantern of the West. Even the clearstory windows are vast in area and these are brought down across the blind story in the style of the late Gothic.

The glory of the building is its fan vaulting, completed in the eastern part of the building before the Suppression and copied over the rest of the cathedral during the last century.

Once the awkward situation of the bishop's choir within the building of the eleventh-century cathedral had been rectified by the extension of its eastern arm, the exterior form of the cathedral took on a completely different aspect. For hitherto this had been seen as an immensely long nave and a humble little eastern arm, not even attaining the proportions of a parochial chancel, which had in fact been merely the sanctuary while the bishop's choir was indistinguishably concealed within the major portion of the church.

Now that the central tower had become the dividing feature separating the bishop's church from that of the laity, all the splendour of Gothic design could be concentrated upon the eastern arm of the building, raising its apparent dignity above that of even the longest nave and making it quite clear to distant observers that within it stood the throne of a bishop.

It should be noted that it is this basic factor which differentiates the lateral elevation of a cathedral, however small, from that of a parish church, however magnificent. For a great cruciform parish church will still only end in a parish chancel while the most humble cathedral will display an episcopal choir clearly taking precedence over the nave.

One may wonder whether it was with any regret that the bishops moved their choirs into the eastern arms of their cathedrals. Did they lament the loss of the lantern's splendour, the soaring cavern of light carrying their prayers towards Heaven? Or dare one suggest that they were glad to escape the down-draughts? Nevertheless the old Byzantine inspiration had gone for ever. The lantern tower had been left, as it were, on the choir's doormat. In this position, however, it began to take on a new aspect. The crossing with its lantern had become an antechamber before the doorway to the bishop's choir. With its spreading transepts it now formed a splendid apartment passing before the choir screen, displaying this and the arcades of the chapels reaching into the transepts as an immense façade to the bishop's church. (Fig. 23.)

The medieval architects had never known the dignity of the frontispiece, that great architectural canvas so nobly developed during the Renaissance. They had discovered the aesthetic value of the west transept and at Wells—and above all at Peterborough —they had succeeded in achieving a Gothic façade. But here was a splendid interior frontispiece presented to them ready-made.

That they accepted the gift there can be no doubt. It was for the purpose of creating the most splendid of all such antechambers, to the choir of the bishops of Ely, that the glorious octagon of the cathedral was built in place of its fallen lantern tower.

In the western arch of the crossing, facing the choir screen, was the rood-screen separating the nave from the bishop's church. The crossing and transepts now formed a no man's land between the two churches, a splendid hall which became known as the 'walking space'.

It is probably this portion of Old St. Paul's, and not, as has been supposed, the great nave—which was no longer than it—which came to be known as 'Paul's Walk'. A hundred yards in length, this covered hall might well have been taken over during weekdays by the citizens of seventeenth century London for their promenade.

A feature which has been lost from our cathedrals is the screen separating the walking space from the nave and providing the reredos to its altar. At St. Albans, until the Suppression a Benedictine abbey, the choir remained west of the crossing and was never moved east of it cathedral fashion. Before the entrance to the choir is the bay known as the retro-choir, which is closed to

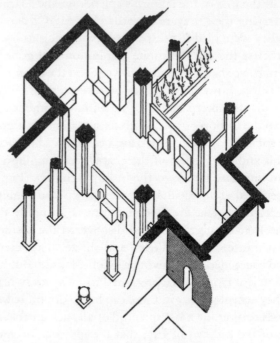

Fig. 23.   *The walking space*
         After the withdrawal of the bishop with his
         choir into the eastern arm of his cathedral the
         whole of the crossing with its transepts became a
         vast entrance hall set athwart the choir doorway.
         This virtual no-man's-land between the churches
         of the bishop and the laity became known as
         the 'walking space'. The most notable walking
         space is that at Ely lit by its splendid octagon

the west by the rood-screen forming the reredos to the nave altar
and pierced by a pass-door on either side of this.

The removal of the choir into the eastern arm of the cathedral
must have been followed by the re-erection of the rood-screen in
the western arch of the crossing in order to provide a reredos for
the nave altar and close the public church from the walking space.

In view of their role as reredos these screens were probably
destroyed during Puritan days. That at Canterbury was taken down
in 1750.

21. SOUTHWELL

22. ELY

During the last two centuries there has been a reckless clearance of obstructions in our cathedrals. The aim has been to achieve that sense of 'unbroken vista' which well-meaning architects sought to introduce into the great buildings so that they might display their size to the full. In consequence much of their screenwork has been removed. Cathedrals such as Salisbury even lost their choir screens, while Canterbury, Lincoln, Exeter, Ripon have all lost their western screens, embarrassing their deans in that no proper situation can be found for the nave altar, which has either to be set out in the open or in a position in which it successfully blocks the choir doorway.

There can be no doubt of course that their splendid choir screens are now seen to fuller advantage than when forming part of the side wall of the walking space passing before them. But when this too has gone, Salisbury and other cathedrals have lost much of their ancient mystery and may even appear as mere over-large parish churches.

The loss of the western screenwork of the walking space has deprived it of a large part of its character as a great apartment in its own right. It is now just part of the east end of the nave and in consequence escapes notice as a separate entity. The significance of its own axis, at right angles to the more prominent one of the cathedral itself, has become submerged. One can no longer appreciate its eastern wall, arcaded throughout its length and concentrated upon the choir screen itself with its sculpture-framed doorway.

The screen was usually designed as a doorway flanked by statues set in niches. But in order to allow for the diminishing of the view by perspective as one passed towards the ends of the walking space, the screen at Exeter is brought forward to form a fine porch flanked by wide recesses for side altars continuing the series reaching away on either hand. The screen had a vaulted ceiling above which was a 'soller' to which access was provided by a permanent stair. Whether or not sermons were ever delivered to persons gathered in the walking space is not known, but the screen was also known as the *pulpitum*.

It might be worth recalling that the Gothic builders employed architecture more as a sacrament than as an advertisement. It did not worry them that a fine frontispiece such as that of the walking space could not be seen to advantage. It was the same with the façades of chapter houses buried beneath the roofs of eastern cloister walks. And to them there was only one justifiable vista— that towards the high altar.

We have been watching the three-storied cathedrals of the eleventh century abandoning aisled construction upon which they had originally depended for stability, raising their main arcades and dispensing with their galleries as masonry technique improved and pillars could be made taller and slimmer. Eventually it was found possible to raise the pillars unsupported from pavement to vault, provided the church was not carried too high. Aisles could be built to the same height as the nave, creating what German architects call the 'hall' church. Amongst the builders of monastic churches not of the largest scale, the Augustinian Order would have been most likely to have brought their architecture to this stage of development.

Bristol Cathedral began its history as an abbey church of Augustinian canons. Its splendid twelfth-century chapter house remains but everything else, including a half-rebuilt nave, was destroyed at the Suppression except, curiously enough, the monastic choir which was preserved by the King to serve as a cathedral. The nave was rebuilt in 1866.

The choir of the cathedral is of unique design being built as a 'hall' church with nave and aisles of equal height. It came late amongst the rebuilt choirs and is of the fourteenth century. There is no blind story and no clearstory, all three aisles have their own pitched roofs, and the aisle walling is thus high enough to enable tall windows to be built in them.

This type of structure was imitated in the parish churches of the West Country from the fourteenth century onwards.

The aisle vaulting of Bristol Cathedral is original in design. In order to make up for the loss of the low aisle vaulting which had stiffened the pillars of the earlier cathedrals, they were joined to the aisle buttresses by strainer arches which were in fact stone versions of the 'flying shores' we see today strutting gaps between buildings —a long stone beam has to be supported by an arch below it. In order to give some weight to the arch and prevent its buckling upwards under lateral pressure from the high vault of the nave, stone king-posts were set upon it and developed into vaulting cones so that the aisle vault is divided into two and there are a pair of vaulting bays to each bay of the aisle.

The device—a *tour de force* of the medieval mason—was copied on twice the scale in the main transept at Gloucester.

The central tower of Bristol Cathedral, not by any means of spectacular height, is panelled in the Western style of the more imposing tower at Hereford.

When we consider that during the thirteenth century Gothic architecture was being developed in the choir rebuildings of the monastic houses, and that their eastern arms were particularly singled out for destruction at the Suppression so that very few indeed are left, we may count ourselves lucky to have been able to retain so many of them in our cathedrals.

9

The Architecture of Transcendency

A score or so of cathedrals helped by some ruins and a pitiful remnant of once lovely abbey churches retained for parochial use are all that we have to tell us the story of one of the most glorious epochs in architectural history.

Gone is the splendid array of buildings upon which for five centuries all the devotion of a tremendous architectural era—and the whole of the building potential of an age—were expended. By a study of a little more than a tenth of what we might have had, we have to try to ressurrect and appreciate the Gothic architecture of England.

From what is left, however, we can at least be sure of one aspect of the Gothic—that the aim of its creators was to build for one purpose only—for the greater glory of God. There were no palaces in Gothic England. Architecture was the sole prerogative of the Church.

Amateurs of architecture are apt to regard as the basis of Gothic architecture the pointed arch. The most acute 'lancet' form of this seems to burst into architecture as though a notice had been issued to all lodges that in future no semicircular arches were to be used. But some of the loveliest and earliest of Gothic—in Lincoln choir, for example—employs an arch which is practically still semi-circular.

The semicircular arch was simply a traditional form of a primitive feature. No doubt even the Romans would have used a pointed arch if they had needed one to rise more than half its span. Moslem architecture—which is also derived from the Byzantine—

has employed the pointed arch in both its acute and depressed form from earliest days. It is true that the two-centred arch is more satisfactory in that it does not sink and drop out its keystone if its abutments begin to spread—a fact which played a large part in the development of the structural aspect of Gothic architecture but aesthetically it is an indication of that striving towards the vertical which is the practical motive of Gothic design reflected in, amongst other features, the tall pointed arch.

French architects call Gothic architecture 'ogival'. This is curious as *ogive* does not mean a pointed arch, or even a serpentine one such as is described by our use of the word 'ogee'. The French word means a pointed cap—probably a pointed dome—and thus suggests a changeover, not from a round arch to a pointed one, but from the normal Byzantine dome to a pointed one such as one finds in the great five-domed church of St. Front at Périgueux, the interior arches of which remain semicircular. So perhaps the term *ogival* does not really indicate what we regard as Gothic architecture but really calls attention to the development from the Eastern Byzantine to its Western counterpart.

Today, alas, *ogive* is . . . the cap of a high-explosive shell!

The Gothic church was offered up as a symbol of worship. In order to achieve the fullest emphasis the building was lifted as high as possible towards the heavens. This soaring sensation—what the Greeks called *hypsosis*—provides the primary element in all monumental architecture, which is to say, all building which attempts to achieve more than mere accommodation, whether for habitation or for congregational worship.

The mere *size* of a building may ignore this monumental element. The vast area of roofing covering a market, for example, is still only serving a practical purpose and is lost among the surrounding roofs. But raise one small church above these roofs and the prayers of the townsfolk rise with it.

This was the underlying principle of Byzantine church design, accepted in Western Europe as soon as it began to build, and remaining as the inspiration of the Gothic age.

Cathedral architecture as we know it may be said to have been founded by the Benedictine Order whose enormous abbeys covered

England at the beginning of the twelfth century to an extent with which, in the field of architectural experience, the few and scattered cathedrals were hard put to it to compete.

But as the century progressed a new element entered the architectural sphere, the Cistercian Order which began building abbey churches in their scores throughout the countryside.

At first austere of purpose, they acquired riches from the flocks they bred, herded and sheared and began to think that they should revise their views upon the virtue of worship from amongst the trappings of humility. In the heart of the fertile valleys of Yorkshire they saluted the thirteenth century by raising lovely churches in the new Gothic style, which they adopted without qualms and did much to perfect.

Able to build their daughter abbeys on fresh sites, or to raze the sometimes unworthy churches of the mother houses without regret, they replaced simple little eastern arms with splendid choirs which may well have encouraged their more distinguished brethren the Benedictines, and even the bishops, to follow suit.

The new Cistercian choirs followed a standard ordinance—a practice always acceptable to this Order—of clustered pillars supporting an elaborately moulded arcade, a low gallery arcade of Gothic biforas two to the bay, and a triplet of lancets in the triforium of the clearstory. The charm of their buildings, all of which are now in ruin, is undeniable. Much of it is due to simplicity of detail, all of which is purely architectural, for they either projected their original views on austerity into the Gothic era or else in their rural retreats suffered from a scarcity of sculptors.

The Cistercian practice of building a daughter house to a standard plan issued by the mother abbey is the kind of organization which assists the development of good architecture. For a sound architectural style depends upon an adherence to a basic ordinance which ensures homogenity and stability, discourages cranks, and yet is in no sense intended to prohibit free expression in the interpretation of ordinance and the development of architectural detail. It is a fact that one does not find ingenious Augustinian experiments in Cistercian architecture. Their Gothic buildings taken as a whole, however, are uniformly enchanting.

They readily followed any clearly acceptable development in the general ordinance of the Gothic style. At Netley Abbey in Hampshire, for example, we find the gallery arcade abandoned and the triforium treatment at the clearstory extended downwards to absorb the blind story, a development completely in accordance with contemporary cathedral practice and executed with confidence and clarity. (Fig. 25c.)

After the almost ludicrous attempt at Gloucester to introduce the basilican type of church into this country, the Cistercians took up the campaign with far more success. Notwithstanding the hold they achieved over parish church architecture, however, they never obtained the smallest hold on the architecture of the cathedral. Their influence was concentrated in the West and they may have affected the design of the nave of Wells, but the restless unpunctuated interior, only redeemed from dullness by the enchanting richness of the clustered pillars and moulded arches, seems to have been the only serious attempt at basilicanism made by an English cathedral.

A horizontal sprawl such as is displayed by Wells would have been out of step with the Gothic emphasis upon the soaring element as represented by the vertical bay with its strong lines of punctuation.

Passing over the spiritual, philosophical and political elements supporting the Gothic achievements, it is necessary to consider in what form these aims were projected into terms of architecture and how they were affected by structural requirements.

We have explained that Gothic architecture is not indicated by the pointed arch but by the elaborate, and unique, systems of mouldings which sweep along it.

Byzantine architecture, out of which the Gothic developed, concerned itself only with structural development and gave little heed to architectural detail. It relied for decoration upon the use of mosaic as a permanent form of wall-painting and restricted this to important areas such as the conch of the apse. Carving was rarely used and was often strangely barbaric in design.

There were no mouldings. These were devised by the Gothic designers to soften the crudities of purely structural architecture.

The basis of every moulding was the 'quirk', a groove cut into the stonework next to an angle, matched by another parallel one, with the angle between worked to a curve. An 'angle-roll' thus created could be given a diminutive 'cubiform' cap and a base, thus completely changing the aspect of the corner of one of those piers upon which Byzantine architecture depended. The roll could be taken round the edge of the arch, and from this beginning developed the Gothic moulding. (Fig. 15b and c.)

The development of the elaborate mouldings of the thirteenth century is not difficult to follow. By chamfering the edge of the order and cutting four quirks, or merely by flanking the two original quirks by others, the triple roll of Wells can be easily achieved. The intention of the carvers was to develop the mouldings from the edge of an order across to the opposite side, and again towards the soffit of the order adjoining it so that all traces of its flat surfaces disappeared. By treating each order in this fashion the ordered arch could be made one compound system of mouldings. It is this moulded element in Gothic architecture, employed in no other style, that is its peculiar characteristic.

One can see the beginnings of the break-up of the Classical soffit at Norwich with its tentative orders. Then at Peterborough we can see the early roll-mouldings and at Ely the duplication of the orders only requiring a little more carved work to convert them into Gothic arches. At Durham there is little left of the orders now almost disguised by primitive but effective mouldings.

The compound pier being the complement of the ordered arch, the mouldings spread equally over both. The result was the conversion of the English pier into the Gothic clustered pillar.

From the elements of the main arcade the mouldings reached other arches including those over windows, which of course were carried down the sides of the jambs.

The aedicular form of the Byzantine duplex bay, the *bifora*, plays a very large part in medieval design and it will be seen throughout the thirteenth century in Gothicized forms employed in many places throughout the cathedral, in particular the gallery arcades. The secondary element of this feature, the little medial colonnette, became replaced by a mullion and this was echoed in the jambs of

Fig. 24.   *The bifora*
Aesthetically, the feature which plays the most
important part in the development of Gothic
architecture. Of Byzantine origin, during the
twelfth century its central baluster became a
slender Corinthianesque colonnette, an enclosing
arch with a pierced spandrel completing the
feature. In order to glaze the bifora for external
use the colonnette became a moulded mullion and
this became swept up into the arch to produce
bar tracery which eventually sprouted cusps on its
way to achieving the foliated Gothic window

the opening and carried round its head. Here again the mullion
had become transformed into an inner order and embellished
accordingly with an array of mouldings. (Fig. 15d.)

With the enlargement of windows and the introduction of
mullions of primary and secondary degree these became as it were
additional orders, the whole incorporated within the system of
mouldings framing the window. Only in the Gothic does one find
openings embellished in this fashion.

The development of the mullioned window resulted in the extension of the mullions into the head to be woven into 'tracery'.

All this Gothic detail, the rich moulding and the traceried window, may be said to have been derived from the acceptance of the
system of construction by orders which replaced the flat arch soffit
of Classical times.

Another of the notable differences between the Anglian style of building which continued to be employed through most of the twelfth century and the Gothic of the thirteenth is the change from the compound pier to the clustered pillar. While this appears as merely an echo of the moulded arch it represents an important change in the technique of building masonry supports. For the pier was planned as a silhouette, the pillar as a solid mass of stone on the lines of a Classical column. Despite its mass the pier had little strength compared with the slender pillar, which was capable despite its slimness of being carried to a greater height.

It will be remembered that the two-storied arrangement of the eleventh-century cathedral was essentially a structural device which made use of the gallery floor as a stiffener so that height could be achieved by building in two tiers instead of a single tall story which might have proved unstable. The gallery arcade was not intended to serve as a mask for the blind story; indeed it left the aisle roof in plain view from below.

When the gallery was abandoned and the main arcade raised, together with the adjoining vaulting—now become a high vault— to the level of the roof of the aisle, the space occupied by the rise of the aisle roof formed a meaningless vacuum in the view from below and would have become a blind story, either—as in the basilica—left as a strip of bare wall, or perhaps decorated with painting or mosaic.

But the Gothic designers decided to let the gallery arcade remain, reduced in height, as an architectural feature, pierced by arcading having its openings small enough, and attractive enough, to relieve the eye from the view of portions of the aisle roof. This band, today incorrectly called the 'triforium', forms the most delightful feature of the Gothic cathedral.

We have seen the rather unimaginative attempts to treat the blind story at Wells, that experimental design which suffered too much from basilican influence. But the eventual Gothic answer to the problem turned out to be a development from the abiding bifora.

This had appeared in impressive form in the old galleries at Peterborough and Ely. The experiment at Gloucester had shown it inevitably reduced in size and set in pairs above the enormous pillared arcade, the arrangement, in fact, which was eventually adopted as standard for the Gothic cathedral.

At Gloucester the biforas were set together in the centre of each bay. But the Gothic masons, anxious to bring the story into line with the main arcade below, arranged the pairs to fill the bay neatly devising a series of dwarf clustered pillars to echo the main supports of the arcade, others in the centre of each bay, and miniature clustered pillars that took the place of the shaft of the Byzantine feature.

At Salisbury an attempt was made to retain the wide arch of the old gallery and set the pair of biforas beneath it in the fashion of a duplex bay. But the area of walling available was inadequate and the scheme was a failure. The Salisbury experiment, however, in a church of notable austerity of design, certainly illustrates the high regard in which this feature of the Gothic cathedral was held at the time. (Plate 30.)

At Worcester the trifora was introduced in pairs to form an elaborate arcaded front to one of the older, taller galleries. But it looks very crowded and is not met with elsewhere. But Worcester is one of those cathedrals in which anything may be forgiven.

For thirteen centuries this venerable cathedral has looked calmly down upon the waters of Severn, and it was an Anglo-Saxon bishop, later to be St. Wulstan, who wept when he had to begin the destruction of the work of his predecessors so that he could build anew on the ancient site. His words are memorable:

'We poor wretches destroy the works of our forefathers that we may get praise for ourselves.'

All that is left of Wulstan's cathedral is the splendid crypt upon which the long eastern arm of the church including its great apse and *chevet* were raised. Its eastern parts have been destroyed but it still appears as a forest of columns like a Byzantine cistern.

Early in the thirteenth century the usual extension was made to the eastern arm of the cathedral, in this case necessitating complete rebuilding. This choir is one of the finest in England, equipped with eastern transepts and with its east wall projecting in the manner of a lady chapel. The architecture is purest Gothic, richly moulded arches rising above thickly clustered pillars incorporating shafts of Purbeck marble. The caps are of that delightful crocketed kind with stylized foliage clearly developed from the small Corinthianesque cap of the twelfth century. (Plate 24.)

The gallery arcade is taller than usual for the thirteenth century but this is possibly due to the wish to ease the junction between it and that of the early church. As it would have exposed too much of the roof of the aisle, it has been closed by a wall leaving a kind of triforium passage.

It is very noticeable that when the east end of the nave was rebuilt in the next century very little attempt was made to improve upon the design of the lovely eastern arm, indicating that the builders of the fourteenth century could appreciate a good design when they saw it and had no wish to appear to criticize it by adding something more 'contemporary'.

The high vaults of Worcester are simple and rise direct from the pavement—in a fashion which was eventually to become standard practice—by way of the tall half-shafts forming part of the pillars. This introduces the principle of combining the high vault into the elevational design on the bay.

The central tower of Worcester seems to be of the panelled Western type but with the number of bays in each elevation reduced to the pair, which in early days had fitted in so pleasantly with the rhythm of the general bay design. It was eventually to become standard practice for the cathedral tower, because nothing assists harmony more completely than the rhythm of the bay.

Worcester had been a great cathedral priory and some of the buildings of this remain adjoining the great church, among them a beautiful cloister, its splendid vaulting elaborately carved.

With the coming of the high vault, into which the shape of the clearstory trifora so neatly fitted and became submerged, the Gothic gallery arcade became the crowning feature of the cathedral walling and the base from which the vaulted ceiling rose. In perspective, the whole of the clearstory, with much of the side vaults connecting with it, tended to disappear from sight, and the cathedral vista assumed a two-storied aspect consisting of the stately main arcades and the scintillating arcading above it.

From the eleventh century onwards interest had been shown in the treatment of the spandrel between the openings of the bifora and its enclosing arch. Sometimes it was ornamented by surface carving as at Rochester. But it was inevitable that it should eventually become pierced by foliated openings as at St. Hugh's choir at Lincoln and that it should thereafter become incorporated into the design system of contemporary fenestration and become fully traceried.

When one remembers that it would have been much easier to have experimented with the design of window tracery when there was no glass to consider, one may suspect that some of the earliest forms of this art were conceived in connection with work on the gallery arcades of thirteenth-century great churches.

And amongst the lost glories of those hundreds of monastic houses 'plucked down' after 1539 are the arcades which carried the roofs of the cloisters round their garths. Many of these were rebuilt late in the Gothic era with large windows, but the earlier ones were much lower and their detail smaller in scale; it was only after the renewal of the cloister roofs with flatter pitches covered with lead that their walling was able to rise to the height we are familiar with. Thus the early arcades would for the most part have been removed even before the Suppression.

This is tragic for they may well have been features similar to those which we see above the main arcades of our cathedrals.

We have commented upon the piercing of the spandrel of the gallery bifora and its development as a fine architectural feature. Yet while this was taking place the windows of the cathedral had attained nothing of this interest. At Salisbury, for instance, with its wildly extravagant gallery arcades, the aisle windows are pairs of plain openings. For an opening having a central shaft cannot be glazed; and thus it was some time before the fenestration could catch up in architectural interest with the internal openings within the cathedral. Comparison between any clearstory and its triforium will illustrate the point. And the exterior of a thirteenth-century cathedral such as Lincoln is not really a preparation for the splendour within.

The best introduction one can have to Lincoln Cathedral is to see it about sunset from a train going from Grantham towards

Doncaster. An unexpected glimpse of it could be taken for a mirage, the three immensely slender towers rising up from the summit of their Roman hill. How must they have soared before they lost their steeples in 1807!

The west front of Lincoln is a most interesting jumble of centuries of endeavour to produce an impressive frontispiece to the cathedral. First are the three great arches of the west transept, later developed into a broad arcaded screen behind which the two tall towers are seen to be climbing. (Plate 19.)

The interior of the cathedral is Gothic at its best, tall, very stately, and in the English fashion extended into a seemingly interminable vista, the glare from the great east window fortunately broken by the silhouette of the splendid organ rising above the choir screen. Above is the long canopy of the vaulting, broken only by the light dropping from the lantern above the great crossing. (Plate 23.)

Although of two separate periods of building, Lincoln choir is one of the most splendid in the country. First one reaches the lovely work of St. Hugh with his eastern transept all in purest Gothic of the days when the twelfth century was beginning to end its splendid reign and become the thirteenth.

Completing the great church is the eastern choir, sometimes called the Angel Choir, built a century after St. Hugh's day on the site of his *chevet* but as his monument. Considered by many to be the finest example of English Gothic, its design seems to include every feature of the style. The main arcade is carried on the developed pillar with its clustered shafts absorbed within it. Above these the richly moulded arches are echoed by those of the splendid gallery story with its array of carved detail. Above in the vaulting are seen the graceful triforas of the clearstory. The ordinance is clearly stated, the mason has done his best with the architectural detail, and the carver has been allowed full rein even to the sculptured angels he has set everywhere to watch over this Gothic masterpiece.

On the exterior, two magnificent portals adorn the cathedral. On the west side of the south transept, in the usual position for the choir entrance after its removal into the eastern arm, rises a turriform structure perched above four arches like a miniature crossing, while the entrance to St. Hugh's chapel on the south side of the Angel Choir, however, seems far more like the transeptal portal of a French cathedral.

To the north-east of the cathedral is one of the loveliest of the octagonal chapter houses so often added to English cathedrals during the thirteenth century. And over all rises the great tower of Lincoln.

Amongst the improvements introduced at the end of the twelfth century in this country one must count the improvement of glazing methods and the consequent enlargement of windows.

There seems no evidence that it was intended to keep church interiors filled with a dim religious light. On the contrary even the windows of the eleventh-century churches were of a notable size, for the country possessed iron in plenty from which to make the 'ferramenti' of stanchions and saddle-bars while native lead for making the 'calms' holding the pieces of glass together had been worked by the Romans.

The bifora had originally been designed as a belfry window for allowing the sound of the bells to escape. Its central shaft prevented its being glazed. Nor would it have occurred to the early builders to have set the windows in their building bays other than singly.

By the end of the twelfth century, however, the tall windows of the period were being set in pairs in each bay as at Lincoln or Salisbury, an innovation probably brought about by the realization that a single opening of the current proportions would have looked odd if set in the middle of the area of walling concerned.

It was reasonable to expect windows so set to approach each other for aesthetic support, and in fact in the end it was possible to dispense with the section of walling separating them and replace it with a shared feature worked in dressed stone. This resulted in the couplet which replaced the older bifora and from which is developed the Gothic window.

From the large cathedral window was undoubtedly borrowed a variation on the bifora which replaced the central shaft with dressed stonework in order that the feature could be glazed. A small window of this type could be set in a single arched recess, with the actual external stonework kept so light that it would have become what is known as a mullion, part of the inner order of a glazed window from which Gothic tracery is eventually developed. It will be remembered that a masonry wall has two faces of dressed stonework. The stonework of a window would form part of the outer face; behind it would be the reveal with its wide 'scoinson' arch. Above the dressed stonework of the window, and within the reveal, would be the spandrel of the bifora ready to be pierced with a trefoil or quatrefoil. The whole feature is simply a development from the old Byzantine form but with this difference, that it is capable of being glazed; moreover the lightness of the stonework forming the actual window as apart from its reveal makes it possible to experiment with the shape of the apertures piercing the spandrel. Gradually the outline of this, instead of being an independent shape such as a trefoil, begins to follow the curve of the small arches below. And in this way the traceried window is developed. (Fig. 24.)

The couplet, child of the bifora and the first major window in Gothic architecture, suffered from what is in the rules of architectural design a major defect, for when one is looking through a window one does not want the centre of one's vision blocked by solid material. Thus the bifora became a trifora, the familiar triplet which is found everywhere in the gables of Gothic buildings of the earlier part of the thirteenth century—though very rarely in lateral elevations—and became the standard east window of the English parish church of the period.

But even in lateral elevations the couplet disappeared under the influence of the containing arch which since the days of the bifora had almost invariably accompanied this. The absolute necessity for a centre light produced the three-light window enclosed within a wide arch and with the large upper part of the window—now the window-head—filled with trefoils and quatrefoils in the style of window which is aptly known as the geometrical.

The projection of the mullion into the window-head, where it became involved in the evolutions known as tracery, led to the traceried window of the fully developed Gothic.

The foliation of window tracery, which appears to be due to the transference of the teeth or 'cusps' of the multifoils met with in the

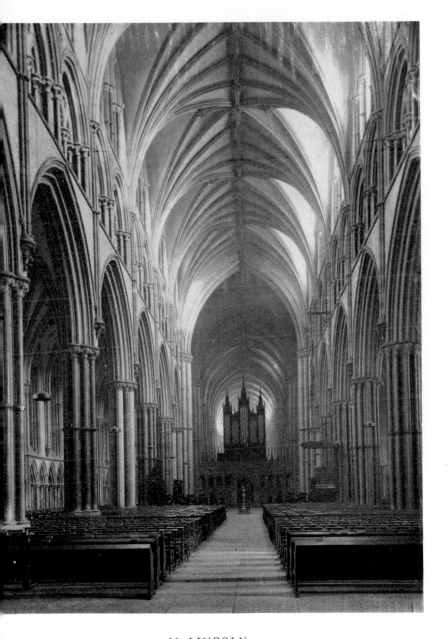

23. LINCOLN

24. WORCESTER

geometrical window to the network of extended mullions forming the bar tracery of windows, is a curious feature which will be discussed in another chapter.

After the discovery of the use of window tracery the designers began to weave the heads of their mullions into interlacing patterns echoing the sweeping lines of arcades and vaulting cones. This is a feature entirely limited to Gothic architecture and was developed from the device of setting out masons' work in 'orders'. Eventually the patterns of window tracery became more restrained, fanciful designs giving place to systems of panelling conforming with those appearing on screenwork contributed by the carpenters.

For the design of a traceried window could be transferred to a wall-surface and there employed as a scheme of wall decoration. Or again a scheme could be so devised that part of the system could be glazed and part left solid, a most important discovery because it brought windows into the design of a wall-face instead of leaving them as mere openings in a wall. It was by this means that the triforium of the clearstory was brought down to absorb the blind story, first by merely extending its mullions downwards and then by designing the whole area as a single unit, part solid and part glazed. (Fig. 25.)

What might be called the 'extended mullion' played an important part in elevational design during the later part of the Gothic era. We have noted the ingenious use of the 'basilican' arcade on the faces of towers in order to bring their windows into the scheme of decoration, as at Lincoln or Durham for example. But this horizontal division of towers—similar to the present-day 'layer-cake' form of elevation—was in opposition to the Gothic aim of achieving verticality in design.

So later towers, in particular the panelled towers of such cathedrals as Hereford or Worcester, show a complete switch of policy away from the arcade and towards the 'extended mullion' which brought the windows together once more, but this time in a vertical direction instead of a horizontal one.

This was a tremendous improvement and revolutionized Gothic design internally by giving the architects an element they could employ to increase almost indefinitely the vertical emphasis of their presentations. And employed externally on the faces of towers, an ordered system of mullions enabled them to create the western towers of Wells and the Angel Tower of Canterbury itself.

By casing early crossing piers—as can be seen begun at Ripon— the walls of a central tower could be thickened and its upper parts recessed in mullioned orders to produce a rich effect never dreamt of by the builders of the early lanterns.

But the tower of the cathedral is one of the latest of its acquisitions and was in all probability a feature which the cathedral builders left until last, not knowing when they began to erect their vast structures what would have happened to the world about them by the time they had reached the base of the tower.

For, probably, their real concern was always with the interior beauty of their house. It is in such cathedrals as Lincoln, Worcester or Lichfield that one is able to sense this force without a shadow of doubt.

Lichfield, during the ninth century the capital of Mercia and thus until 827, when this kingdom was subjected by Wessex, virtually the capital of Anglo-Saxon England, is also a very ancient episcopal see. But even the twelfth-century cathedral has vanished, swept away relentlessly in the course of rebuildings. Thus Lichfield today is an entirely Gothic cathedral, and a very splendid example of a medieval great church, perfectly designed and unhampered by that strange, probably Cistercian, restraint so clearly sensed at Salisbury. (Plate 16.)

There is a similarity in effect between Lichfield and Worcester, the same clustering of pillar-shafts and the same opulence of arch mouldings. Above are the large and impressively designed gallery arcades and the same confident inclusion of the high vault in the complete design.

The choir of Lichfield, a Gothic cathedral, is naturally in the eastern arm, a splendid structure unbroken by any eastern transept and clearly a prototype of the perfected eastern arm built as one vast apartment with all traces of Byzantine cruciform forgotten. There is a splendid lady chapel raised in height to form a prolongation of the sanctuary and ending in a semi-hexagonal apse, an interesting survival not only of the apse, but of this in its Anglo-Saxon form.

Seen from the south-east, the eastern arm of Lichfield presents a most impressive architectural spectacle of a bishop's choir of exceptional length and ending in a great apse recalling earlier days.

The west front of Lichfield is a curiously naïve composition with its interesting arcading and its attempts to get as many sculptured saints as possible into frames ill designed and too big to accommodate them comfortably, or balanced in a somewhat Continental fashion up the central shafts of two-light features. This close-set Western-style arcading is carried right up the faces of the towers and the uncomfortable little figures follow it to the end. It seems as though some determined sculptor had forced his output upon a master mason who had no idea where to put them, which is a pity, as the three western doorways of the cathedral are charming and the tiers of arcading immediately above them so well suited to include sculptured figures.

The famous spires of Lichfield, like all those of English cathedrals which appear to have been converted from timber to stone without the enthusiasm displayed by hundreds of competing parishes, are mediocre in design but with their tiers of dormers help to prevent the elaboration of the arcaded towers from running out at their summits. The central spire was destroyed during the Civil War and subsequently rebuilt.

Externally it is the splendid eastern arm which makes Lichfield architecturally notable. But it cannot be denied that the whole exterior forms one of the richest in our cathedral architecture.

It was in the interiors of their cathedrals that the Gothic builders were creating their architecture of transcendency. Their ordinance was now clearly established and recognized. It comprised a main arcade, an open gallery-like arcaded story representing the space between the vaulting of the aisle and its roof, and a high vault with the clearstory windows set in its cavernous side bays.

In section this produced a building some fifty feet high to the springing of the vault which rose in a great ribbed tunnel some thirty feet higher. In perspective one saw the ranging arcades and above these very richly moulded bands of serried shafting forming the foundations of the elaborate modelling of the high vault. The architectural strength of this part of the interior was prevented from becoming oppressive by the light entering through the windows of the clearstory.

This formed the general picture of the cathedral interior. But it still had to be built up out of a series of individually designed bays placed end to end, and it was the architecture of these units which provided the master masons with sources of competition. There was the design of the pillar and its caps, the section of the moulding of the great arches. The shaftings, mouldings and ornament of the gallery arcades provided unlimited scope for ingenuity and artistic inspiration. It was however not until a later stage that the thoughts of the masons began to turn towards the rescue of the clearstory, bereft of its triforium since the introduction of the high vault in the folds of which it had become smothered.

We must remember that the change in the section of the cathedral brought about by the introduction of the high vault had actually deprived its interior of a surprising amount of its ancient dignity. No longer did the great piers tramp two-deep down the length of their interminable naves: along them the Gothic pillars now tripped far more daintily but with less conviction. And the visible height of the interior had been reduced by a quarter when the clearstory vanished into the high vault. The Anglo-Saxon builders had their last laugh over the Gothic architects. The great cathedral would never be the same again.

The designers of the thirteenth-century cathedrals had concentrated much of their effort on the embellishment of the gallery story, a feature which, although descended from the Byzantines, had created the 'basilican' effect of drawing a long horizontal line down the building; and this, though it linked the bays together in a satisfactory manner, was nevertheless in opposition to the Gothic aim of striving for verticality.

So before the end of the thirteenth century we find a clear change of attitude towards the gallery arcade, involving its disruption as a horizontal feature in order to reconstitute the individuality of the bay, that basic element of Gothic design upon which the aesthetic effect of the compositions was so dependent.

This was not due to a sudden whim. We have been ignoring what had been happening to the exterior of the cathedral, but in point of fact there had been a complete change in roofing methods. The principal problem facing church architects as far back as those of Constantine had been what to do with the blind story where the aisle roof met the main structure. But the change in pitch of the roofing system had abolished practically the whole of the blind story, as will be explained in the next chapter, and this had made the architects of the late-thirteenth-century cathedral consider whether they could use this discovery to improve the lighting of the cathedral by enlarging the clearstory.

For a start they dropped the old triforium passage to what had been the level of the gallery below, the back of the lowered passage being blocked by a wall which was in fact a recessed blind story. The triforium element was retained but lowered so as to include the blind story as well as the clearstory. Some most attractive compositions were to evolve from this innovation. (Fig. 25.)

Such a development undoubtedly represented good design. Unfortunately, however, its effect was not as satisfactory as might have been hoped, for although verticality had been restored to the design it had been at the cost of abandoning what had long been the most glorious architectural feature of the cathedral's interior. Cathedral architecture had, in fact, been abandoned for that of the great parish church of the end of the Gothic era. As will be seen later, it was only by raising the whole building that its cathedral dignity was restored.

Much of the glory of the cathedral was due to the opulence of its carved ornament. This was of two kinds. The architectural ornament was represented by repetitive motifs forming running ornaments in the mouldings of pillar and arch. The purely decorative ornament was provided by the skilled carvers of such features as caps and corbels, canopies and vaulting bosses. All this, however, forms a subject for the art historian and critic and is beyond the scope of a book concerned with architectural construction and elevational design.

Whether inspired by Byzantines or Romans, the principal feature of the interior of the cathedral was bound to be an arcade. It therefore became probable that the arcade in its aedicular form would play a large part in the architectural ornamentation of the cathedral, especially in early times before the discovery of other forms of wall decoration such as the panelling of the late-Gothic era.

We have seen the arcade used in many cathedrals of different periods as a dado, and at Wells to cover the blind story between main arcade and clearstory. (Plate 15.)

When it was needed to ornament large areas of walling the arcading rose in tiers. The west front of Ely is the most notable example of its use in this fashion and illustrates dramatically the manner in which it could be varied at will to create indefinite interest. And for the faces of contemporary towers, tiered arcading varying in design, such as at Norwich Cathedral, created façades of immense richness which, though they were primitive in design compared with the later Gothic treatments, gave undoubted distinction to structures so treated.

The most important advantage of aedicular arcading was the facility with which it could be adjusted to fenestration so as to bring this into the design of the elevation. And with an increase in the size of windows one finds the scale of the arcading increasing to suit, until compositions of great dignity and charm could be undertaken, especially on the west fronts of cathedrals. Perhaps the most perfect example of the arcaded façade incorporating windows is the west front of Ripon Cathedral.

Ripon is one of the oldest surviving cathedral cities in England. Its first minster was founded by St. Wilfrid during the seventh century and below the existing building is a tiny room said to have been a crypt connected with his cathedral.

The present cathedral, however, was built in the eleventh century and again after 1154. Throughout the Middle Ages it was a collegiate church similar to that of Southwell and was with it regarded as a pro-cathedral in an outlying part of the large York diocese. It was William IV who at last raised it to full cathedral status.

The principal remains of the twelfth-century church are the transepts and the portions of nave and eastern arm which adjoin the crossing. The nave was built without aisles, a practice often followed by quite large churches though not, however, those of the first rank. In the case of Ripon, however, the builders anticipated the long choir arms of the following century and provided the church with an eastern arm six bays in length. This remains basically as it was when built, but having been modified by successive generations makes an interesting study of the developing fashions of medieval taste.

In the thirteenth century the nave, still aisleless, was provided with a western transept raised to form a pair of towers, the whole composition, including a splendid west front, being covered with graceful arcading designed with great care, and the front itself properly terminated with broad clasping pilasters in the style of the twelfth century. Although the west front of Ripon lacks both the scale and the majesty of Wells, it forms nevertheless a charming medieval frontispiece not easily forgotten.

In the middle of the fifteenth century the lantern tower collapsed to the south-east. The pier at that angle was rebuilt and its neighbour re-cased but the intended rebuilding scheme was never completed. The half-finished work is of great interest as illustrating how old work was brought up to date—as at Exeter, for example—merely by applying the new design on top of the old and concealing it from view.

It was not until the sixteenth century that the old aisleless nave was removed and a new aisled nave built in its place. The day of the great churches, however, was over, and the masons were more familiar with the ordinance of the parish church. This is reflected in the design of Ripon nave.

There is an unmistakable air of antiquity lingering about Ripon; especially every night at nine o'clock when the cathedral towers are silhouetted against the sky above the great square with its rows of ancient houses. For then one may see a strange figure in a long brass-buttoned coat, appearing from among the houses carrying a great curved horn. He sounds four blasts, each starting as a mere breath, then swelling in crescendo, then dying away gradually into silence. The four quarters he salutes in this fashion, moving then to the door of the mayor's house to announce the end of his task with another long lowing blast before vanishing into the shadows whence he came.

On a winter night the square is given up entirely to the solitary ghost from the long past of Ripon . . . its 'Wakeman'.

The west front of Ripon is doubtless only one of many such which were erected during the thirteenth century as entrance façades to monastic churches now long forgotten. As a solitary survivor of these it is of great value in giving us some idea of the level of elevational design attained at the time by English masons.

Its basic element is the 'lancet' opening employed in arcading, the size of each unit being attuned to that of the window required. The church behind had no aisles; thus the normal three-storied elevation was not present to control the design of the façade, which is set out freely in three stories the proportions of which have been decided independently.

First comes a basement containing a pleasant group of three entrance doorways. Above this is a splendid west window to the nave arranged as two tiers of quintuplets of which the upper group is raised towards the centre. These two tiers are carried across the towers as triplets of which the centre lancet is glazed. In each tower the belfry stage is filled with another triplet matching that below. The whole design is perfectly assembled and could not have been bettered. Even without its steeples it is most impressive and serves to draw attention to English architects' already advanced conception of elevational presentation by the second quarter of the thirteenth century.

But they were seldom able to employ their ability in the direction of elevational design. A west front or a transept end provided their only canvas. The lateral elevations of the cathedral remained as rows of bays, incapable of being assembled into an architectural composition. So the architects of the age had to approach the problem not as architecture but as scenery.

It was the buttress, originally a unit of punctuation indicating the architectural bays of the building and having nothing to do with abutment, that began to play an ever-increasing part in the exterior presentation of the cathedral.

The development of arcading in tiers led to the projecting 'buttresses' of the thirteenth century being included in the design plan, and to the width and projection of the features being adjusted so as to fit in with the dimensions of the units employed. In thirteenth-century west fronts such as those of Salisbury and Wells the buttress is designed so as to accommodate a single unit on its face and a pair on the flanks.

As elaborate schemes such as these became more restrained the buttresses retained their arcaded fronts, now arranged as a form of vertical decoration replacing the original horizontal role of arcading. Here again one can see the concentration upon the vertical which was always behind the Gothic design.

Lincoln and York employ the arcaded buttress, often with its arches recessed into niches for statuary. As the head of the niche becomes expanded into a pinnacle the developed feature can be used in connection with the decoration of towers and their angle features as at Gloucester.

Salisbury Cathedral is one of the few equipped from the start with a proper west front. This might be explained by the fact that when it was being built its splendid predecessor was still standing close by. There are reasons for supposing that this was a fine example of twelfth-century architecture. It certainly had a western bell-tower flanked by transepts and thus a proper west front. In the new cathedral the tower was omitted and its place taken by a detached bell-tower which was destroyed by Wyatt. The west transept too was omitted but its west wall was retained as a screen wall which could be converted into a frontispiece.

However one may regret the austerity of Salisbury, one has to respect the confidence of the architect for the manner in which he planned his cathedral and set out the basic elements of its elevational scheme. Unlike the builders of so many of our cathedrals he had no intention of being caught with a 'sawn-off' end to his nave; hence his provision for a proper screen wall to be spread athwart it. As completed it turned out to be a most un-Cistercian piece of architecture, even going so far as to include statuary in considerable array. But in its general design it shows quite clearly a complete understanding of what might be called 'drawing-board technique'.

There is a pronounced central motif, properly flanked by lesser areas which enhance its dignity, and sturdy terminal features to complete it. The main gable has been allowed to project above the line of the screen to stabilize the whole design by establishing its axis.

The horizontal punctuation is perfectly co-ordinated with the vertical features. The great central triplet, which could have created a gap in the system of arcading which is the basis of the treatment, has been tied to it by strong bands of diagonal panelling.

The arcading of the lower two stories is close-set, but above the sill of the great window it is lightened for the next stage and then lightened again, which is very advanced design. The arrangement of the short buttresses which frame the main doorway is carried up to include the west window in the central motif, but dies away before reaching the gable and becoming obtrusive.

As at Ripon Cathedral, the builder was able to complete his façade to the original design; and it is pleasant to be able to recognize his competence at his craft.

It is a great pity that we cannot discover the intentions of the designer of the west front at Wells, contemporary with Salisbury but far more enterprising in conception. It was clearly intended to terminate in towers—the pairs of buttresses make this fairly certain —but its period was not one for tower-building and we have no examples for comparison. We can just imagine pairs of immensely tall lancets, two stories of them perhaps, not so very different from those we see today, with tall steeples crowning them.

What is left of the original design is splendid indeed. The richly arcaded basement story leads to a magnificent *piano nobile* of great lancet arches the central triplet of which forms the west window of the nave. What should have happened above? (Plate 17.)

The west front of York Minster seems to be reminiscent of a similar technique but more restricted and with its arcading scheme lacking the nobility of that of Wells. Again we cannot tell what the original design might have been, for the earlier work has been quite overwhelmed by the tall parochial-type towers, very inferior in design to those which were added to the splendid front of Wells.

It is a sad pity that this was never finished, especially as it provides such clear evidence of the skill behind the design, which seems to have no equal anywhere in the world. Such of the Continental west fronts as belong to the Gothic age are mere essays in the piling up of towers with no thought for the broadening of the frontispiece on the lines of Wells or Peterborough.

But then the Continent seems to have completely missed the splendid grounding in fine architecture enjoyed by the builders of St. Edmundsbury and the great Anglian churches of the eleventh century.

10

The Carpenters

It is difficult to look back along a whole millennium to the time when all the architecture of this country was supplied by its carpenters, and at the same time to appreciate that their buildings were regarded as the finest in Western Europe. But wood is easy and quick to work. And as it is vulnerable to the elements it may have a short life and need frequent renewal, thus providing fresh experience for the carpenters. It makes for an active building trade. Was it not observed by a chronicler during the Hundred Years' War that the destruction of villages mattered little to the inhabitants who 'with a few poles and some thatch will soon have their homes back again'?

So perhaps, like cities destroyed in some earthquake, the churches built by Anglo-Saxon carpenters and converted into bonfires by the Danish army were soon raised again more splendid than before.

It is a pity that the art of the Anglo-Saxon carpenter seems to have perished so completely before the advance of the quarryman and the mason. But as time goes on the trained observer will doubtless be able to recognize in English architecture those features which owe their characteristics to him.

When we come to the great stone cathedrals we can say that three crafts contributed to them in a major sense. There were the masons who built the walling. Then there were the carpenters who not only built the roofs but before they could do so had to 'attend' upon the masons with a great deal of temporary timberwork such as scaffolding and centering for arches. Then there were the carvers

who embellished the building with the enrichment to which it was
entitled. And many of these would have been carvers first in wood.
The day of the carpenters was the tenth and eleventh centuries.
But we can remember them when we admire the splendid carvings
on the elaborate doorways of the eleventh and twelfth centuries,
noble survivals of their craft.

But while the Anglo-Saxon woodcarvers had to turn their
chisels to the stones supplied to them by the masons, the carpenters
still had the timbering of the cathedral roof to prepare and raise.

The English roof was covered with shingles split out of hardwood and laid like the clay tiles of today. But shingles can warp in
dry weather and snow may blow under them so that it is necessary
to keep the pitch of the roof steep enough to prevent this from
happening. The steep roof is one of the principal factors dividing the
Western Byzantine architecture from that of its homeland.

The Anglo-Saxon carpenters had nothing to learn about the
construction of roofs. The basic component of the roof is the rafter
which rests on the wall-top and rises to the apex of the construction.
Arriving there, it meets a rafter rising from the opposite wall and
is there pinned to it. Thus the roof consisted of a series of these
pairs of rafters, known as 'couples', which were simply set side by
side from one end of the building to the other.

To counteract the tendency of each couple to spread at the foot,
its components were joined together at one or more levels by
horizontal timbers known as 'collars'.

Since the couples forming the roof were set very closely together
the timberwork as seen from below in perspective composed three
planes, two sloping and one flat, the upper part of the roof above
the lowest collar being practically invisible.

In the wall-top was set a wide plank of timber, called today a
'wall-plate', to provide a sound foundation for the rafter-feet. At
right angles to the wall-plate short lengths of wood were set across
the wall with the rafter set on the outer end of it, and balancing this
inside the building a short vertical timber known today as 'ashlaring'. Thus the foot of each rafter was stiffened by a timber
triangle and the ashlaring contributed a short vertical plane to the
silhouette of the roof and concealed the top of the masonry wall.

As roofs developed to cathedral scale the problem of the strength of the rafters increased, and it had to be met by the addition of diagonal timbers known as braces passing across it from side to side and introducing the well-known principle of triangulation. Thus the cathedral roof became a forest of beams, retaining, however, the general shape of its underside.

In a roof of forty feet in span the feet of the rafters had to be very securely mounted upon the wall-top and this was assured by widening the masonry out with projecting stone 'tablements' both inside and, more important, on the outside. The undersides of the projecting tablements were chamfered off. As eaves were of the utmost importance for preventing the stormwater passing down the slope of the roof from running down the wall-face and soaking through into the building, the outer tablement was brought well forward of the face of the wall and carried between corbels fixed in the wall. This is the familiar 'corbel-table' with which the tops of all large eleventh and twelfth century buildings were finished.

During the thirteenth century the tablement was supported by a series of small arches, often trefoiled, springing from the corbels, another familiar and most attractive method of forming the eaves of the cathedral.

At the middle of the thirteenth century the roof of the English cathedral had its shingles replaced by sheets of lead, a material of which this country produced most of that used in Europe, as it had supplied at one time the Roman Empire, from the mines of Derbyshire and the Mendips. Lead cast into sheets provides a permanent and waterproof roof covering but is a very difficult material to handle satisfactorily.

One of the first major buildings to be covered with lead was the newly finished cathedral at Salisbury. The masons' lodges on the south side of the nave were still standing and these were taken over by the lead-workers and became the 'Plumbery'. When the cloisters were built they had to be planned away from the nave wall as the plumbery was still in operation.

As time went on the plumbers began to learn more about their very troublesome material. Its high co-efficient of expansion made it move about and strain the timbering of the roof, and its great weight made it liable to 'creep' down the roof slope and land on the ground. The writer has seen a whole church roof lying like rolls of linoleum at the foot of the walls where it had arrived in one swoop! Complete redesign of the roofs became necessary. The Gothic roof, now no longer needing a steep pitch to keep snow from blowing under the shingles, was abandoned for a roof with practically no pitch at all so as to discourage the lead from 'creeping.' In order to lessen the chance of the lead diving completely off the roof its eaves were abandoned and the wall-face carried up as a parapet, with cleverly designed lead gutters behind this to collect the water and lead it away through spouting.

This completely changed the outward appearance of the Gothic building. What remained of the once tall roof began to disappear completely behind the new parapets.

The internal section of the church was completely altered. The lowering of the pitch of the roof brought its apex down on top of the vault so that the silhouette of this had to be made less acutely pointed. Towards the end of the Gothic era the arch had adopted the familiar four-centred shape. This is quite incorrectly called 'debased'. The architecture of King's College Chapel at Cambridge could in no circumstances be described as 'debased'—it may have lost the acutely pointed 'lancet' arches regarded by the 'Gothick' artists of the Regency as so romantic, but it has raised its walling to counteract the lowering of the apex of the roof and by so doing has preserved that vertical effect expected of the Gothic style. It was merely a case of an ordinance revised to accommodate new structural systems demanded by new materials.

Externally, the top of the wall changed its appearance completely after the arrival of the lead. The eaves vanished, though the tablement remained and was used to support the new parapets. Below the tablement spoutings or gargoyles appeared to give the successors of the twelfth-century carvers a chance to quiz the world with their grotesques.

The parapet broke out into pseudo-military crenellations sometimes panelled and fretted in the style which was being developed by the carpenters in their screenwork. Crocketed pinnacles began to appear on the skyline of the cathedral in place of the great tall roof of the past. Formerly the whole of the elevations had been dominated by the great Gothic roof. This was now in subjection and the architecture of the cathedral wall could be given a chance to display itself.

The best example of the new ordinance may be seen in the choir at Norwich. Here the apex of the new roof has been kept at the same level as the old but the walls of the clearstory have been raised high in the air so as to keep the low roof—which is barely visible— away from the top of the new vault. The interior effect of the huge clearstory windows is of course most impressive and the whole scheme of remodelling has been carried out with the greatest skill and now enhances the dignity of the eleventh-century apse.

With the coming of lead, the roofs of the aisles could be lowered to a suitable pitch, which enormously increased the height of the clearstory and enabled it to be redesigned with tall windows. At the same time the old blind story which had for so long troubled the architects—though it had of course produced the lovely gallery arcades of the thirteenth century—became practically obliterated. It was thus the introduction of lead for roofing which caused the interior ordinance of the cathedral bay to be reduced to what was in fact the same two stories as could be found in the large parish church; a situation which was appreciated by the Gothic architects too late in the cathedral age for them to be able to rectify the resultant loss of dignity in the interior of the greater church.

The main roofs of the cathedral, however, remained as originally designed. Their eaves, though, were removed and the corbel-table beneath it elaborated to produce a greater overhang and enable the new parapet to be set well out from the wall-face so as to get a wide gutter behind it. And anyone who has ever walked along the gutter of a cathedral roof will be able to appreciate the great width needed to accommodate its 'falls'.

Beneath the now attractive corbel-table with its foliated arches carrying the parapet of the main roof one could see the development of the clearstory into a range of windows approaching the size of those in the aisles below. With the aisle roof now lost to view its parapet was becoming one of the most outstanding features of the exterior of the cathedral, fortified as it was by the

25. YORK

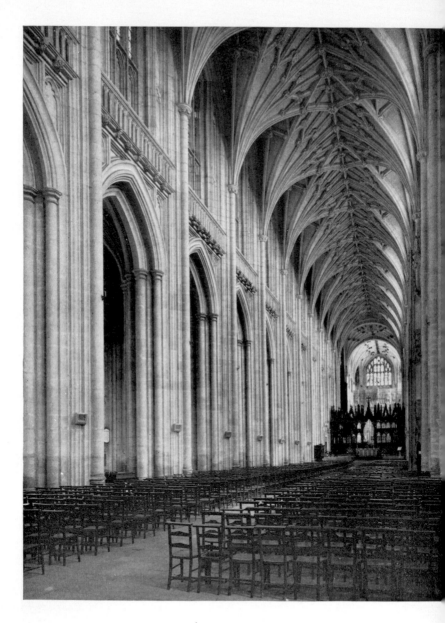

26. WINCHESTER

buttresses with their pinnacles which were becoming a kind of stone forest seeming to advertise the presence of the forest of pillars within.

The design of the parapet itself was becoming an important feature of the cathedral by reason of the influence which was being exerted upon the masons of the late Gothic period by the carpenters. In addition to their labours upon the great structure of the roofs, they were also being called in with increasing frequency to design what today would be called 'joinery', that is to say finished work of the nature of furnishings. This meant that in addition to being builders in timber they were by way of becoming craftsmen in their material and developing the same artistic skill in using it as that of the stonemason at his banker.

The carpenter's earliest efforts at producing finished—as opposed to 'carcasing'—work would have been concerned with the erections of partitions inside a building. It may not be generally appreciated that a masonry wall cannot be less than some thirty inches in thickness. Thus, quite apart from the expense of building a wall that was not carrying a roof, such walls were practically never used as internal partitions.

In the same way that an assemblage of laths is called a lattice, so was an arrangement of boards called a 'brattice', a term which is still used in mining engineering for partitions in a shaft. The walls of Anglo-Saxon timber churches were formed in bratticing. Only one example remains, at Greensted church in Essex.

This external screenwork was formed of the off-cuts left from squaring logs into beams, each rough plank being trimmed at each end and set upright between grooves formed in a ground-sill and a head-beam. The rounded side was faced outwards so as to give a smooth interior. Interstices could be daubed with cob of clay and chopped straw.

Judging by later developments, it may be that the joints between boards were covered with narrower boards trimmed from smaller beams. And to this day small barns are built in the country districts of two skins of off-cut boards set 'breaking joint' in this fashion.

Medieval boards were very much wider than those used today, eighteen inches to two feet being quite common. As developed into a piece of joinery, the screen was framed up from a sill, a head, and a series of vertical 'studs' between which were the wide boards set into grooves in the framing.

It is interesting to note the fundamental part played by the groove in the timber beam into which could be set the 'wattling' of a cob partition or the boards of a better-class one. A development from it is the 'glazing groove' for converting an opening in the framework into a window.

Screens of medieval type are still to be found in considerable numbers in old farmhouses, especially in Devonshire. It was probably screens of this type which first enclosed the choirs of the early cathedrals.

But as solid screens would have cut off some of the light from the aisle windows the horizontal member called the 'transom' was introduced. It separated a solid lower part of the screen from an open part of it, while the screen remained to a height that was thought to give an adequate element of enclosure.

With the 'foliation' of the head of the open part of the screen following the transference of moulded orders from the fenestration, the screen was on the way to becoming a fine piece of furnishing. Taking the panelled arrangement of the vertical studs and the transoms as a basis, the carpenters began to elaborate their designs in conformity with Gothic detail until they had created a style of panelled architecture which was eventually to be copied in stone, both in the form of screenwork and as panelling applied to the solid wall-faces and even the jambs and soffits of arches. At the end of the Gothic era the panelled architecture reached up over the cones of the vaulting to embellish the splendid 'fans', and with this last flourish its glories came to an end.

The cathedral has a number of internal partitions. Called screens, they are for the most part solid below and open above, barriers yet not intended to assure complete privacy. They separate chapels from each other and from the main area of the cathedral. They completely surround the bishop's choir. A bay west of this was the only impassable partition, the rood-screen, completely shutting off the bishop's church from that of the laity.

During the last two centuries these two screens, the rood-screen and the choir screen itself, have been steadily whittled away to provide the 'unbroken vista', that view of the east window from the west door which the ecclesiologists of the period have regarded as the only acceptable presentation of the interior of a cathedral. The idea has been taken up by the modern cathedrals. Such fine examples of architecture as those of Truro, Liverpool and Guildford fail to recall to us the cathedral of the Middle Ages for the plain reason that the bishop's choir has been omitted so that we see just a large church with its chancel for surpliced choristers.

For a cathedral is not a large church. Nor is it an assembly hall or a concert hall. It is a very special building, and size is the least of its requirements. It is a church in which daily prayers are offered up by priests appointed for the purpose. The greater part of the building, added to increase its size and thus advertise its magnificence, can be a promenade for the laity who can assist in public prayers, listen to a preacher, or to an organ, a choir or an orchestra.

When we enter the choirs of Canterbury, Winchester or Exeter it seems we find the ancient spirit of the place present within them. At Salisbury, Worcester or Lichfield there is only a sense of loss.

Now that congregations vary in numbers with each occasion upon which the cathedral is used, it might seem reasonable to separate choir and nave once more—if only to economize in lighting and heating.

The stately stall-lined halls of ancient days have long been cluttered up with extra rows of seating for congregational use.

It makes one realize how fortunate we are to have been able to preserve some of the splendid choir screens such as those at Exeter and Ripon. Let us hope that no enlightened Chapter of the future will decide to bring some cathedral into line with 'contemporary' fashion by sweeping away yet another anachronism!

As befitted the ecclesiastical significance, the entrance to the bishop's choir was always treated as a major architectural feature. Within, the first two or three bays were lined with the choir seating, eventually to become splendid examples of the carpenters' art with sculptured sides and traceried and pinnacled canopies soaring high into the arches overhead. Between the end of the stallwork and the altar stretched the side screens of the choir with their side doorways leading into the transepts, and behind the altar itself the vista was brought to an end with a splendid reredos.

Beyond the choir screens, on its flanks and behind the reredos, lay a maze of side chapels. They were sited in the eastern aisles of the main transepts and in the eastern transepts if these existed. Eastwards were the chapels of the ambulatory.

When admiring the pillars and arches of a Gothic building it is sometimes as well to stop to consider the function of these beautiful features. For all were simply to support a roof. Their architectural presentation may be supremely lovely. Functionally, however, they were simply the skeleton of a building. Thus for any kind of internal plan to be established this had to be set out in the form of screen-work—what in a house would be partitions. An eastern aisle by itself would be like a cart-shed beside a transept without the screens dividing in into its chapels and other screens with entrance door-ways in them set between the pillars of the arcade.

It was the carpenter who had to provide all this screenwork. And in a cathedral it had to be of the finest craftsmanship. Later on in the Gothic era the masons began to copy the designs of the carpenters in stone, so that the screenwork of the choir and side chapels gradually became replaced by stone copies. It was this borrowing of the carpenters' designs that resulted in the stone panelling which characterizes late Gothic architecture.

The only styles of architecture to have been considered by the historian hitherto have been those illustrated by buildings of an imperishable nature, the trabeated in which the timber beam has been replaced by a stone lintel, and the arcuated which is developed around the arch formed of stone voussoirs.

But while timber architecture cannot be considered in the light of great building for the reason that its productions must always have been small in scale compared with those of stone, both the arcuated and trabeated styles may well have been influenced by timber forms long perished and forgotten.

Influences of this sort are unlikely to have been connected with the structural aspect of architecture, because structural matters are difficult to translate from timber to stone. Indeed the whole of the trabeated style eventually disappears to be replaced by the arcuated. But it may well be that there have existed features of timber building sufficiently admired for them to have merited some attempt to convert them into stone.

It has for some time been realized that the forms of Gothic architecture are surprisingly sympathetic with those of the 'cruck' style of building.

The cruck or crook was a timber form well known to the medieval builder and we find it surviving in cottage architecture into the seventeenth century.

The cruck of the builders had an aedicule in an object very much in use during the Middle Ages—the packsaddle.

The packsaddle used by the Duke of Wellington's troops during the Peninsular campaign was called a 'Devonshire crook'. An old horse only fit to carry a packsaddle was called a 'crock'.

In considering the architecture of other days, it is often a valuable exercise to contemplate contemporary circumstances which might have affected the attitude towards aesthetics. In the matter of common transport we accept without thought the motor car and truck. The oldest amongst us can remember the twilight of the 'horse and buggy' era of trap and waggon. But the wheel itself, familiar to our ancestors during the last two or three centuries, was even then far from being in universal use throughout the countryside, for the simple reason that there were few all-weather roads upon which it could turn.

During the Middle Ages it was the horse itself which provided transport, not only for the rider but for all kinds of goods and materials. The essential item of horse-furniture is the saddle: the riding-saddle for the man and the packsaddle for a load. The former in its contemporary form is still with us, while the latter may yet be retained for use with military mule companies as in the last war. Fine locally made examples, less than a century old, may still be found in museums.

Saddles of all descriptions would have been seen everywhere during the cathedral-building era.

The structural basis of every saddle is the saddle-tree. In the riding-saddle this is a piece of wood shaped like a wishbone, set within the saddle. The packsaddle has two miniature 'crucks'—called in fact 'crooks'—serving as pommel and cantle.

The purpose of the saddle-tree is to transfer the weight of man or load upon the ribs of the animal while at the same time keeping it off the spine. Thus the curve of the tree is shaped to the horse's back until the two sides approach each other; the curves then go into reverse and meet at a sharp apex. No one can glance at the front of any saddle without realizing instantly that the double curves of the tree form the perfect 'ogee', a graceful shape which must in the Middle Ages have been before everyone's eyes.

In medieval architecture the ogee is found in two forms. Most familiar is the arch, set over small openings such as niches or the tops of window lights. But the ogee is also employed convexly as a gable, in the hood-moulds above such niches for example, or the ends of early pews. Such aedicular forms of the ogee gable usually end in elaborate finials, trilobar like clumsy fleur-de-lis. As these features were called in medieval days 'pommels', their origin can hardly be in doubt. One may note that the pommels seen in the 'Western' film display knobs now vanished from the English saddle.

It is pleasant to think of the architect jogging to his new church contemplating the pommel of his saddle and at the same time some detail of a finial to the hood-mould of a piscina.

One of the lesser but very prominent features of the Gothic is the practice of 'foliating' the heads of arches in window lights, niches and other small objects. Foliation seems to be of native origin and appears in no uncertain form about the middle of the twelfth century in the upper stories of the west front at Ely. It would seem that it must have developed from the designing of multifoil openings in such situations as the tympanum of the bifora. One can imagine a mason 'doodling' with his compasses and in so doing designing multifoil openings.

But there is a major aspect of foliation which may also be seen at Ely in the splendid processional doorway on the south side of the nave. This is not likely to represent an enlargement of the ordinary foliated design, nor is the latter likely to be an aedicular representation of it.

The trefoil-headed doorway of the twelfth century, very often ornamented with Anglo-Saxon carving, has almost certainly a timber origin, very probably a development from the cruck.

Nowhere is the form of the timber cruck more forcibly suggested than in the transept of Hereford where the arches rise from their springing at an angle entirely at variance with the most fundamental ordinance of arcuated architecture. In the gallery arcade above one sees an inner order added to the smaller arches, this order being set out with a 'cusp' so that the whole silhouette forms a tall trefoil. This looks very much like the stone copy of a timber design, especially when one compares it with the ordinary mason-like quatrefoils over it. So possibly we have here an aedicular representation of a house-cruck with an inner order added to it having this central cusp and converting the whole silhouette into a trefoil.

When one considers the amount of experimental work upon models which must have been engaged in during the Gothic period and how this has all disappeared without trace, one can imagine the vast store of experiments in the far more perishable material of the carpenters which would in like fashion have long rotted away, taking with them a great deal of information that would have helped us to understand far more about the origins of Gothic design.

For there must have been an army of carpenters working around a rising cathedral, engaged in preparing not only roof timbers but the vast amount of temporary timbering required by the masons. A strong scaffolding was needed to rise to a great height and there support the temporary wooden centering of the great arches while they were being turned.

The scaffolding would have relied upon softwood poles or hardwood posts set vertically in the ground and probably tied one against the other as they rose. Between these the rails would have to be shifted for each 'raise' of the wall. The medieval carpenters would be familiar with the need for bracing their scaffolding to prevent its collapsing sideways. Over the rails the 'putlogs' would be set into the wall at each raise, the 'putlog holes' being filled up as the building rose. On the putlogs would rest the planks upon which the masons worked and which carried their materials.

One can with difficulty imagine the enormous amount of scaffolding required to build the eighty-foot-high wall of a cathedral, to say nothing of its tower.

One may reflect also upon the scaffolding needed to support the centering of a vault over a forty-foot span.

It will be appreciated that a vault could not have been erected without a section of centering for each of its main ribs. Every piece of this centering had to be constructed on the ground, taken to pieces, transported up to the scaffolding and there re-erected. One may therefore suspect that the vault plan was in fact devised by the carpenters, the masons merely cutting the stones to suit.

The triumph of the carpenters is undoubtedly represented by a vault which was not only designed, but entirely made by them—the noble octagon at Ely Cathedral.

As one travels away from Cambridge across the empty Fenland upon the road to Ely the time comes when one is aware of a kind of presence slowly materializing upon the horizon—the great tower of Ely. As one approaches it, the long mass of the cathedral begins to dominate the scene, lying along the skyline and looming above the roofs of the little city clutching at its skirts. (Plate 7.)

There is no church in all England to compare with Ely Cathedral. Its tall west tower has no fellow, nor has the splendid octagon, unique amongst those central features around which Western churches were once built.

The absence of the northern wing of the west front is a sad loss, as one realizes when one has examined the elaborate architecture of the remaining wing, not a square foot of which is left without that carved ornament the Anglo-Saxon churches were once famous for. The great tower itself is not lacking in architectural charm and remains as the sole survivor of a race of great west towers.

Inside the nave one cannot but be struck by the immense dignity which could be displayed by these primitive buildings with their two-storied arcades so clearly designed to achieve height combined with stability. While the main arcade had to be reduced to an unspectacular scale and capacious galleries provided above it which were probably never used, the strength of the bay design remains undoubtedly impressive and a proper verticality of effect is achieved through the strong lines of the half-shafts punctuating the bays and endowing the interior with a proper monumental emphasis. Thus without being too much broken up into bays the splendid length of Ely nave is able to present us with a noble vision of a primitive hall.

Ely choir, also, is one of England's noblest architectural achievements. Although of the thirteenth century, its ordinance is an anachronism owing to the sensivity of the designer who sought to repeat the story heights of the nave rather than to create a sense of irritation by changing to the Gothic ordinance employing the taller main arcade and the lower gallery one. Thus the galleries are repeated, even filled with the most ingenious Gothic versions of the Byzantine bifora, the whole lavishly embellished with carved ornament. (Plate 22.)

This, by the way, could well supply an example to the modern architect by encouraging him to adjust his own elevation to fit courteously and in neighbourly fashion with adjoining house-fronts in the same street.

The central feature of Ely Cathedral, its amazing octagon, is of course unique in architecture.

After threatening for some time to succumb to the pressures from the eight arcades abutting against them, the original crossing piers collapsed in 1322, bringing the lantern down. The choir had already moved into the new eastern arm and the transept had become a 'walking space'. So instead of rebuilding the central tower the Chapter decided to remove the remains of the four piers and construct an octagonal hall, crowned by a lantern, before the doorway to the bishop's choir—a plan only made possible by the fact that the transepts had aisles on both east and west sides.

It is this octagon, built entirely by the carpenters and in such fashion as can hardly leave any doubt that it was they alone who had designed the high vaults of English cathedrals, which was the glory of the noble church of Ely. (Plate 29.)

The lady chapel, built as a separate structure joining the north transept at its angle—the kind of position often favoured by the Augustinians—is a splendid building of the fourteenth century. Its wide span is covered by a lovely vault rising from abutments designed so as to leave space for large windows with elaborately traceried heads. The whole of the interior is lavishly ornamented with intricately woven carving.

The fall of the central tower having wrecked the choir, a new set of stalls had to be provided. These stalls remain today and, with the vaulting of their glorious antechamber, make a lasting memorial to the skill and versatility of the Gothic carpenters.

11

Glades of Stone

Most of what is written today in defence of what is called 'contemporary architecture' takes the form of exhortation to perform abstract actions as though they were positive actions. 'Spatial' is a word often used as though it were describing a solid rather than its absence. High-sounding aims are suggested, but never the means of attaining them.

Great architecture needs two inspirations, one spiritual, one practical. The architect needs to be aiming at some achievement. And he has to know by what means to attain his goal.

There is of course no doubt that the inspiration of the Gothic architect was the desire to create the most glorious architecture in honour of the Supreme Deity. This would have been the same with the gods of ancient days—the awesome gods who inspired Luxor, the heroic figures in whose honour was created Baalbek.

In what form was the Christian God of medieval England honoured? It would seem clear that in common with all great monumental architecture the cathedral was reaching for the sky.

Here we have an inspired dimension. But we are still a long way from giving the architecture of the cathedral a form.

It is said that in the flat plains of Sumer the aim of the temple builders was to achieve height by building brick copies in stylized form of the mountains which rose each dawn into the eastern mirage.

In the England of a thousand years ago, height would not have been represented by its rolling downland, but by another natural form, unknown to the great builders of Classical days—the forest of tall hardwood trees.

Height as suggested by a hill would be that of the tall mass of the exterior of a building. But enter a forest ride and you are *within* a tall temple, lined with pillars and covered with a high vault, and with the light from tall windows filtering through the trees.

It is possible that a bishop of the later Middle Ages, quizzing his master mason, might ask whether his new cathedral was meant to resemble a forest glade. In which case he would probably be met with a blunt, possibly embarrassed, denial. But all the same he might have guessed the mason's secret.

But it would have been many decades before the cathedral designer could allow himself to think along philosophical lines. His concern was to get the building safely erected. And for him design was structural, with aesthetics looking after themselves.

Although the basis of the cathedral design was the bay, the dependence of its forms upon structural requirements makes it a matter of speculation as to whether each story, represented as this was by a row of bays, was the limit of its particular unit of design, or whether the pile of three stories forming each bay was designed as an entity and the resulting effect of setting them beside each other a product of chance.

The construction of a cathedral, or even a major portion of it such as a new nave, would have taken many years, perhaps a generation or more. The lower story, comprising the main arcades and the aisle walls with their vaulting over, would have contained the most material, but the stories over would have had to lift everything up to the scaffolding and so they also would take many years to complete. During all this time ideas might alter considerably. There might even be a serious change in ordinance. It would seem that it was not until well into the thirteenth century that we could have found the mason sure of being able to follow a cohesive design from pavement to vault.

Even the design of Salisbury, a cathedral built on a virgin site, seems to lack conviction. We know that the aisles were first built and thatched with straw and that the eastern chapels were built and roofed so that the building could be brought into use that far, five years after it had been founded. But we are then clearly shown that either the next story had not been designed or, if so, that the design had been abandoned and another substituted. And it was at this stage that it had been decided to cover the main span with a high vault—a finish, by the way, omitted by the early Cistercians. At the triforium stage, however, the designer—perhaps a newcomer—returned to the established ordinance and executed it in Gothic to match the rest of the cathedral.

Thus, although the intention of the English architect had been to design by the bay, the exigencies of his constructional programme had resulted in the building being assembled upon horizontal or 'basilican' lines.

The architects may indeed have had to wait for the constructional programme to reach a higher state of reliability, and for design intentions to represent a greater assurance of stability, before being able to design a complete bay with a reasonable chance that in the end it would be built as designed. Only then could they be assured that their Gothic inspiration of the soaring bay could be achieved.

After the transformation of the gallery arcade the next story to suffer modification was the triforium. This had continued in its original eleventh-century form with the arches becoming pointed during the thirteenth century. Its pyramidal shape enabled it to fit into the side bays of the high vault without any need for adjustment.

A tendency seen as early as the Ely triforium, however, was to omit the two shafts and construct the feature as a single wide opening. This form enabled it to accommodate the new broad traceried windows of the Gothic clearstory, and towards the end of the era the whole feature was omitted and the side vault carried right through to the clearstory wall as at Oxford.

The actual cleaning passage, as has already been noted, dropped to the level of the old thirteenth-century gallery the arcading of which was abandoned; and the two features combined into a single one which must in future be described as the clearstory, the triforium treatment having been lost during the various attempts at assimilation of the blind story. This had become, through the

Fig. 25.   *The trifora*
Of Byzantine origin, it became employed to
carry the inner face of the wall of the
clearstory of the twelfth-century cathedral, the
centre arch being raised to increase the light
from the window beyond. It gave its name to
the triforium, today wrongly applied to the
gallery arcade below. During the Gothic era
the trifora became extended downwards to
enable it to emerge from the shadow of the
high vault and replace the lovely but expensive
arcading of biforas which had covered the
blind story against which the aisle roof abutted

advent of lead roofing, no longer a major problem, and for the
same reason the cleaning passage for the triforium windows was
now situated at no great distance below them. The passage may
have had a parapet, as in Lichfield choir, or may be concealed by a
blind-story treatment as at Exeter where each bay has four trefoil-
headed arches in it. (Plate 32.)

The recession of the clearstory windows behind the great cones
of the vaulting was met at York Minster by bringing them into the
inner fade of the wall with a cleaning passage outside the building
—but apparently none inside which would provide direct access to
the glass—so that temporary scaffolding would have had to be
rigged when required.

The parapet over the outer passage at York was carried by a
series of mullions. Inside the building a system of open stone

panelling, similar to that at Gloucester, was run across the passage.

By the virtual obliteration of the gallery or blind story the interior of the cathedral had lost one of the horizontal elements in the design which had been militating against the desired verticality. This, however, was at the cost, unfortunately, of losing what for long had been the most lovely feature of the interior, crowning the arcade and forming a superb architectural base for the high vault. Indeed it was only this last tremendous firmament which saved the interior ordinance of the cathedral from appearing as though reduced to parochial status. Both the danger and the remedy may be seen at the splendid cathedral of Exeter.

Until a lapse on the part of the citizens of Exeter raised a multistory department store on the skyline of the ancient city of Exeter, its remarkable cathedral church dominated the surrounding buildings as it had done for eight hundred years.

The absorbing mystery of this splendid Western cathedral lies in the fact that its design runs contrary to all the churches of its age in omitting the essential central feature of a lantern tower over the crossing and indeed seems to have deprived this of all light by raising its transepts to form a pair of towers flanking the church like panniers. The present transept arches are later than the towers themselves so we cannot be sure just what their relationship to the interior of the church was intended to be. The only analogy is that of the western transept raised to form a twin-towered west front.

The pair of towers presents the sole visible remains of the cathedral of which they formed part, buried in the splendid Gothic building which displays one of the most perfect cathedral interiors in architecture, designed as an entity and carried out accordingly.

The present building dates from the middle of the thirteenth century and is notable for a novel approach to the design of cathedrals in that the traditional emphasis upon a monumental height was abandoned in favour of providing an increased opulence of architectural detail, the high vault in particular completing the interior of the building in a decisive fashion.

The charming gallery arcades so universally admired during the thirteenth century were abandoned in favour of a return to the low story first seen at Wells. This economized in interior height and at the same time provided space for exceptionally large traceried clearstory windows of advanced design and of great value in lighting the tremendous vault, which was clearly intended to be the principal architectural feature of the interior.

The fine vaulted hall, unbroken by any lantern, the vault itself intricate without being elaborate, is Exeter's notable contribution to English cathedral architecture. The choir is in the eastern arm and is approached through an exceptionally fine screen above which the Renaissance organ case is silhouetted against the space beyond without in any way breaking the line of the great vault.

One of the best times to enter a cathedral of this kind is when snow is lying on the ground outside and one sees all the beauty of the vaulting with its shadows driven away by the glow from the clearstory. At Exeter a similar effect has been created by setting clear glass in the spacious windows of the clearstory. With its glorious vault now shining as lovely as ever on any day in the year, the interior of Exeter Cathedral has been presented as one of the most beautiful churches in the world. (Plate 32.)

It will probably be appreciated that there were aesthetic disadvantages attending the covering of a cathedral with a vault of this magnitude.

One of the reasons for the tremendous dignity of the large Anglian naves is the fact that the walling is displayed to its full height of three stories. (Plate 3.) The advent of the high vault, and its general acceptance as the standard form of ceiling for the great church, completely transformed the proportions of the interior. The shape of the wall-surface of the bay was now changed at triforium level from a rectangular area to an arch framed by the wall-ribs of the vault.

We have discussed the loss in height, due first to the shrinking of the gallery into the line of arcading so popular during the thirteenth century; then the further loss following the absorption of this into the clearstory, making the church below the vault little more than the height of the main arcade.

The section of the building changed from a flat-ceilinged hall to a tunnel, the walls of which were some five-sevenths of their former

27. CANTERBURY

28. CANTERBURY

height. The old Byzantine grandeur had been lost, and little attempt was made at first to replace it with any kind of soaring arboreal effect: Exeter was a case in point.

It was in an attempt to recover this lost dignity that the later Gothic architects tried to raise the heights of their main arcades when they dispensed with the gallery arcades of the thirteenth century. But stateliness and charm seem to have suffered equally, and it can hardly have escaped the notice of the architects of the end of the thirteenth century that they were failing to maintain the standard of dignity set by the cathedrals of two centuries earlier.

York Minster added twenty feet to the old standard height of eighty feet when rebuilding, but this meant rebuilding the central tower also. The result, however, was that it was able to recapture much of the old dignity and by skilful handling of the elements of the pillared interior succeeded in creating a real glade of stone, a Gothic rival at last to the tremendous naves of the Anglians.

Chester Cathedral is humbly proportioned in comparison with some of the great cathedrals of this country. It was not originally of cathedral rank, having been a Benedictine abbey church preserved by Henry VIII at the Suppression and provided with a bishop in place of its abbot. Thus among its most interesting features, perhaps, are the remains of the buildings of the monastery, in particular the Gothic vestibule leading to the chapter house of the monks.

Very little is left of the original abbey church, and the existing building is of interest as an illustration of the development of the church of a monastic house not of the first rank, not of cathedral degree, but considerably finer than the parish church of the period. The kind of church which once existed in scores throughout the country, and in scores perished after 1539.

It is probable that from a study of these great churches of the second rank we could have discovered more of the modifications which were tending to reduce the earlier cathedral architecture to something more economical, perhaps less impressive, yet abandoning nothing of the Gothic spirit, the Gothic charm.

The history of Chester abbey church follows the normal programme of development. We have the choir rebuilt at the beginning of the thirteenth century and after this the rebuilding of the eleventh-century nave. The abbey was not a wealthy one and the whole of the work progressed piecemeal.

The choir with its diminutive gallery arcade stopped with the roofing of the aisles and a high clearstory was added later. In the nave, begun during the fourteenth century, the design is plain and bordering on the parochial, a clear indication of things to come, with the blind story absorbed into the clearstory above.

An unusual feature of the cathedral is its enormous south transept, like the nave of a late parish church. Most abbeys provided a parish church alongside their abbey church and this curious transept appears to have replaced one such church. It is said that the parishioners took over the great transept against the wishes of the monks, but it may well have been intended for parish use and not simply to add to the architectural dignity of the church.

On the south side of the choir may be seen a group of four elaborately carved sedilia in a style recalling the reredos at Durham Cathedral. But the glory of Chester is the splendid array of four-teenth-century choir stalls dating from the days of the Benedictine monks. There is no choir screen or pulpitum, but worked into the scheme of decoration is a tall pinnacled porch leading out of the walking space under the crossing. It is a sad thought that so much glorious carpentry of this description must have been thrown onto the bonfires of 1539.

The cloister is simple, but has an interesting feature in the walk next the church where the outer wall of the cloister has been provided with arched recesses in which the monks could read and write.

One of the lessons of Chester Cathedral is the manner in which the lesser churches were able to profit from the abandoning of those horizontal divisions which had for so long broken the vertical lines of greater churches and hindered the development of the Gothic expression of verticality.

If the division into stories was obstructive to Gothic aims, so too was the traditional interruption of the arcading by an insistence upon indicating the impost with a moulding or a row of carved caps to form a compound capital.

From the fourteenth century onwards we see a determined effort to limit the number of interruptions made by unnecessary impost treatments, as many shafts as possible being allowed to rise unbroken, not only to join the mouldings of the arches but even up into the vault.

By the fifteenth century word had no doubt reached the cathedral architects that the Renaissance was appearing on the horizon. That may explain the abandonment of the clustered pillar and a return to the rectangular pier, together with that essential feature of Gothic architecture, the moulded arch, and the reappearance of the flat soffit. For the surfaces of such features could now be redeemed from some of their inherent dullness by the use of the stone panelling learned from the carpenters.

But such treatments are not found in the major ordinance of the cathedral which continued to follow the Gothic ordinance of the clustered pillar and moulded arch, the individual members of which were, however, becoming much broader in their detailing, probably due to the influence of the moulding practice of the carpenters based on the chamfer rather than the arris.

It will be remembered that in the eleventh-century cathedrals the inner member of the compound pier had often been carried up as a pilaster or half-shaft—the 'vaulting shafts' of the Victorian antiquary—in order to punctuate the design by indicating the bay units and helping to maintain their rhythm. These had been in some cases neglected during the twelfth century in the course of various attempts to 'basilicanize' the churches but now came back in strength, this time as real vaulting shafts, joining the pillars of the arcade to the springing of the high vault. They seem to be helping to create the impression of tall tree-stems rising and meeting overhead. It seems not unlikely that it was this sensation of being in an architectural glade which was inspiring the Gothic architects of the fourteenth century. (Plate 28.)

One of the last of our cathedral works is the nave of the metropolitan cathedral of Canterbury lying in the shadow of its graceful Angel Tower, itself one of the last achievements of English Gothic. As befits the dignity of the church below, it is the finest of all our cathedral towers; though perhaps in both design and detail it could be well matched by some of the smaller towers which adorn the parish churches of Somerset. But the stone-less south-east of England could never have hoped to compete in enterprise with the centuries of masonry experience long nurtured in the shadow of Glastonbury.

The towers of the west front are of little more than parochial quality, and are moreover individually hampered by that duality which makes it impossible for a monumental structure to achieve a distinction such as that possessed by hundreds of parish church towers, and above all by the lonely tower of Ely. The towers of Wells succeed through having been constrained, not to become monumental structures, but to serve as terminal features completing a frontispiece of exceptional complexity.

Within, Canterbury Cathedral may be seen as a glade of stone, its pillars rising almost unbroken towards the springing of a vault which sweeps across overhead like the vault of a forest ride. Midway along this vaulted firmament is the splendid lantern with its eight tall windows and its fan-vaulted ceiling lifting high overhead.

Passing through the choir screen, the English architect of today might well be disappointed that no English architect of the twelfth century could have been found to design the choir of Canterbury. For William of Sens, admirable though he may have been, was so deplorably Continental! Here we can see what we escaped—and how easily we might never have experienced the loveliness of English Gothic. Here are the exotic Corinthianesque columns— sign manual of 'basilicanism'—so unsuitable for carrying the ordered arches by means of which the architecture of Byzantium was becoming transformed into the English style. Similarly, in the Île de France, one can see the 'vaulting shafts' trying to balance on Classical *abaci* and the most extraordinarily inept arrangements of assorted pillars and shaftings, which no Anglo-Saxon would have been so gauche as to inflict upon his architecture.

The most satisfactory portions of the design are the eastern transepts where skill and ingenuity in elevational design are clearly displayed. Here the Corinthianesque cap in the aedicular form suited to the Gothic is used to advantage and here the arrangements of the arcading are simpler, less muddled, and altogether more confident.

An interesting choir, but in no way comparing with those of the great English churches developing their exquisite Gothic at stately Lincoln or even humble Wells.

Architectural designing takes two forms. There is the hard work with the T-square, making things fit and getting proportions right. This completed, there is the pleasant doodling, with compasses or with idle freehand, filling in areas in which pure ornament may be used. To this latter phase may be assigned the design of window tracery.

Not that this is entirely undisciplined. The mullions have to be joined by arched heads to complete the lights they separate. Only then can the tracery begin to unfold. But afterwards there are unlimited devices for shaping the lights over, and owing to the Gothic system of designing in two or more orders several systems can be woven into a single window-head.

As the design of the high vault was certainly a creation of the carpenters and owed nothing to the masons except in so far as they had the skilled task of converting the wooden ribs into stone, so must the tracery of the Gothic window have owed much to the carpenter.

We can possibly detect the early efforts of the masons in experiments with circles and multifoils out of which the geometrical style of window tracery was created. But until his own panelled schemes became part of the decorative ordinance of the cathedral, it may have been the carpenter who swept the window mullions here and there, crossing, joining and separating them again. And he may have drawn his inspiration from shapes seen in the tanglewood of English converts from the depths of which he hauled his material.

He was of course able to reproduce his own technique of craftsmanship when creating the lovely screenwork of the cathedral choirs. But it seems hardly conceivable that when he was making twisted shapes he was copying them from those of traceried windows; far more likely, he was reproducing the tracery of the hedgerow.

Window tracery is a good example of that element in architecture which while being essential—in this case for the purpose of reinforcing the glazing of the window—is nevertheless in the manner of its presentation entirely the province of the artist, able to hand over his curves, without any fear of control by practical objections, to the mason at his banker.

No great church in England conveys such a profound atmosphere of antique dignity as the Wessex cathedral of Winchester. It stands on the green turf of its close, huge, stern and immovable. It is in fact one of the largest churches in the world.

Its antiquity becomes evident when one enters a transept and sees the primitive architecture, pure Byzantine as in some church of Anatolia or Syria. The transepts were to have been aisled all round but the end galleries seem never to have been built. (Plate 11.)

The sanctuary was raised over a crypt which still remains and shows that the eastern arm was, as in most of the greatest of the eleventh-century cathedrals, four bays in length and ending in an apse. It seems that there may have been a *chevet* and that this was destroyed at the end of the twelfth century and replaced by one of those extensions which in the case of existing long presbyteries were a substitute for rebuilding the whole eastern arm.

Though a common form for these extensions was a transept two aisles in width having a row of four chapels leading out of an ambulatory in the western aisle, the Winchester extension, perhaps one of the earliest, took the form of a single-story extension continuing the line of the existing presbytery but divided into three equal aisles. These may have had their own roofs but the whole structure is now covered by a late lead roof.

The extension seems to have represented an ambulatory, a chapel for St. Swithin, and three other chapels the central one being extended to form a lady chapel. It subsequently became a splendid mortuary chapel and place of sepulture for bishops of Winchester.

After the eleventh-century apse and chevet had been removed the whole cathedral, save for the transepts, was completely re-cased in Gothic stonework, the galleries being ripped out and the aisles raised and given new high vaults at a height which would allow for tall windows to be pierced in their walling. The clearstory was re-modelled and its treatment carried down over the blind story.

The original presbytery had never been lengthened and so the bishop's choir had to stay in its original position at the east end of the nave and under the lantern. A flight of steps leads up to the choir entrance and then out of it again to rise up over the top of the crypt upon which the sanctuary is raised. The stalls are of the fourteenth century.

Anyone interested in discovering just how the design of the cathedral nave had changed during three centuries can see it displayed before him at Winchester, for at the middle of the fourteenth century all the bays of the nave were simply knocked out leaving the supporting piers, the aisle vaulting being of course included in the demolition.

The new design was basically two-storied in place of the former three. The springing of the new arcade—which of course corresponded with that of the new aisle vaulting—was fixed at the level of the old gallery floor. This brought the top of the vaulting to the level of the springing of the old gallery arcade, so that this became the level of the upper story of the new elevation.

Above this new first-floor level everything was absorbed into the design of the clearstory. A kind of triforium arcade, lofty and with massive mullions, was carried up from the inner face of the wall to the vaulting. Behind this a somewhat unimaginative clearstory window with its system of wall-panelling occupied the wall of the triforium passage, which was at the level of the top of the aisle vaulting. Its front was protected by a balustrade arcaded in the unexciting fashion of the period. (Plate 26.)

The vertical element of the wall-shafts of the eleventh-century building was retained in the new work as far as the springing line of the new vault, set in accordance with normal Gothic practice at the level of the original triforium passage, well above the level of the new.

The heavy-handed detailing of Winchester nave places it below the architectural level of those of Canterbury and York which belong to the same design era. The most noticeable and unattractive innovation in Winchester nave is the introduction of the square head above the main arch of the arcade, acceptable in the case of small doorways but unsympathetic when enlarged to the scale of a great arcade, as well as introducing an unwelcome horizontal element at variance with what elsewhere was the prevalent aim at verticality.

The piers are designed with little care for their appearance and are simply the downward projection of the arches over. Both have curiously coarse mouldings, with their orders separated by wide 'casement' hollows derived from the concave splays of windows, and very different from the deep rich mouldings of the thirteenth century.

Is the square head over the arch the first submission to the Renaissance and is the coarsening of the mouldings the beginnings of the rejection of the barbarism of the Gothic?

The lierne vault, in any case, is splendid indeed and was certainly designed by traditionally minded carpenters whose vault above the presbytery was never replaced in stone.

The design of Winchester nave poses a number of problems, first of which is its date. Its conception was about the year 1360 when the eleventh-century work is said to have been pulled down and the new work begun; thus it is difficult not to assume that the design for the new work dates from this period. But the work was soon abandoned and not resumed until a generation later, in 1394, about the time of the nave of Canterbury which is believed to have been begun about 1400. This is a splendid Gothic cathedral, of the reformed proportions of Winchester but with none of its crudities.

For more than a century after the building of Winchester nave the most beautiful Gothic buildings were being erected in Westminster and Cambridge which again seem of assured architecture, though it is true that neither was hampered by aisles.

Is it possible that William of Wykeham, Bishop of Winchester and Surveyor of the King's Works, was able to impress masons for work on his palaces and the cathedral, and may this be the reason for the absence of that feeling of devotion which is the soul of Gothic design? Looking at the detail of Winchester one seems to be seeing parochial architecture, as produced by a local builder, applied to a church of cathedral scale.

Not that the architecture of the fifteenth-century parish church was not of a high order. It is just that the old charm has disappeared and the detail has become coarse and spiritless. The old race of masons who had struggled to build Peterborough and put their soul into Lincoln had died away.

A century after the nave of Winchester the new cathedral at Bath follows, its design more sophisticated but its detail sadly lacking in sensitivity.

Thus it is that the parish churches, increasing in size and pomp of architecture as the fleeces filled their coffers, took up the mantle of Gothic architecture and produced it, not on the bankers of devoted masons, but in the yard of the 'local builder' who was only waiting for the year 1539 to divert his efforts towards building great houses and eventually those in which we live today.

Canterbury upheld the Gothic tradition to the end, as did also its northern sister at York.

In few English cathedrals, even those of much earlier origin, can one fail to appreciate the importance to the medieval cathedral architect of the towering central feature bequeathed to him by the Byzantines. At Canterbury its Angel Tower, at York its lantern tower, of no dramatic height, and indeed almost certainly unfinished, more than holds their own as they bestraddle with their great mass the roofs of the cathedral.

It should be remembered, when we see today a cathedral having but a low central tower, that this was certainly intended to be the base only of some splendid tower such as that of Lincoln or Canterbury, or at least a timber steeple soaring high towards the clouds.

We can see how the tower at Durham was raised, possibly after the steeple had been removed and its place taken by an upper story roofed with lead.

York Cathedral externally represents Gothic at its most massive. Instead of the tall transept gables of the twelfth century we find the façades of its aisled transepts developed into compositions resembling west fronts. The west front itself, towering high above that of Wells, has none of the charm of the Western façade. Everything about York Minster seems to be on an over-large scale.

Inside the building, however, one receives the full benefit of the splendid lantern, the sunlight pouring into the centre of the cathedral and lighting the sculptured screen leading to the bishop's choir.

The interior of the nave shares with Canterbury that effect of the architectural glade, with everything calculated to lead the eye upwards to the high vault sweeping overhead. For horizontal punctuation only the traditional string-course marking the top of the aisle vaulting has been retained. The blind story has been completely absorbed by a downward expansion of the clearstory windows.

With the advancement of the bishop's choir into the eastern arm, the walking space in the transepts has become an area meriting a special entrance from the close. At York this has been contrived not in the usual place in the west wall of the transept but in an elaborate façade contrived of the transept end; but the composition lacks the charm of earlier simpler ones, seemingly more of a Continental character than English and in any case illustrating the impossibility of making a façade out of the end of an aisled building without adding a transept or at least a screen wall.

Such west fronts as those of Rochester or Worcester show the extreme difficulty of coping elevationally with a wall which is not rectangular and cannot be composed into the series of bays which is the foundation of vertical design. Even the architects of the Renaissance were unable to solve the problem.

The interior of York Minster is one of the noblest in the world. The long vaulted glade-like hall with the clearing in it where the sunlight breaks through from above, the fine choir screen with the organ case over it steadying the whole vista without checking it, all in pure Gothic with the panelled clearstory gently indicating that it will be the last of a great race of buildings. (Plate 25.)

It is a pity that the Gothic was never able to master the task of designing an exterior elevation. Building by adding bay to bay in lateral progression could never have done this. An elevation has to be built up from the ground and that is what the Gothic builders could never have done.

What they did achieve, however, was something no other architectural style has ever done—an external presentation without an elevation.

One might almost venture to say that the principle of elevational design was completely unknown to the Gothic architect and that such west fronts as those of Wells or Peterborough were entirely fortuitous and not consciously designed as elevations.

We have ventured to suggest that the interior of the Gothic cathedral might have been inspired by the glade. It seems that the exterior, also, might have been intended not as architecture but as scenery, similar to a stage setting for a pageant.

The fundamental feature of the cathedral exterior is the buttress; after the thirteenth century it provided essential abutment to the vigorously arcuated structural system and introduced the desired vertical element in the aesthetic presentation. Its system of set-offs helps it to pile up without appearing top-heavy and its crowning feature, the pinnacle, developed from a conical cap, must be a copy in stone of the timber steeples of the past, a perfect example of the aedicule. And the buttress itself appears in aedicular form passing up such towers as that of Gloucester and, reduced still further, incorporated into window mullions. Combined with tracery it becomes introduced into the design of the glorious screenwork and stallwork of the bishops' churches.

During the later Gothic era the aesthetic function of the buttress is for concealment. The ugly lean-to roofs of aisles are masked by close-set buttresses helping in perspective to convert the building into a cluster of craggy pinnacles rather than a building. No other historical architectural style has ever created such remarkable structures disguised as scenery, buttressed like rock formations and capped with stalagmites.

This is not elevational design. Simple though they might have been, the Byzantine churches and their English descendants had been surrounded by elevations in the traditional manner. But by the end of the thirteenth century the great Gothic buildings had lost their elevations, these having become obscured by a large number of accessories quite foreign to traditional architectural development. It should be noted that the abutment systems employed by the Romans and Byzantines, and by the architects of the Renaissance, were always sited internally, behind the elevations.

Is it possible that the Gothic builders were trying to design not architecture, but scenery? We have seen the creation of glade-like halls resembling nothing else in architecture. Was this piling-up of turrets, buttresses and pinnacles, together with the constant penetration of the masonry with niches—more like a rocky hillside than a building—could this have been, perhaps unconsciously, a tribute not only to God, but to the inescapable glory of His works, ever before the eyes of medieval man?

The great architectural styles of the past had been developed in arid lands or in bleak plains, where any building was an asset to the view and a horizontal presentation might not be monumental but fitted easily into the landscape.

The countryside of England is one of the most beautiful in the world and almost any building is in fact an intrusion into it. Anyone having a feeling for art in any form, even a rude forefather who lived six or seven centuries ago, would surely have been conscious of this.

So perhaps the medieval builders believed that the whimsicalities of their elevations and silhouettes represented a greater asset to their sites than the sterner lines of more formal architecture might have done.

12

A Vaulted Firmament

The basic requirements of any building are four walls and a roof, the last more commonly of timber. Even the finest cathedral—a poem in masonry perhaps—had to be content with a roof framed in this humble material.

Apart from the spanning of openings in a wall—in monumental architecture regarded as a task for the stone lintel—the other principal task for the timber beam was that of supporting an upper floor.

In this country it was the practice until about three hundred years ago to live at the opposite end of a single-story building to one's livestock, houses being built across the contour so as to keep the upper or living end well drained.

The Byzantines lived on upper floors, their domestic animals being generally housed on the ground below the living quarters.

As one begins to follow history through the era of the great Classical civilizations and into that period which we call the Dark Ages in this country, one begins to appreciate that the timber floor, whether in the interests of architecture or simply for sanitary reasons, would not have been suited to public buildings, let alone those of a monumental character.

In such buildings, provided the span was not too large, ordinary arched construction could have been expanded longitudinally to form a 'tunnel' or 'barrel' vault, the upper surface of which after being levelled off with stone rubble mixed with mortar would make a permanent floor which could even be paved and thus kept reasonably clean. Thus we have the beginnings of the stone vault, and

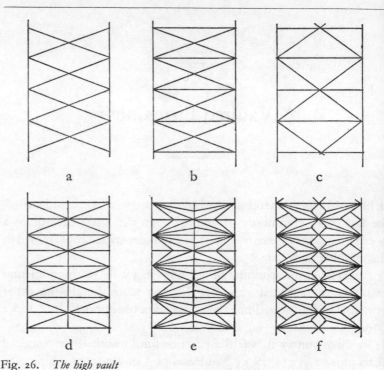

Fig. 26. *The high vault*
(a) shows the simple 'quadripartite' vault, which in (b) has
had its larger areas of 'web' halved by the introduction of
transverse ribs separating the structural bays. (c) shows the
'sexpartite' vault by means of which the building is vaulted
in 'great' bays. In (d) the areas of web are reduced still further
by the introduction of ridge ribs. The process is repeated at
(e) by the provision of intermediate ribs or 'tiercerons'.
At (f) the introduction of short lengths of rib called 'liernes'
enables the pattern of the vault to be developed into stellar designs.

also its first task, that of providing what the medieval architect
called a 'stone soller'.

The tunnel vault was a troublesome form of construction in that
it filled up such a large amount of space in the apartment it covered.
The early semicircular vaulted ceiling had to be sprung from close
to the floor so as to get it into the story height, and this made it
difficult to raise a vault above an arcade or even a row of windows.
The answer was to divide the length of the apartment into bays

each of which was approximately equal to its width and run vaults across each bay as well as a main longitudinal vault. This is the 'cross vault', sometimes called a 'groined' vault because the diagonal lines where the vaults meet is called a groin. This type of vault was used in the Roman Empire to cover buildings of huge spans.

But that was monumental building of the kind which ended with the Romans. The Byzantine church architects continued to use the groined vault, but as a 'stone soller' for carrying the galleries surrounding the central area of the building. Though it might be thought that these vaults would have exerted an overturning pressure against the tall crossing piers, the weight of the roofs and domes the architects placed upon them easily counterbalanced the lateral thrust and stabilized the structure, while the vaults themselves actually acted as stiffeners to the tall piers. Everything of course depended, as in all arcuated structure, on not 'striking the centering' until everyone was satisfied that the structure was balanced.

The outer walls of the building were also subject to pressure from the gallery vault. But these too were raised to a sufficient height to 'load the abutments'. To this we owe the neat cubical form of the Byzantine church.

The eleventh-century English cathedral followed the same structural principle; 'stone sollers' had to be built over the aisles and the walls of these kept high until the introduction of the buttress.

A stone vault has to be turned upon strong and elaborately framed centering, fashioned on the ground and then lifted up to the springing level of the vault and mounted upon a scaffolding. The actual form-work consists of timber ribs cut to the exact shape of the vault; below this is the system of struts and braces forming the framing.

In a groined vault the form-work is represented by two wooden ribs crossing in the centre, on which the stones forming the groins are set up.

All this elaborate timberwork had to be left in position while the arch was being turned and then moved to the next bay. But before the end of the eleventh century the masons discovered how to make the ribs of the centering in stone, which could be left in position and the vault 'web' turned upon them while the centering was moved to the next bay and the ribs there built up.

The result was the 'ribbed vault', which is that used in the eleventh-century cathedral. It added a great many new arches and enabled the Anglo-Saxon carvers to indulge themselves in creating chevron and other types of running ornament, making the vault an architectural feature instead of a mere masonry surface.

The interesting conversion of the timber centering into a perpanent feature of the architecture of the cathedral would not have escaped the attention of the carpenter. One can imagine him making his own vault of ribs moulded with the skill he had no difficulty in displaying, and with a web formed of simple boarding.

The ceiling was a feature unknown to early architecture. In the monumental building of Classical days it was the underside of a vaulted roof. The vaults and domes of the Byzantines, thrown over far smaller spans, continued the tradition.

In England the only ceiling would have been the underside of the tangle of timbers required to carry a wide and high medieval roof. In some cases the roof was boarded in with what was called 'wainscot', a name given because the underside of the roof was sometimes shaped with curved timbers so that the ceiling could be curved like the tilt of a waggon.

It will be appreciated that the 'stone soller' which covered the aisles of the eleventh-century cathedral was not intended to be a ceiling but the underside of a structural floor. The idea of using the architectural form as a ceiling over the main span so as to hide the roof timbers and protect the church from leaks may very well have been first thought of by the carpenters who had for years past been making the masons' centering.

It is quite within the bounds of possibility that the first high vaults—that is to say vaults which were purely ceilings and not supports to floors—were constructed by the carpenters. They would in due course have been replaced in stone—not all, however, for the elaborate lierne vault over the presbytery at Winchester remains in wood.

One of the great advantages of the stone high vault was that it

29. ELY

30. SALISBURY

was fireproof. Throughout the Middle Ages one hears of disastrous fires, often started by lightning in the timbers of roofs or steeples. When a blazing roof fell into the church its pillars became so calcined and cracked that the whole of the main structure might have to be pulled down and rebuilt. A high vault in stone prevented this and saved the building. The writer remembers seeing photographs of Rheims Cathedral after German shelling had destroyed its roofs. The stone vault still rose above the walls and had kept the interior of the cathedral inviolate.

The vaulting of the eleventh-century cathedral aisles with its four compartments separated by diagonal ribs is known as quadripartite vaulting.

The arms of the Byzantine cruciform church had been covered with wide-span barrel vaults or, in the case of large churches with arms projecting the whole of a 'great' bay, with another series of domes of lesser height than the central one. The Byzantine dome died out as it entered Western Europe, but there are cases where its place was taken by a wide-span quatripartite vault.

Something of the sort may have been intended at Durham Cathedral, for the nave has been divided into great bays by heavy arches spanning across it. As it turned out, however, the masons constructed the vault in bays corresponding to the normal bays of the elevation, and thus each great bay of the nave has a pair of quadripartite vaults rectangular in plan.

The great arches do not appear elsewhere, and the rectangular bay becomes established for the main span of the cathedral, appearing in such early vaults as those of Wells and Salisbury. In Canterbury and Rochester, however, a Continental form of vault may be found which is a compromise between the normal English vault and the quadripartite vault covering the great bay. The bays are coupled and their diagonal ribs form a square, but an extra transverse rib has been introduced to accommodate the intermediate bay. This is the 'sexpartite' vault of the great churches of the Île de France. It was an ugly device as the side vaults had to be twisted to meet in pairs at the centre of the bay, the intermediate 'cone' of each being so thin that the vault is sometimes called a 'ploughshare' vault.

A Vaulted Firmament

We have suggested that a very large part in vault design was played by the carpenters. Anything in the nature of a vaulting rib must have been characteristically a timber object rather than something built up out of pieces of stone.

We explained in the last chapter the primitive system of roof construction based on the 'cruck', whereby a pair of rafters joined at their tops formed a 'couple', these being set closely side by side to form the roof. It will be noted that something is missing from this structure which is always seen in the roofs of today—the ridge.

Vaulting construction was also on the cruck principle in that the sides of the arched rib rose from the springing to meet at the top, there to be locked by a keystone often raised to form a boss and subsequently carved. The boss takes the place of the treenails pinning the two halves of the cruck or couple together.

About the middle of the thirteenth century someone, probably a carpenter making a centering, introduced a ridge rib into his timberwork. Thenceforth the vaults—now become high vaults over the main span—took to including ridge ribs in their stone framework.

It was a revolutionary feature for the masons, like the carpenters who may well have been instructing them, discovered that they could reduce the size of each 'severy' of the vault web by introducing intermediate ribs between the diagonal ones. When this was achieved they began to box the compass by introducing still more ribs, called 'tiercerons', between the intermediate rib and the diagonal.

The vault now began to take on a major aspect of the interior view of the cathedral. The side vaults leading to the clearstory windows were becoming prominent features and were separated one from the other by elaborately moulded features formed by the 'cones' of the vault.

The vault cone is seen at its most splendid in the polygonal chapter houses of such cathedrals as Salisbury, Wells and Lincoln. These fine Gothic apartments are vaulted from the side walls with their large windows towards a central clustered pillar, the shaftings of which are designed to line through with the clustered ribs of the immense cone.

Developing further the principle of reducing the areas of web, the next stage was the introduction of short lengths of rib called 'liernes'—corresponding to the English 'ties'—which join the ribs to form patterns, often of a stellar form.

As it had become customary to mask the junctions of the ribs in some fashion, especially now that far too many ribs were meeting the ridge at the same point for their mouldings to be properly fitted together, the vault began to accumulate a considerable array of carved bosses depicting coats of arms, initials and rebuses of bishops, or simply conventional or naturalistic sculpture. Although of considerable interest individually as sculptural achievements and occasionally as historical evidence, these punctuations have not improved the aesthetic smoothness of the vault; and it is noticeable that early vaults such as that of Worcester which uses them sparingly have a greater charm and dignity than the over-elaborated vault of, say, Gloucester, which looks a little like someone wearing too many finger rings.

It is perhaps in less dignified situations such as the cathedral cloisters, where the vaulting is less in the nature of architecture and takes on the mantle of interior decoration or furniture, that the stellar vaulting is most successful. At Worcester, for example, or at Norwich, the vaulting becomes a complete firmament which may have seemed most homely to the monk or canon spending much of his time beneath it.

But looking down the tremendous vista of the cathedral one can sometimes regret the breaking-up of the crown of the vaulting by the restless liernes.

When looking up at a cathedral vault, let us sometimes think of the masons who made it first on the ground, took it to pieces and coded each piece of stone, sorted it all out on the scaffolding eighty feet in the air, and at that height and in all weathers, put it together for our delight.

Anyone with over-imaginative susceptibilities should never go upon the high vault of a cathedral. For one thing there is the realization that there are only a few inches of stone between oneself and the pavement eighty feet or so below—and a stone might drop out! And as one balances along the ridge-rib one observes beside one the disconcerting vision of deep cones diving down towards the springing of the bays, waiting to entrap the traveller should he miss his footing. Getting back again up the smooth sides of the trap could be an exceedingly difficult and lengthy operation.

The earliest vaulting, as employed by the Imperial Roman engineers, was of concrete cast on 'shuttering'. The form of the vault, however, was first set out in bands of brickwork, similar to the Gothic ribs but more in the nature of profiles assisting the formation of the subsequent shuttering, and membranes separating the various vaulting severies in order that these could be cast separately. The miniature vaults covering the Byzantine aisles had no need for such devices.

It is well to separate these 'stone sollers' from the high vault over the main span, for this is in reality quite a different type of structure both as regards its purpose and in respect of its conception and development.

The high vault is in reality a reproduction of the curved roof formed by the primitive timber cruck. There is in fact evidence that the crossing of timber churches had an arrangement of timber crucks set diagonally across it—the device may still be seen in the twelfth-century churches of Essex.

But even by fixing boarding to the back of the ordinary series of crucks forming the roof of an early timber hall one could produce a vault. This would have no relationship at all to the 'stone soller' carrying a floor; it would simply be a ceiling, which is the purpose of a high vault.

The indigenous trees of England are for the most part deciduous and provide not only the moderately straight stems from which the Anglo-Saxon churches were built but also a great variety of 'lop' —those curved branches which could be converted into any number of features of timber architecture such as crucks, struts, braces, and minor curved items such as window tracery.

No one will ever be able to make a reasoned study of Gothic architecture without deep consideration of its timber origins and achievements. A glance into the octagon at Ely will make this clear beyond a peradventure. Only a race completely familiar with timber building in the highest form ever achieved could have even considered such a task. The beams upon which it is founded are enormous. They have to carry across the span of the octagon and support in their centres the weight of the lead-covered lantern. This is the structural side of the problem. The aesthetic treatment of the octagon comprises a series of eight great cones like the heads of trees rising from the pillars below and spreading inwards to meet the base of the lantern. This is surrounded by eight large windows and is covered with a vault. The whole is entirely constructed in timber. It seems quite clear that the design was not copied from the masons and is much more likely to represent the results of experiments in carpentry supplied as models for masons to copy in their high vaults and lanterns.

The final development of English vaulting—a development, incidentally, met nowhere else in the world—shows more clearly than anything the influence of timber building upon English architecture.

The introduction of the ridge-rib and the subsequent multiplication of the intermediate ribs and tiercerons had changed the character of the high vault completely.

It had begun as a tunnel, with side tunnels provided to accept light from the clearstory windows.

It was now a series of cones spreading from the top of the cathedral's main supporting elements, closely resembling a row of trees with their branches spreading to meet across the ride.

This presentation had come to stay and had to be accepted, so that any future development of vaulting design had to take this into account.

Thus after the fourteenth century the high vault ceased to be a ceiling thrown across the building and became a prolongation upwards of the supporting elements of the wall and a part of its bay design. Hitherto the bay had been regarded as the space between two supports. Now it was the supports between the bays which had to be designed.

The treatment took the form of bringing up the vault cones in ordinary masonry corbelled out from the wall; completely semi-circular in plan and meeting each other across the span in the form of horizontal fans, thus giving the name of 'fan vaulting' to this type of ceiling. Between the fans were almost flat areas of ceiling ornamented with panelling.

Across the cones of the fan vaulting spread the panelling which now covered all wall-surfaces, the heads of each panel foliated in accordance with current taste.

Considering the lack of knowledge in medieval times of the elementary mechanics of building construction, it is remarkable that early high vaults such as those of Durham are still standing. The development of the pointed arch certainly helped to divert the bursting tendency of the arch into something less susceptible to ordinary gravitational pressure, but an overturning stress was always present to a considerable degree.

The eleventh-century cathedral was safe from such stresses up to the top of the aisle vaulting, and by adopting the Byzantine device of building arches across the gallery to join the main and aisle walls together, the main walls could be rendered safe as far as the sills of the clearstory windows. But thereafter the upper part of the building had to stand on its own and was quite unprovided with abutment against a high vault.

Our observations concerning stability, however, all depend upon one vital factor—the proper loading of all abutments to provide sufficient downward pressure to neutralize the lateral thrust of the arch. Often the heavily timbered roof would supply this, but only if it was sufficiently well tied together to prevent its spreading at the foot and adding to the overturning pressure on the wall.

One may wonder how long it will be before some early high vault collapses because someone has idly removed the roof for repair. The writer remembers being shown by a distinguished church architect a very fine cloister he was restoring. Since he was proposing to remove the story above it which had been damaged by enemy bombing, he had to be reminded that the loss of this top weight from the unbuttressed inner wall of the cloister would certainly bring the vault down.

The high vault is today a lost feature of architecture and one can quite appreciate the ignorance of the modern architect concerning the problems of its mechanics. But what one wonders most forcibly is how the architects of eight hundred years ago, in their far greater ignorance, managed to raise these tremendous firmaments of masonry in the first place.

The cause of failure in the 'sleepless arches' of an arcuated structure was failure of the abutment, resulting in the spreading of the arch and sagging of its crown. This caused cracks to appear in the haunches of the arch, indicating both that the arch was failing and exactly where pressure was needed to check the movement.

With the principle of the timber 'raking shore' in mind the masons could build up a piece of walling in a direction away from the abutment, tapered off from the ground upwards by means of 'set-offs'. This is the origin of the buttress and its familiar tapering outline.

A more sophisticated masonry interpretation of the raking shore was the half-arch built across the gallery of the eleventh-century cathedral to stiffen the supports of that story. As the top of this arch had to be sloped away to the angle of the aisle roof its resemblance to a raking shore would have been marked.

Until the invention of the buttress this was as far as the twelfth-century builders could get with their abutment systems. But the arrival of the mid-thirteenth century buttress set against the aisle walls completely altered the situation. By then the builders would certainly have discovered the point in its haunches where the high vault was likely to fail, and from those points could carry their half-arches above the aisle roof to the new buttresses. In this fashion they developed the 'flying buttress' which is simply a 'flying shore' in masonry.

The buttress was prevented from overturning by the rake of its outer face through a series of 'set-offs'. The danger that the flying buttress might push the top of the buttress away from its seating was counterbalanced by the provision of a heavy pinnacle as a counterweight. Thus that splendid Gothic feature, the crocketed pinnacle which is the aedicule of the English steeple, was introduced entirely as a structural device.

But to go back a century or two, it has to be remembered that it took many generations to perfect the buttress itself, first as a mere pilaster indicating the bay design, then as a more prominent feature of early-thirteenth-century Gothic, and only in the end as an adopted structural device.

The angle of a building having an adequate foundation and with its stonework bound together with proper quoins forms a perfectly stable structure and has no need for any abutment feature. Nor do angles require any aesthetic assistance from buttresses except when closing an elevation formed of a number of bays. But the thickened angle formed by the clasping pilaster of the twelfth century was invaluable for accommodating the spiral stairs so essential for reaching the upper parts of a cathedral. Spiral stairs were, however, of course, in no way to be considered as buttresses.

The development of the pilaster during the thirteenth century made it necessary not only to include pilasters at the angles of the building but to set them in pairs to give the end of the elevation aesthetic strength. Short lengths of wall were then set splayed between the projections and between them and the adjoining wallfaces, so that the stair could now be accommodated in what had in fact become a clasping pilaster set diagonally.

During the fourteenth century the pair of angle buttresses was replaced by a buttress set diagonally; it was known as a French buttress and therefore presumably of Continental origin. Again splayed walling had to be provided if a stair should be needed in the angle. It will be seen that these buttresses were solely decorative and that the angle was in fact weakened by the stair within it.

The popularity of the buttress was undoubtedly affected by appreciation of the value of its strong vertical emphasis.

The principle of shoring must have been well known to the timber builders. The failure of many eleventh-century crossing piers to withstand the lateral thrust of the arcades pressing against their middles must have been observed at an early stage by builders whose churches had never known the thrust of an arch against the timber posts.

It was not until the fourteenth century that the masons learnt from the carpenters the principle of the 'flying shore' by means of which a beam is fixed between two structures so that each may support the other.

Transformed into masonry the beam becomes an arch, which has to be sprung from its impost but which can have a flat upper surface like that of a beam and can thus serve the same purpose, provided the whole feature is heavy enough not to be burst *upwards* by any lateral pressure.

At Salisbury and at Canterbury, what are called 'strainer arches' —which are in fact masonry flying shores—have been set between the pillars of the crossing to prevent their being bowed inwards.

The arched stone saltires at Wells are firmly built against the tops and bottoms of the pillars supporting small circles of stonework which press against their centres where pressure is needed to prevent bowing. (Plate 15.)

13

Steepled Landscape

Since the end of the pagan period in history, all major religious architecture has been indicated by some prominent vertical feature.

As the minaret is to Islam, so is the campanile to Christendom.

The muezzin calls the faithful to prayer while in Christian lands the same summons is performed by the call of the bells.

The tower is all-important to the Christian church, first as the church itself, and then as an obligatory attachment to it.

As we look from the hilltops out over the vales of England and count the church towers rising everywhere beneath us it is of interest that at one time or another practically all of them had steeples. Steeple-chasing was merely a way of saying going from village to village, and there was a popular sport of steeple-flying, now long forgotten, which consisted in sliding down a rope tied to the top of a steeple and held away from the foot of the tower by a group of people to keep it taut.

Many church steeples, assaulted by high winds or lightning-strike, were removed during the later Middle Ages and replaced with lead flats. After 1539, the King expressly ordered that the steeples of the abbey churches should be destroyed without trace—steeple in this case meaning the whole tower.

And when trying to imagine the steepled countryside of England with its hundreds of parish churches let us not forget the great host of abbeys and priories each with its tall spire rising above its lantern tower. Some of the great abbey churches may have had steeples matched only by that of Salisbury. In the same county the abbey of Malmesbury had a great steeple which fell like a tree straight down the high street of the town. The spot where the weathercock landed is remembered to this day.

The cathedrals all had their steeples. During the seventeenth century—the most difficult period in the history of the cathedral—Ripon and Durham lost their steeples. Try to imagine the soaring tower of Durham leading up to a steeple. Hereford's steeple succumbed to Wyatt in 1790, about the same time as he was pulling down the huge bell-tower of Salisbury. Lincoln's steeples—imagine them—were removed in 1807.

The tower seems to have originated in Classical days as a military structure attempting through its great height—like the red coats of the old soldiers—to terrify the enemy.

Apart from this aspect, the tower was not a feature of Imperial Roman or Byzantine architecture. But with the development of church-building, the tower entered into architecture in two forms.

First, as a campanile. The ringing of great bells being a feature of Christian worship, special towers had to be provided to carry them. The Byzantine campanile was a tall slender tower, devoid of any architectural treatment, simply a tall tower with the belfry story indicated by openings to allow the sound of the bells to reach out over the countryside. Each opening was, of course, a typical Byzantine bifora. Towers of this description can be found scattered all down the eastern side of England.

But in the course of their development of the architecture of the Christian church the Byzantines found themselves building towers of a different character. These were towers proper, actual buildings which from the ground upwards were intended for use, in this case for congregational worship. And each tower was roofed over, quite simply, with a dome. The purpose of building a tower instead of merely a square apartment was to introduce that monumental element of height which is essential for a building that required to command respect and, in this case, reverence.

We have seen how the Byzantine turriform church developed when its tower came to be carried upon piers and arches and surrounded by additions which increased its size and eventually led it to become the nucleus of the English cathedral, of course after its dome had been replaced by a tall steepled roof.

It has to be remembered that to the eleventh-century English cathedral builder the term 'tower' was not something associated with the cathedral. To him the tower was a military structure such as the Tower of London, built by the Conqueror to overawe the citizens.

The ecclesiastical tower was the 'steeple', a tall structure rising from amongst surrounding roofs and capped with a tall timber spire which differentiated it completely from the crenellated summit of the military tower or keep, the roofs of which would have been concealed behind walling so as to protect them from damage by fire or missiles.

Indeed the steeple may have taken its name from the steepness of the sides of its roof.

The steeple rose from a low base brought high enough above the roofs to provide space for windows to light the centre of the building. It was this story which gave it its designation of 'lantern'.

Translated into masonry, the lantern became an elevated prolongation of the clearstory, rising above a blind story against which the roofs impinged and which might sometimes be embellished with arcading inside and out. The interior arcading often included an arcaded wall-passage as at Norwich. In the simplest form of central feature there was no proper lantern, windows being set in the blind story beside the roof slopes.

After the lantern tower of Norwich had been raised to accommodate a belfry story, its exterior presented a most elaborate system of architectural ornament incorporating tier after tier of every kind of ornamental device known to the designer. And when one realizes that only about half the tower is visible above the roofs one can appreciate that it forms a splendid monument to the skill of the twelfth-century English builder.

For a tower to be properly appreciated it should be seen to rise from the ground. This is what the great west tower of Ely is seen to do. Its detail is far more restrained than that of the Norwich tower and we can clearly see displayed in its elevations the Anglo-Saxon exuberance settling down into the English Gothic.

The curious pair of transeptal towers—they were not originally joined to the church internally—at Exeter are good examples of towers in the hands of the ecclesiastical architects of the twelfth century and are ornamented in their upper stages with tiers of arcading.

After Norwich had set the fashion for the belfry over the lantern, the central tower often took upon itself the duty of carrying the cathedral bells. With the larger windows filling the transept ends of Gothic days the lantern was sometimes eliminated as an anachronism, relic of the windowed drum of the Byzantine churches of the East. But it had been for some time the principal feature of the interior of the building and was restored to all its glory in the late rebuildings at Canterbury and York. At Salisbury the sealing-off of the lantern and the carrying of the high vault through from end to end of the cathedral were merely one of the attempts made to stiffen the sorely tried central tower after it had been riven by the spread of the lantern vault.

But there seems to have been a style of tower-building, especially in the West of England at such cathedrals as those of Wells and Hereford, Worcester and Gloucester, where the tower was regarded solely as a belfry and its old task of lighting the crossing abandoned. Sometimes, as at Worcester, there is simply the belfry stage rising above the blind story, but more frequently a ringing floor is included, for this is generally regarded as an essential element of even the parish tower.

In a class by itself is the enormous tower of St. Albans Cathedral, built entirely with Roman bricks from despoiled Verulam in the style of a Norman keep but with the usual ecclesiastical lantern with large windows, an external gallery forming a range of biforas, and a belfry stage. It was only intended to be the base for a huge and elaborate timber steeple, descriptions of which remain.

Similarly in its own class at the other end of the scale is the tower of Salisbury Cathedral. There has never been a belfry in it for the bells were hung in a detached tower which has now vanished. But after the collapse of the original lantern the present tower was built as though with a ringing floor and belfry, each with eight windows around it. And above, of course, was set the stone spire, its cap over four hundred feet above the pavement. The summit of this tremendous monument to Gothic England suffers such a battering from the elements that the upper part of it has to be taken down in every generation and renewed.

The Byzantines used the tall slender campanile for carrying bells, but the great tower exposed as a major feature of the exterior of the building was unknown to them. The basilican school was even less able to assist in the development of the architecture of the tower. Its only contribution could have been the aedicular arcade, and in fact this form of treatment was applied to the elevations of the Western tower; it was employed in exactly the same fashion as in the modern skyscraper in which horizontal stories are just piled one above the other, the difference being that the twelfth-century architects had the sensitivity to vary each story, alternating the heights and occasionally as at Norwich introducing a tier of something quite different such as a range of circular panels.

The face of the tower was practically the only opportunity offered the medieval architect for displaying his skill at the designing of elevations. That given an opportunity he could take it, may be detected in the unfinished west towers at Lincoln, where the windows are contained in wide arches but between them the arches are reduced in width to create the effect of richness. There could of course never have been any doubt as to the Anglo-Saxon builder's skill in the use of arcading, for the west front of Ely as an example of the use of arcading as wall-decoration is possibly unsurpassed in architecture.

A masterly piece of design may be seen in the west towers of Durham which contrast so perfectly with the plain walling of the transepts upon which they have been raised.

By the thirteenth century it was becoming apparent that the layered elevations of the towers broke up the vertical emphasis of the tower and also that over-elaboration produced a restless effect. So the designers reduced the number of tiers of arcading so as more nearly to equate the exterior elevation with its interior arrangement, one tier only to each story, with the windows enlarged to suit the new scale of the treatment. The thirteenth-century towers at the west end of Ripon Cathedral illustrate the new system and how it produces an elevation of great dignity and repose.

From now on the story with its windows controls the elevational design of towers. The system of arcading remains up to a point, but ceases to control the window arrangement and becomes subjected to this in the form of panelled surfaces. The towers of Wells and Hereford show clearly this system and how with the development of wall-panelling the tracery of the windows could be combined with this so as to facilitate the design of a very sophisticated elevation.

The bifora remains the basis of the tower window, Gothicized in treatment and set in the elevations in two or three bays, four in the elaborate tower of Hereford.

The curious situation of the tower of the English cathedral, as it were perched upon the roofs around it, makes it the most unfortunate of great architectural structures for the reason that its lower half is concealed from view.

The curious circumstances connected with the development of the west end of the English cathedral and the possibility of the retention of part of a predecessor—the 'west work'—have been discussed earlier in this book. There is still much interesting research to be done into the remains of such structures and consideration to be given to the probable effect they had upon the development of the west tower, the west transept and the great west front, unique in the world, of St. Edmundsbury out of which grew Ely. The origins of the lovely west front of Wells, to say nothing of the wonder at Peterborough, have yet to be explained.

One day we may be able to appreciate the exact significance of those three great arches at Lincoln, and the ghostly remains of something similar at Durham. (Plate 6.)

But for the present there is only the great tower of Ely to remind us of something lost.

The raising of a tower must have represented a tremendous sustained effort on the part of the medieval builder—to say nothing of the expenditure of vast sums of money. Thus one must expect most towers to have been built up to a stage, left for a while, and completed when funds and energy had been restored. For this reason, perhaps, we can seldom be sure what the original design of any tower might have been. St. Hugh's tower at Lincoln may have been a magnificent piece of work matching his choir, but only its stump remains.

It would have been interesting to have known what the complete design of the west front at Wells was to have been. How fortunate we are to have had an architect for its completion who could make such a splendid substitute for this. Not only are the towers perfect in themselves—though of course today lacking their steeples—but they rise with perfect smoothness from their thirteenth-century foundation in dignified acceptance of the skill and devotion of its designer. (Plate 17.)

The most important feature of a tower, and therefore its most interesting, is the treatment of its uppermost story. Originally this served merely as the base of the steeple, but after the introduction of lead roofing the top of the tower with its fretted parapet and its pinnacles became silhouetted against the sky. It is remarkable how well most of them stand up in the circumstances, without their steeples, sometimes even without their upper stories.

There are two important aspects of Gothic tower design. One is the fenestration of its elevations, the other the degree of importance attached to angle treatments.

The clasping pilaster developed from the pilaster indicating the bays of an early building has been discussed together with its use for accommodating a spiral stair. The obvious development from this was to make the angle treatment circular on plan. This could not be done in the building itself without interfering with the rhythm of the bays, but the isolated angles of the tower could assimilate the change without difficulty.

It is noticeable that the angles of the belfry story of the St. Albans tower have been changed from the normal square of the story below. In the base of the unfinished central tower at Lincoln the projecting angles are round, a clear rejection of the military type of tower angle and a promise of a developed angle treatment for the church tower.

There were, however, factors affecting this. After the development of the thirteenth-century buttress set in pairs at the angle of the building and adjusted to suit the requirements of a staircase, it became possible to introduce such features at the angles of towers,

31. SALISBURY

not, of course, as buttresses but in order to give an impressive element of Gothic verticality.

The early timber steeple, like its contemporary roofs, would have projected at its base in the form of overhanging eaves, complete with the usual corbel-table. This would have had the effect of restraining the projecting angle feature within the compass of the eaves. But with the coming of lead, and the recession of the base of the steeple behind a parapet, the situation at the angle would have changed completely.

For a start there would have no longer been any necessity for tucking in the angle treatments under the main eaves. At the same time the corners of the tower roof between the angle features and the side of the octagonal spire would need some kind of filling. Thus any development of the angle feature would actually have been welcomed.

Parallel with the introduction of lead roofing with all its benefits, therefore, was the introduction of the pinnacled tower-top, with or without a steeple, in the latter case an attractive aesthetic link between tower and spire.

The later Gothic architects seem to have displayed considerable aesthetic sensivity concerning what could have been an abrupt junction between these two very different objects, the square tower and the pyramidal spire. In parish churches the transference was often made through an octagonal turret or lantern. This does not appear in our cathedrals but the central tower of Durham shows a recession in the faces of the belfry story behind those below, obviously to ease the aesthetic junction between tower and spire.

One of the last and grandest of the lantern towers is that at York begun about 1400. Below its lierne vault eight tall windows pour the sunlight down into the heart of the stately church below. The exterior view of the tower suggests that it was intended for another story, probably a belfry. Thus it looks a little short of what it might have promised, and it certainly seems to lack a finished summit.

Last of the great towers is the 'Angel Steeple' of Canterbury, begun a generation after the tower of York and lifted another story higher so that it is seen as an entity, designed in one composition and built in one operation. It is completed at the summit by a quartet of tall pinnacles. Its lovely lantern can compare with that at York. (Plate 27.)

Although the tower at York is almost certainly unfinished, when compared with the design system of the Angel Steeple it is seen to be entirely different in conception. At York we see the Western type of tower with the design concentrated upon its elevations, whereas at Canterbury we have the sophisticated Somerset type of design, deeply moulded and with strong angle features designed to end in tall pinnacles.

We can see the two types together at Wells. The central tower was designed in the first quarter of the fourteenth century and is of the Western type with panelled elevations, while the western towers followed just half a century later and are deeply scored, with the windows set between heavily mullioned treatments. These towers, and their glorious protégé at Canterbury, represent the finest achievements of the English tower builder.

It is particularly in the design of towers that we can detect the decline of cathedral architecture, and at the same time appreciate that of the parish church developing in its place. A combination of wool-riches, Ham Hill stone, and the lodges of Glastonbury produced a splendid series of parish bell-towers amongst the hills and marshes of ancient Somerset. Wells Cathedral benefited, but even its lovely towers are equalled in beauty by that of St. Cuthbert's church nearby.

Not all the cathedrals seem to have possessed that spirit of enterprise essential for launching upon the considerable building programme involved in building a central tower—which it must be remembered might cost three or four times the value of a western tower only a quarter of the area.

Norwich had raised its splendid tower during the twelfth century, while several fallen central towers had been rebuilt in feeble fashion—at Winchester and Ripon for example. The explanation may partly be reliance upon tall steeples now lost.

It is the actual elevational design of the later cathedral towers that is so disappointing. Even the prince-bishops of Durham could produce only a parochial elevational design for what is otherwise a splendidly proportioned central feature. The great tower of York, also a product of the Age of Towers, rules by virtue of its tremendous scale rather than the excellence of its architecture.

The success of the twin-towered west front displayed by the cathedrals of Lincoln, Durham, or even such originally non-cathedral churches as Southwell or Ripon—and there were a number of monastic examples, mostly Augustinian—seems to have encouraged few imitators. St. Albans began a long west front similar to that at Wells but never finished it; in fact few of the Benedictine abbeys showed any interest in their frontispieces. The splendid portico of Peterborough owed nothing to towers. Late in the thirteenth century Lichfield began a twin-towered west front but it progressed very slowly and uncertainly and might not have achieved a notable degree of dignity, despite the elaboration of its elevations, but for the stone steeples which fortunately remain.

Every parish church of the later Gothic era had to be provided with a bell-tower at its west end. The design of these was standardized as a ground story continuing the nave, a ringing floor with a small window on each elevation, and a belfry stage with a large window on each face. The heights of the parish towers varied, and where stone and masons were available there might be some degree of elaboration.

The monks, who like the bishops had moved their choirs into the eastern arms of their churches and surrendered their naves to the laity, sometimes provided these with western bell-towers of parochial pattern but on a larger scale. The architecture of these towers was nevertheless entirely of a parochial character.

Cathedrals such as York and Canterbury followed the example of the abbey churches in building western bell-towers but reverted to the earlier system of providing a west front flanked by a pair of towers. However, there was no longer the inspired architectural skill capable of designing such a monumental composition. Thus what we see is a large west window flanked by a pair of heavily buttressed and pinnacled, but nevertheless frankly parochial, bell-towers.

To be fair it should be recorded that the English architects had never set out to become tower-builders. Their original central features had been primarily lanterns for lighting purposes and externally were to have been taken for bases for steeples. To have so quickly in history embarked upon a tower such as that of Lincoln was a remarkable feat.

The true church tower of the early-medieval church was its timber steeple. The word for the actual spire was 'broach' meaning a spit, the whole construction, tower and broach, being the steeple.

Judging from those examples of early timber architecture left to us it would seem probable that the early steeples were tent-like structures of inward-leaning rafters divided into stages each with its lean-to roof. Some of the more elaborate ones would have been octagonal, founded upon beams laid across the angles of the tower-top.

We know from illustrations and descriptions that some of the cathedral steeples were so exceedingly elaborate that their extravagances could not possibly have been repeated in far less tractable masonry: only the tent-like core came to be copied when the era of stone spires came into being.

Once more we can see how these were regarded as suitable ornaments to the parochial bell-towers—there was a spire-building zone in Northamptonshire—but were apparently too much for the average cathedral, with its far larger tower, to attempt, especially as in almost every case it already had a timber steeple. It was at Salisbury, where the original tower and steeple had to come down and be rebuilt, that the replacement was achieved in stone. In 1361 the timber steeple at Norwich fell into the choir and wrecked it—hence the splendid vaulted clearstory—and was rebuilt in stone. The three stone spires of Lichfield are also mid-fourteenth century in origin.

We need not suppose that the top of the early tower was always brought to a level line with eaves passing all round it, for it is possible that in some cases the four walls might have been carried up as gables. The Byzantines had no gables, the pitch of their roofs was unspectacularly low. The English roof, however, high-pitched and exposed, could end in gables. But the end of a roof, the 'verge', is usually regarded as a weakness and a source of trouble where the wind could get under the covering. So the timber churches may have had their roofs carried all round the building without gables, as may be seen in the timber tower-churches of Essex.

But in masonry architecture the gable becomes prominent in the elevation. In the Rhineland there are examples of towers which are carried up into four gables before being covered with a steeple. The well-known tower of Sompting church in Sussex has a steeple known as a 'helm' in which the angles of the roof rise from the tops of the gables instead of the corners of the tower, in what was probably the normal practice. (Fig. 18a.)

Since any form of pyramidal steeple would have exerted a certain amount of bursting thrust upon the angles of the tower, the construction might have been strengthened by setting beams across between the gables and helping to support the raking rafters of the steeple.

The external effect of such a form of construction would have been to create a steeple of pyramidal form having four roofs impinging upon it; which, curiously enough, is exactly the standard design of the Gothic pinnacle. (Fig. 18b.)

It is tantalizing to dwell upon the lost timber architecture of England set in its steepled landscape. And it seems a pity that the English architect of the Middle Ages, with such a great tradition behind him, was never able to build—possibly for lack of funds— tall stone steeples to compare with the elaborate features which rose throughout the Continent. Even the tall spire of Salisbury seems to match its cathedral in an austerity that seems to have played no part in the Gothic architecture of Europe. (Plate 31.)

Deserted now on its wind-swept down is the site of the old city of Salisbury, once a splendid medieval spectacle of castle and cathedral surrounded by walls of fortification.

The cathedral had a central lantern and a western bell-tower flanked by transepts. It was covered with the most elaborate twelfth-century ornament.

Below it in a green meadow by the Avon rose the new cathedral begun in 1220. Completed within a generation, it is seen to be in a single architectural style except for the tower and spire of a century later. The cathedral belongs to a period during which the lively architecture of the twelfth century had been tamed by the Cistercians, an Order which Bishop Poore, the cathedral's founder, admired so much that he was not buried there but in a Cistercian abbey church which he had founded some miles away in Dorset.

The austerity of the Cistercian Gothic, not yet developed into the lovely style of the Yorkshire abbeys, is reflected in every line of Salisbury Cathedral.

The bishop's choir was sited from the first in the eastern arm and has its own transept. At the east end is a charming aisled chapel, a miniature church, called the Lady Chapel but more probably the chapel of St. Edmund, the cathedral itself being dedicated to the Virgin.

The architecture is simple, the only striking feature being the shafts of Purbeck stone, in Victorian days coloured black. The lantern has been sealed off by carrying the vaulting across from nave to choir as one of the series of structural precautions which have been applied to the base of the tower during the centuries.

During the course of a drastic restoration at the end of the eighteenth century by the architect James Wyatt the cathedral was stripped bare, the screens being removed and all the tombs lifted from above the graves they commemorated and set in rows along the arcades. (Plate 30.)

Outside the cathedral the scene is unsurpassed for the grandeur of the soaring spire of Salisbury. That it is still standing is a complete miracle. For it was raised upon a base already riven as a result of ignorant thirteenth-century design which set a vaulted lantern high up in the air without any abutment. Today one can see flying buttresses put up in an abortive attempt to save the old lantern, and iron bands added by Christopher Wren.

The scaffolding upon which the spire was built is still built up inside it. At its foot is a great man-wheel or windlass, worked by a man walking inside it as in a treadmill. To get a stone from the pavement to the base of the spire takes a quarter of an hour, after which it has to be carried up the scaffolding. No other way of getting it up exists.

Below the spire are the two vast chambers of the tower. Each is lit by eight immensely tall windows. They are quite empty. To pass by them up the winding stair is a moving experience. For on the calmest day they are filled with strange sounds, a kind of deep booming, almost inaudible but of immense volume, like the murmurings of a great host of voices echoing through six centuries of England.

How many scores of thousands have assembled from time to time within the cathedral. A place of prayer, that has been offered up without pause and in perpetuity, fulfilling the purpose for which its stones have been piled so high—as though towards the heavens.

The cathedral purpose has been loyally observed by the canons of Salisbury, nothing being allowed to break the continuity of prayer, said in the cathedral twice every day. Not long ago the Avon flooded the nave. The canons procured a boat, rowed through the nave, up to their stalls in the choir—and said their prayers.

The centuries pass and the winds of change sweep through the lovely halls . . .

      but the prayers still rise . . .

      and the cathedral abides.

Glossary

===

abacus: the topmost member of a capital which actually carries the load

abutment: the foundation upon which an arch rises and which has to support both its weight and its overturning pressure

aedicule: literally a building in miniature, a structural feature such as a gable employed on a miniature scale for ornamental purposes as in a pinnacle

aisle: a lateral extension of a building reached from it through an arcade or colonnade. (The Latin *ala* from which the word is derived referred to a wing or transept and has been misapplied.)

ambulatory: a passage provided to enable persons to pass behind an altar

apse: a semicircular or semi-hexagonal end to a building

apsidiole: a small apse, usually an apsidal chapel at aisle level

arcade: a row of arches

arcading: an arcade applied to a wall-face for ornamental purposes

ashlar: thin stones set on edge and used as a facing to a rubble wall

ashlaring: vertical timberwork set internally beneath the feet of rafters

banker: the heavy baulk of timber upon which, as on an anvil, the mason dresses his stones

basement: the lowest story of a building, often an architectural story rather than a part of the accommodation

basilica: literally a regal apartment. Applied to Greek and Roman assembly halls and to the first Christian churches built in Rome

bay: a longitudinal division of a building or its façade

bifora: an Italian word used to denote a two-light window

blind story: an architectural story displaying no openings through it

bolster: the wide chisel used by the banker mason when dressing his stones

boss: a lump of stone left to accommodate the junction of vaulting ribs and carved with an ornamental design

buttress: a section of walling projected from the wall-face to withstand a thrust from an arch behind it. A flying buttress is an arch transferring a thrust from one buttress to another set at a distance from it

capital: the topmost feature of a column or pillar

cap: a diminutive capital crowning a shaft (q.v.)

centering: the removable timber framing upon which an arch is turned

chancel: the building attached to the east end of the nave of a parish church and housing the altar

chapter house: the apartment, usually octagonal, in which the chapter of the medieval cathedral met

chevet: a French word denoting the eastern termination of any church, used by English antiquaries to describe the ambulatory surrounding a great apse and giving access to a ring of chapels

choir: properly the enclosed apartment in which the cathedral canons met to say their prayers. Also used to denote the eastern arm of the cathedral

clearstory: an upper tier of windows lighting the upper part of the cathedral

collar: short length of timber joining the upper parts of couples (q.v.)

colonnade: a row of columns

colonnette: a diminutive column

column: a supporting member, usually of Classical origin, built up in drums of stone

corbel: a stone bracket carrying an arch or vaulting rib, sometimes carrying a statue

corbel-table: a tablement (q.v.) supported out from the wall-face on a series of corbels

core: the centre of a masonry wall lying between its two faces

couple: medieval roofing device comprising a pair of rafters joined together at the apex *crossing:* where a transept crosses the main structure

cruck: a medieval roofing device comprising two heavy bowed timbers meeting at the apex

cubiform cap: cap formed of a cubical lump of stone with its four lower corners shaved away

cushion capital: capital formed like the half of a square cushion which has been split into two

dormer: window formed in a roof

dressings: stones worked to details instead of merely forming part of wall-face

duplex bay: a great bay supported by piers divided into a pair of normal bays carried by a medial pillar

elevation: the vertical presentation of a building

foliation: development of the soffit (q.v.) of an arch or window-head by dividing it into 'foils' separated by 'cusps'

four-poster: a type of church having a central feature such as a tower carried upon four piers or timber posts

gargoyle: a water-spout projecting through a parapet and discharging the stormwater from the gutter behind, usually carved into a grotesque

groined vault: a simple cross vault constructed without a framework of ribs, the intersections of the vault being known as groins

haunch: the curved side of an arch

impost: the point whence an arch springs

keystone: the centre stone of an arch which locks it together

lancet: a window of the thirteenth century, very tall and slender and with a sharply pointed head

lantern tower: a tower built over a crossing having windows in it to light this

Glossary

lierne: short length of vaulting rib tying major ribs together

moulding: running ornament consisting of a series of grooves and shaped projections ornamenting such features as the soffits of arches

mullion: stone feature separating window lights

narthex: a portico passing across the entrance front of a church

nave: the main body of any church

niche: a small ornamental recess

ogee: term used by English antiquaries to denote an arch having serpentine sides

order: Gothic system of building arches in a series of superimposed rings expanding in size, later introduced into window tracery

pendentive: structural device supporting a dome above the interior angle of a square tower and appearing as a spherical triangle

pier: an isolated masonry support

pilaster: a half-pillar projecting from a wall-face

pillar: a slender masonry support

pinnacle: a weight set above a buttress to increase its stability, generally developed into a decorative architectural feature

pole: the medieval unit of length, usually about sixteen feet

porticus: a portico flanking an early church, sometimes walled up to contain interments and known as a solid porticus

rafter: a sloping roof timber

reredos: a stone screen forming an ornamental backcloth to an altar

respond: the pilaster (q.v.) or corbel (q.v.) carrying an arch or the end of an arcade

rib) the slender masonry arch upon which the 'web' (q.v.) of the vault rests

roll: a simple moulding passing round arches or up the angles of piers

saltire: a St. Andrew's cross

sanctuary: that part of the eastern arm immediately before the high altar

set-off: the sloping portion separating the diminishing stages of a buttress

shaft: tall slender colonnette, usually either an angle shaft, a nook shaft, or perhaps a long vaulting shaft (q.v.)

soffit: the underside of an arch

soller: an upper floor, if carried by a vault a stone soller

span: the width of a building over which the roof has to be thrown

spandrel: a triangular area, usually above the sides of an arch

springing line: the level at which an arch springs from its impost (q.v.)

squinch: arch thrown across the angles of a tower to carry an octagonal steeple above

steeple: strictly any church tower (tower having been used in medieval times to denote a military structure) but nowadays used for a spire (medieval 'broach')

story rod: a length of light timber employed as a gauge to control the height of a story and assure its height being equal throughout

string-course: a tablement (q.v.) provided between stories for purposes of vertical measurement or merely for horizontal punctuation

tablement: literally a stone plank and in fact lines of these set at various levels around a building from the plinth to the corbeltable (q.v.)

tetrapylon: a feature formed of a group of four piers (q.v.) joined by four arches

tracery: the pattern of glazing bars in a Gothic window

transept: lierally the area 'beyond the screen', i.e. the screen filling the western arch of the crossing and separating the laity from the bishop's church, today used to denote any structure crossing the main building or projecting laterally from its eastern arm

trifora: an Italian word denoting a three-light window

triforium: the feature at clearstory level supporting the inner wallface and during the twelfth century formed of a series of triforas; wrongly applied today to the gallery below

turret: a small tower, usually containing a spiral staircase

vault: either a stone upper floor carried upon masonry arches or a high vault forming a stone ceiling carried upon a system of ribs

vaulting shaft: a shaft (q.v.) carrying the line of a high vault down the wall-face towards the pavement or to the springing line of the main arcade

walking-space: after the transference of the bishop's choir into the eastern arm of the cathedral the area covered by the crossing and transepts became known as the walking space

web: the masonry of the vault carried by its ribs

west work: a German expression denoting a feature at the west end of a cathedral and often representing the remains of an earlier building

Index

Index